# Inside Investment Banking

# Inside Investment Banking

**Ernest Bloch**

C. W. Gerstenberg Professor of Finance
New York University

**DOW JONES-IRWIN**
Homewood, Illinois   60430

ISBN 0-87094-899-7
Library of Congress Catalog Card No. 86–71212

*Printed in the United States of America*

1 2 3 4 5 6 7 8 9 0 DO 3 2 1 0 9 8 7 6

In memoriam
Gustave L. Levy
Teacher and Colleague

# Preface

This book grew out of necessity and opportunity. The necessity was forced on me when I began to teach a course on investment banking and could find no text on that subject. The opportunity came from that very necessity, for it was my good fortune to team-teach for six years an undergraduate seminar on investment banking with Mr. Gustave L. Levy, senior partner, Goldman, Sachs & Co. After Mr. Levy's untimely death in 1976, Mr. John C. Whitehead, senior partner, Goldman, Sachs & Co. continued the course. During the entire period the seminar was conducted, Mr. Jonathan L. Cohen, now a partner of Goldman, Sachs, was an active and creative participant. To all of them I owe an intellectual debt, and to this day Mr. Cohen remains my intellectual lender of last resort.

In the seminar that Gustave L. Levy and I ran, we made do with various reading materials, memoranda, newspaper and journal articles, and so on, but the students learned the most from Mr. Levy and from the partners and other financial experts he brought to class. By this book's dedication I want to thank Gus and to suggest that even after a decade, he remains a vivid memory to me as he does, I am sure, to many others.

During the past four years, I have been teaching a graduate lecture course. In running that course, the assistance of the

Securities Industry Association, and particularly of Ms. Judith Cutler of Goldman, Sachs & Co. and of Messrs. Bruce S. Foerster of Paine Webber and Robert J. Kase of L. F. Rothschild, Unterberg, Towbin was very important, and their intellectual contributions to the course and to the book were essential.

The present version of the book is structured to discuss the many functions performed by investment banking firms. The book highlights the market-making functions of these firms, for that is the expertise they make available to their clients. Included in these functions are, for example, participations in large-scale and frequently innovative deals with institutional clients; mergers and acquisition; and the entire panoply of the new-issues process. The pressure of time precluded a discussion of the globalization of finance—that is, the spread of U.S. firms to foreign markets, and the increasingly large-scale entry of firms from abroad on the U.S. capital market.

The industry is a very dynamic one that, in the recent past, has shifted from a partnership type of organization to a corporate structure. And it is this very dynamism of the industry that makes it difficult to set it into the freeze-frame of the covers of a book. For this reason, we shall emphasize the innovative activities of investment bankers as well as their clients' more permanent needs for the services they provide. Indeed, some of the innovative activities of investment bankers are developed in some detail to indicate how these new activities are themselves part of the dynamism of market making; that as the industry promotes new types of deals, it is changing itself. In the discussion of mergers and acquisitions, the emphasis is on the industry's own activities as it participates in the merger game. And in the discussion of these innovations an essential source has been the research output of Salomon Brothers Inc., which the reader will find throughout the book. The permission to use these materials is gratefully acknowledged.

The plan of the book is to discuss the several market-making functions of investment banking in Part I and the new-issues process in Part II. Part III covers the public-policy issues regarding regulatory changes in the new-issues process (such as shelf registration), and Part IV deals with some investment management issues raised by the institutionalization of security markets. Finance and investment banking have developed a jargon all their own; to assist the reader a glossary of technical terms is provided at the end of the book.

In closing, I would like to acknowledge financial support from the Henry and Elaine Kaufman Foundation, Inc., and the NYU Schools of Business Research Fund. This is also an acknowledgment to the patience of our secretaries, Ms. Diane Shand, Ms. Maureen George, Ms. Diana Greene, and Mrs. Selma Rabinowitz, for while their patience was often tested, it never broke. And finally, many thanks should go to my wife, Amy W. Bloch, whose drafting skills the reader will appreciate and whose general encouragement made this book possible.

Ernest Bloch

# Contents

# PART I

# Market Making

# 1

# Introduction

Investment bankers perform two closely interrelated functions:

1. In the *primary* market, they *float* new securities for cash.
2. In the *secondary* market for existing securities, they assist buyers and sellers by acting as a broker or a dealer.

It is the first function named, the sale of a new issue to raise cash, that most people have in mind when the subject of investment banking comes up. The problem of pricing and distributing a new issue—that is, a security that has never been traded—is most important to the corporate issuer because it sets the firm's cost of capital. At the same time, the U.S. legal system restricts the issuance of publicly traded corporate securities to investment bankers. The price of the new stock or the interest rate on the new bond (and its other characteristics, such as maturity) must necessarily be related to the prices and other characteristics of comparable (existing) securities currently trading in the (secondary) markets. Setting the appropriate price and nonprice terms on a new issue is the all-important information step in the investment banking process. That process, in turn, must be based on active and large-scale trading in the secondary market—hence the necessary linkage between the two.

More recently, in the 1980s, investment bankers (and others) have developed new products by repackaging already existing securities. This type of market making produces financial innovations and new types of securities, and raises funds for the asset holders with far greater ease and lower cost than direct sale. Innovating bankers can place the new securities with investors because they have the expertise in finding investors and in structuring and pricing the new securities so they can be readily sold.

In discussing the purposes and functions of investment bankers, this book concentrates on two major themes. The first of these is market making, which requires a set of trading skills that involve finding institutional buyers for large-scale sales and (less frequently) assembling large-scale blocks of securities for a potential purchaser. These trading skills are maintained and tested in secondary markets where existing securities trade on a continuous basis. Because investors' large-scale sales are not predictably matched by other investors' desires to buy on the same large scale at the desired price, the market maker must often take a substantial position, and, accordingly, he must be backed by an equally substantial amount of capital. Not many brokers can be dealers because the risk-capital required is greater than most brokerage firms can raise.

The second theme is new-issues finance, perhaps the most significant subset of the overall market making process. I will deal with the problems of new-issues finance in some detail because that is the market area in which investment bankers provide the information skills, as well as the trading skills, that give them their unique position in the American capital market.

In the last part of the book I discuss institutionalization's other implications for American financial markets. As noted above, this situation requires not only larger trades and larger capital positions by market makers, it may require as well a new way of looking at market theory. For example, the prevailing theory of corporate governance (known as agency theory) assumes conflict between the firm's stockholders and its man-

agement. But what if the stock is held by institutional portfolio managers who use indexing as a portfolio management
technique? What are their interests in corporate governance?
 Finally, beyond looking at the market-making activities of
investment bankers, this book will examine the industry structure of investment banking.

## THE MARKET PROCESS

The dealer, or market-making, function involves placing capital at risk, carrying financial inventories, and for those firms
that play a leadership role in the industry, performing these
services *on a large scale.* As noted, one of the special functions performed by investment bankers is the placement of
new issues on the market. However, other financial institutions that are not called investment bankers also engage in
new-issues financing. For example, many commercial banks
are syndicate managers for new issues of municipal securities
(also called tax exempts) or are involved in new-money flotation of U.S. government securities. In addition, banks and
insurance companies (as well as investment bankers) place
new issues of corporate securities directly with institutional
investors.

 Under the 1930's Glass-Steagall Act, U.S. commercial
banks were not permitted to underwrite new issues of corporate stocks, although they began to underwrite some corporate
debt issues in the 1960s. Nor were banks permitted to act in
the secondary corporate markets as dealers in stocks, although
they were permitted to act as agents for customers. Perhaps the
most significant new-issues function performed by commercial banks in the 1970s and 80s is the flotation of industrial
development bonds. Technically, these are municipal issues,
but they are specifically designed to finance industrial—that
is, corporate—projects.

 Under the regulatory umbrella of the SEC well-established
investment banking firms can engage in every type of underwriting and trading. Today they have entered the new satellite
markets such as options and futures, international activities,
and asset management.

 Not only do investment bankers offer multiple financial
services, but different firms in the industry offer different

combinations of these services. The investment banking industry, moreover, is more adaptable and flexible than most of its competition to substantial outside shocks and market changes. Among these, the data processing revolution permitted the industry to raise its equity trading capacity roughly tenfold during the period 1968–1984.

In discussing the scale of the industry, one important aspect is industry leadership—specifically, the handful of companies called special-bracket firms.[1] One (or more) of these firms is usually the syndicate leader in every major flotation. In addition these firms are considered an elite group that plays a similar leadership role in takeovers, mergers, and acquisitions. Is that leadership position based on the results of objective performance tests in specific industry outputs? With the exception of data concerning underwriting leadership by types of security (e.g., corporate bonds, municipal issues, etc.), few output measures are generally available.

Still, the perception that some firms have certain specialties that they do particularly well persists, in part because those services are identified with certain well-known individuals. For the major firms, market expectations are that they will participate in a leadership role in all of the basic outputs of investment bankers. For the next group of firms, one or more areas will tend to represent a predominant factor.

Nevertheless, *all* investment banking firms, large and small, do some of the same things.[2] All of them engage in new-issue underwriting, private placements, and block trading; in bond swaps and principal transactions; and in brokerage activities for individual and institutional clients. Finally, at this writing, other financial industries, notably commercial banks and insurance firms, are increasingly entering (and for the banks, reentering after 50 years) some of the same brokerage/investment banking areas. Everything is getting more complicated.

---

[1] These are, in no special order, Merrill Lynch, Goldman Sachs, Salomon Brothers, First Boston, and Morgan Stanley.

[2] This is roughly equivalent to the argument that the average country club hacker and John McEnroe practice their serves. The statement is true; the results are very different.

## A QUICK GLANCE AT HISTORY

A little more than a half century ago, a speculative frenzy on all financial markets was followed by the great Wall Street crash of 1929 and the Great Depression of the 1930s. In that decade Congress passed a great deal of, it hoped, remedial legislation.

In 1947, many of the investment bankers that survived the Depression were hit by an antitrust complaint filed by the Department of Justice under the Sherman Act. The government brought suit against 17 major investment banking firms and the Investment Bankers Association (IBA) (see Table 1–1 for a list of the firms involved)[3] charging monopolization of the securities business and, most notably, of about two thirds (69 percent) of publicly offered syndicates. The case came to trial in late 1950 before Judge Medina sitting without a jury. After a lengthy trial, Judge Medina dismissed the charges in September 1953 on the grounds of insufficient evidence.[4]

Following that trial the investment banking and related broker-dealer industries suffered further disruption to the organization and regulation of the financial system.

1. A surge in corporate (as well as state and local) debt financing in the 1960s and 1970s.
2. A surge in stock-market prices and volume until 1968 and subsequent dislocation of trading capacity.
3. A rise in inflationary finance 1968–81.
4. A sharp widening in amplitude of security prices and rates of return and the advent of negotiated commissions.
5. As a result, a sharp rise in price volatility in secondary and primary markets even as commission rates receded (at least in equity markets).

But the industry has a rather unusual capacity to respond to market, technological, and regulatory shocks. In part, this

---

[3] Compare this list to the appendix to Chapter 2 to identify survivors among today's major firms.

[4] For an interesting discussion of the trial and the issues and personalities involved see V. P. Carrosso, *Investment Banking in America* (Cambridge, Mass.: Harvard University Press, 1970).

**TABLE 1–1**

Concentration of Control in the Investment Banking Business:
Security Issues Managed* January 1, 1938, to April 30, 1947
(in millions)

| | Issues Registered with SEC | Rail Issues (Exclusive of Equipment Trust Issues) | Total Issues Managed | Percent of All Issues |
|---|---|---|---|---|
| Morgan Stanley & Co. | 2,783.6 | 578.8 | 3,362.4 | 16.1% |
| First Boston Corporation† | 2,592.4 | 133.6 | 2,726.0 | 13.1 |
| Dillon, Read & Co., Inc. | 1,460.1 | 26.0 | 1,486.1 | 7.1 |
| Kuhn, Loeb & Co. | 762.1 | 618.0 | 1,380.1 | 6.6 |
| Blyth & Co. | 838.9 | 63.3 | 902.2 | 4.3 |
| Smith, Barney & Co. | 804.0 | — | 804.0 | 3.9 |
| Lehman Brothers | 604.3 | 36.0 | 640.3 | 3.1 |
| Harriman, Ripley & Co., Inc. | 611.6 | 6.7 | 618.3 | 3.0 |
| Glore, Forgan & Co. | 418.7 | — | 418.7 | 2.0 |
| Kidder, Peabody & Co. | 364.0 | 28.9 | 392.9 | 1.9 |
| Stone & Webster Securities Corporation | 352.1 | — | 352.1 | 1.7 |
| Goldman, Sachs & Co. | 287.8 | — | 287.8 | 1.4 |
| Harris, Hall & Co. (Incorporated) | 240.6 | — | 240.6 | 1.2 |
| White, Weld & Co. | 233.5 | 4.8 | 238.3 | 1.1 |
| Eastman, Dillon & Co. | 212.0 | — | 212.0 | 1.0 |
| Union Securities Corporation | 181.8 | — | 181.8 | 0.9 |
| Drexel & Co. | 90.2 | 23.4 | 113.6 | 0.5 |
| Total—17 defendant banking firms | 12,837.7 | 1,519.5 | 14,357.2 | 68.9 |
| Total—1 nondefendant investment banking firm | 2,097.7 | 1,050.3 | 3,148.0 | 15.1 |
| Total—257 nondefendant investment banking firms | 3,190.8 | 146.2 | 3,337.0 | 16.0 |
| Total—275 investment banking firms | 18,126.2 | 2,716.0 | 20,842.2 | 100.0 |

*Co-managed issues shown pro rata for each co-manager.
†Includes issues managed by Mellon Securities Corporation.
SOURCE: *U.S. v. Henry S. Morgan et al.,* "Copy of Complaint," 49.

may be due to the relatively small number of major firms in the industry and their manageable size (see following chapter). The industry has also survived the disappearance of more than half the firms deemed to be major underwriters in 1950.

## THE ANTITRUST CASE

Judge Medina held it "preposterous" that investment banking firms had "entered into a combination, conspiracy, and agreement to restrain and monopolize the securities business of the United States" at the time of World War I.[5] To the contrary, he concluded, the pyramidal shape of syndicate organization was a characteristic structure for performing new-issue management in the United States and abroad since the 19th century. Medina suggested that the market-making needs that shifted somewhat with each issue gave the process its peculiar organizational structure.

Broadly put, Medina's argument is that the flotation mechanics are not a specific technical process (as, say, the formulation of a patent medicine) but a combination of security valuation and price forecasting techniques and market-making and management skills that he described as the sum of many different "banking services." In Medina's words, these services were "the product of a gradual evolution to meet specific economic problems created by demands for capital which arose as the result of the increasing industrialization of the country and the growth of a widely dispersed investor class."

Hayes et al.[6] argue that the 1930's legislation (the Exchange Act, Securities Act, and Glass-Steagall) in combination with the relatively small volume of business then done led to more competitive offerings, to narrower spreads, and, in turn, to greater concentration of lead position in syndicates by established firms. Hayes[7] then quotes Carrosso's data and com-

---

[5]U.S. District Court, Southern District of New York (Civil no. 43–757), *United States v. Henry S. Morgan et al.*, pp. 350 ff.

[6]S. C. Hayes III, A. M. Spence, and D. V. P. Marks, *Competition in the Investment Banking Industry* (Cambridge, Mass.: Harvard University Press, 1983), especially pp. 22 ff.

[7]Ibid., p. 23.

ments as follows: In the four and a half years between January 1, 1934, and June 30, 1938, 40 investment banking houses headed 94.6 percent of all managed issues in terms of value and held 82.6 percent in terms of value of all underwriting participations. The real point, though was not whether the pyramid still existed but whether it was being misused."

Hayes et al. further point out that the pyramidal structure of syndicate management and the persistence of a small group of lead firms, seemed to support the popular (and populist) folklore that an "anticompetitive money trust" existed and persisted. Hayes argues further that such beliefs were not supported by evidence of secret plots or back-room collusion but were the product of "professional incompetence, irresponsibility, and out-and-out fraud" that characterized a well-publicized group of broker-dealers and led to the legislation of the 1930s. Because these criminal and venal acts were individual and unorganized, the chosen regulatory remedy—full disclosure—reflects the notion that the broker-dealer community can be relied on to control an excess of organized greed. (Similar misfeasance and malfeasance were discovered in the banking system, although there the chosen regulatory remedy took on a different, and confidential, aspect.)

## COMPETITION FOR SYNDICATE BUSINESS: POSTWAR FINANCE

During World War II and the immediate postwar period, the new-issues business was slow, owing partly to the liquid financial position of the corporate sector and partly to its strong cash flow. To some extent some geographic dispersion of financial power away from New York also began. As a result, many new firms began to enter the distribution business, especially as members of syndicate selling groups.

The adjustment of the major investment banking firms started off quietly in the 1950s, when new-issue financing contributed only a small share to financing of corporate real investment. At that time a few old-line, lead underwriters did the main originating work; they expended little effort on either distribution (retail or institutional) or secondary market making. Specialization was the name of the game; retail ("wire") firms were included in syndicates exclusively as members of the selling group. To overstate the case somewhat, the large, old, mainly New York originating firms were corporate underwriters and advisers to issuers; the distributing (selling) firms were newer, smaller brokerage firms that emphasized relations with security buyers (at new issue).

Everyone could see that the big profits at new issue accrued to syndicate leaders (originating firms), whose management fee came to 20 percent off the top of gross spread (as it still does today). Further, large syndicate leaders also earned substantial underwriting fees by taking down large portions of new offerings and placing them with large institutional buyers. Private placements to the same buyers were also a substantial source of new business. During the 1950s and the early 1960s, moreover, the comparative stability of the financial markets held down the riskiness of the underwriting process, thereby giving originating firms an especially good base for their total profits. This situation did not escape the attention of distributing firms in the syndicate process—especially when these firms became more prosperous and acquired more capital with the bull market of the 1960s.

## The 1960s

In fact, the very prosperity of the stock market began to open cracks in the system from the brokerage/distribution side of the new-issue process. To begin with, the "paper crisis" overwhelmed the record-keeping and transaction capacity of the New York Stock Exchange, resulting in the bankruptcy and forced merger of some firms. Further, the partnership organization of many brokerage firms turned out to be a weak link in the chain of trading relationships. Some older partners thought the sharp price drops in equities in the late 1960s and the breakdown of market processes were all too reminiscent of the Great Depression. Fearing a similar collapse, they withdrew from the business and took their money out of the firms. For many of the firms suffering from flight capital, this set of events brought the very debacle the departing partners were eager to avoid for themselves. This situation also led a number of firms to broaden their capital base by going public. By reorganizing as corporations, such firms as Bache, Merrill Lynch, Dean Witter, E. F. Hutton, Paine Webber, and Shearson

Hayden Stone brought in a more stable capital base as well as a larger volume of public (and permanent) capital.

## INFLATIONARY FINANCE

The decade of the 1970s opened with the back-office crisis on the New York Stock Exchange and a transition to negotiated—that is, expectations of lower—stock trading commissions. In addition, the decade brought on in full force the problems and opportunities of inflation finance and the associated price volatility of securities. Underwriting became a riskier game while market-making expertise in the secondary market became a more significant component of all securities-related activities. Institutional traders, for example, needed and wanted capacity to swap large blocks of bonds. The ability to place securities—either in inventory or with an institutional client—made many institutional and retail firms increasingly valuable as syndicate members to old-line syndicate originators and managers. Their value rose further as the financial environment became riskier and more difficult.

And, as the increasingly more strategic role of distributors became apparent to the firms themselves, they developed their own capacity to manage syndicates. Corporate financial officers and new-business representatives of the most eager major-bracket firms saw that something had fundamentally changed. With more active competition and less tradition in syndicate leadership, greater competition to run syndicates might lead to better performance for new issues. The traditional tie between a corporation and a specific investment broker was broken. On the buying side of the market, the capacity to deal on a large scale was increasingly in demand by institutional investors. As a result of such jockeying, substantial readjustments of major-bracket firms occurred between the beginning and the end of the decade as shown by Hayes.[8] (See Figure 1–1.)

Meanwhile the forces of competition were pressing in on all firms by the move from fixed to negotiated brokerage commissions for equity trading. Although May Day 1975 was

---

[8] S. L. Hayes III, "The Transformation of Investment Banking," *Harvard Business Review*, January–February 1979, p. 165.

**FIGURE 1-1**
Equity Underwriting Syndicate Positions: 1971 versus 1978

| 1971 | 1978 |
|---|---|

**Special bracket:**

| 1971 | 1978 |
|---|---|
| Dillon, Read & Co. Inc. | — |
| The First Boston Corporation | The First Boston Corporation |
| Kuhn, Loeb & Co. | — |
| Merrill Lynch, Pierce, Fenner & Smith, Inc. | Merrill Lynch, Pierce, Fenner & Smith, Inc. |
| Morgan Stanley & Co. Incorporated | Morgan Stanley & Co. Incorporated |
| Salomon Brothers | Salomon Brothers |
| | Goldman Sachs & Co. |

**Major bracket:**

| 1971 | 1978 |
|---|---|
| Blyth & Co., Inc. | Bache Halsey Stuart Shields Incorporated |
| Drexel Harriman Ripley Incorporated | Blyth Eastman Dillon & Co. Incorporated |
| Du Pont Glore Forgan Incorporated | Dillon, Read & Co. Inc. |
| Eastman Dillon, Union Securities & Co. | Donaldson, Lufkin & Jenrette Securities Corporation |
| Goldman, Sachs & Co. | Drexel Burnham Lambert Incorporated |
| Halsey, Stuart & Co. Inc. | E. F. Hutton & Company Inc. |
| Hornblower & Weeks—Hemphill, Noyes | Kidder, Peabody & Co. Incorporated |
| Kidder, Peabody & Co. Incorporated | Lazard Frères & Co. |
| Lazard Frères & Co. | Lehman Brothers Kuhn Loeb Incorporated |
| Lehman Brothers Incorporated | Loeb Rhoades, Hornblower & Co. |
| Loeb, Rhoades & Co. | Paine, Webber, Jackson & Curtis Incorporated |
| Paine, Webber, Jackson & Curtis | Smith Barney, Harris Upham & Co. Incorporated |
| Smith, Barney & Co. Incorporated | Warburg Paribas Becker Incorporated |
| Stone & Webster Securities Corporation | Wertheim & Co., Inc. |
| Wertheim & Co. | Dean Witter Reynolds Inc. |
| White, Weld & Co. | |
| Dean Witter & Co. Incorporated | |

**Major out of order:**

| 1971 | 1978 |
|---|---|
| Bache & Co. Incorporated | Bear, Stearns & Co. |
| Paribas Corporation | L. F. Rothschild, Unterberg, Towbin |
| | Shearson Hayden Stone Inc. |

**FIGURE 1-1 (concluded)**

| 1971 | 1978 |
|---|---|
| Mezzanine bracket: | Oppenheimer & Co. Incorporated |
| | Thomson McKinnon Securities Inc. |
| | |
| Submajor bracket: | Ladenburg Thalmann & Co. Inc. |
| Bear, Stearns & Co. | Moseley, Hallgarten & Estabrook Inc. |
| A. G. Becker & Co. Incorporated | |
| CBWL—Hayden, Stone Inc. | |
| Clark, Dodge & Co. Incorporated | |
| Dominick & Dominick Incorporated | |
| Equitable Securities, Morton & Co. Incorporated | |
| Hallgarten & Co. | |
| Harris, Upham & Co. Incorporated | |
| E. F. Hutton & Company Inc. | |
| W. E. Hutton & Co. | |
| Ladenburg, Thalmann & Co. | |
| F. S. Moseley & Co. | |
| John Nuveen & Co. (Incorporated) | |
| R. W. Pressprich & Co. Incorporated | |
| Reynolds & Co. | |
| L. F. Rothschild & Co. | |
| Shearson, Hammill & Co. Incorporated | |
| Shields & Company | |
| F. S. Smithers & Co., Inc. | |
| Spencer Trask & Co., Incorporated | |
| G. H. Walker & Co. | |
| Walston & Co. Inc. | |
| Wood, Struthers & Winthrop Inc. | |

SOURCE: S. L. Hayes III, "The Transformation of Investment Banking," *Harvard Business Review*, January–February 1979, p. 165.

the date when all brokerage commissions became subject to negotiation, pressure from Congress and the SEC had pushed institutional-sized trades into negotiation of commission as early as 1971 and into some other forms of informal negotiation (through give ups) even earlier.[9]

## A FEW CONCLUSIONS

The investment banking business is often called dynamic and for good reason. With a few exceptions the group of leading firms has involved a changing cast of characters—namely, those firms that managed to adjust best and fastest to a substantial set of shocks. One shock was the retooling of the major market place, the NYSE. The Exchange, once a paper-based retail operation with a daily trading volume of 15 million shares, was threatened with collapse and required to close one trading day a week. Today the electronic market has traded 150 million shares a day, or nearly 10 times the volume of the late 1960s, without major interruption. At the same time the broker-dealer firms that in part competed with and in part supplemented floor trading by upstairs block trading made that rise possible because average trade size was rising with growing institutionalization of the market.

Finally, large-scale institutionalization moved into the new-issues market, and the SEC proposed its shelf-registration rule. But because that issue has many ramifications and raises many other questions, it will be discussed separately in Part II.

---

[9] For further discussion, see SEC's *Institutional Investor Study Report,* 82d Congress, 1st Session, Washington, D.C.: U.S. Government Printing Office, 1971.

# 2

# The Investment Banking Industry: Size and Structure

## INTRODUCTION

Little quantitative information is readily available about the investment banking industry's size or the structure of its current outputs. Few people appreciate the fact that this is a cottage industry located on the island of Manhattan and concentrated primarily in the area around Wall Street. This section provides quantitative estimates based on comparable and consistent Securities and Exchange Commission (SEC) data.[1]

## INVESTMENT BANKING FIRMS: SOME PARAMETERS

In its role as regulator of broker-dealer firms engaged in providing secondary-market trading services (under the Securities Exchange Act of 1934), the SEC classifies firms by trading function and location of head office. Altogether some 5,700

---

[1]The data to be discussed are compiled by the SEC primarily from an analysis of FOCUS reports, which are regulatory reports filed by broker-dealers with self-regulatory organizations (such as the organized exchanges) or the SEC. Over 5,700 broker-dealers filed such reports in 1981, the latest full-year data available.

**TABLE 2–1**
The U.S. Securities Industry and Its Major Components by Number,
Assets, and Equity Capital, 1981 (dollars in millions)

|  | Number of Firms | Total Assets | Equity Capital |
|---|---|---|---|
| NYSE member firms: | | | |
| National full line | 11 | $ 36,004 | $2,600 |
| Large investment banking | 10 | 58,042 | 1,881 |
| New York based | 35 | 7,334 | 395 |
| NYSE regional | 126 | 9,252 | 872 |
| Other NYSE carrying | 65 | 10,563 | 1,230 |
| NYSE introducing | 206 | 1,160 | 344 |
| Non-NYSE firms: | | | |
| Securities brokers | 272 | 1,206 | 151 |
| Securities dealers | 315 | 2,844 | 657 |
| Other non-NYSE carrying | 226 | 2,326 | 303 |
| Non-NYSE introducing | 1,207 | 1,068 | 415 |
| Total firms doing a public business | 2,473 | $129,799 | $8,847 |

SOURCE: SEC, *The Securities Industry in 1981* (Washington, D.C.: 1982).

firms report to SEC via FOCUS reports; less than half (about 2,500) do business directly with the public. As Table 2–1 indicates, among the 2,473 firms reporting to the SEC, only the first 21 firms are involved primarily in investment banking. The national full-line firms are those (such as Merrill Lynch) that have an extensive network of branch offices. Firms included under "large investment banking" are engaged mainly in large-scale underwriting and trading (for example, Salomon Brothers). The terms *clearing* or *carrying* mean that such firms "cleared" securities transactions (for themselves and/or other firms) or maintained possession or control of customers' cash or securities (as, for example, through margin accounts). Most of the remaining NYSE members that carry customer accounts are classified as New York–based firms if their head office is located in New York City or NYSE regional firms if the head office is outside New York City. NYSE introducing firms are members who neither clear nor carry securities for customers; the unclassified group are NYSE members who carry public customer accounts but fall outside the other classifications.

Firms classified as large investment banking houses by the

SEC in consultation with the Securities Industries Association (SIA), a trade association, constitute a small industry even within the financial-services universe. At the end of 1981 (the latest date for which complete data are available), total industry assets were about $94 billion—roughly equal to the size of a single large money-center bank, (i.e., Bank of America).

Financial transactions considered investment banking are not conducted exclusively by the two groups mentioned; many broker-dealer firms are involved in such activities. But if we group all broker-dealer firms that do business with the public, that group's total assets at year-end 1981 were about $130 billion, a total just slightly larger than Citicorp's, the nation's largest single bank holding company. (See Table 2–1.)

The most easily identifiable activity of investment bankers is the flotation of new issues, although other financial industries (for example, commercial banks) are involved in new-issues financing as well. Investment bankers also perform typical broker-dealer transactions in secondary markets (many of these transactions require special handling because of their large scale).

What, then, is investment banking? To paraphrase a famous quote, investment banking is what investment bankers do. And because the increasingly volatile price and interest-rate environments compel quickness of decision and response in financial markets, investment bankers have learned (1) how to use satellite markets to lay off risks and (2) that innovation in products, markets, and services may provide an important, even if temporary, boost to their own rates of return. This proposition may help to explain the stimulus to innovation and the quick (and defensive) response of other firms in the industry to the innovation of any pioneer, thereby producing a series of competitive readjustments in a set of firms that could conventionally (and probably erroneously) be thought of as an oligopoly. More on this later.

## THE SEC CLASSIFICATION OF INDUSTRY GROUPS AND SIZE COMPARISONS

All classifying schemes, although useful, are somewhat arbitrary. Accordingly, the following section peels down the statistical onion, hopefully without tears.

The analysis begins with data for what the SEC calls carrying/clearing firms. These are firms that both:

a. Do business with the public.
b. Are members of an organized exchange.

This means that excluded are all firms that are not exchange members as well as those exchange members that do not do business with the public (such as exchange-floor traders or specialists) and all member firms that do not clear, or carry, customer accounts.

The investment banking industry is rather concentrated (refer to Table 2-1). Following the SEC's classification, in terms of total assets, the 11 national full-line firms,[2] and the 10 large investment banking houses together aggregate $94 billion of the total $130 billion security-business universe. Put slightly differently, the assets of 21 firms out of 2,473 (or less than 1 percent by number) constitute about 70 percent of the security industry's total assets. Within that group of 21 firms, the assets of the 10 investment banking houses alone add up to almost half the assets (those of the 11 national full-line firms add up to about 30 percent) of the securities industry as defined. If only for that reason, the investment banking industry bears separate examination.

## WHICH ARE THE MAJOR FIRMS?

The SEC classification system uses firm size, type of business done, and location of the firm to establish subsets of the industry. The 11 national full-line firms are large broker-dealer firms that are involved in all aspects of the securities business and that have a nationwide network of branch offices. The 10 large investment banking houses are large firms that are known mainly as syndicate managers or leaders (other than those that operate extensive branch networks and are therefore placed in the first group). Most of the remaining NYSE members that do a public business are placed into a group called New York–based firms if their main office is in New York City

---

[2]In the past these firms were identified as "national wire houses" because of the private wires that connected their many retail-oriented branch offices.

or into NYSE regional firms if their main office is located outside of New York City. (See Appendix for firm names.)

## MAJOR REVENUE COMPONENTS

Pre-tax revenue components indicate the variety of outputs and/or services produced by major firms doing investment banking. Based on the data in Table 2–2, several preconceptions may need adjusting. For example, figures on revenues from underwriting (that is, revenues from new-issue flotations) show that full-line firms earned twice as much from that source, and even NYSE regionals earned more, than the large investment banking houses. More surprising, in 1981, before the NYSE bull market pushed up trading volume, the large investment banking houses earned twice as much from securi-

**TABLE 2–2**

Comparisons of Primary Revenue Items among Three Major Groups of Firms Engaged in Investment Banking, 1981 (dollars in millions)

|  | Full Line | Investment Banking Houses | NYSE Regionals |
|---|---|---|---|
| Security commissions: |  |  |  |
| Listed equities | $1,753 | $ 567 | $ 646 |
| Other | 673 | 95 | 333 |
| Total | 2,426 | 662 | 979 |
| Margin interest (income) | 1,707 | 232 | 503 |
| Profits from underwriting | 722 | 318 | 324 |
| Gains (losses) trading A/C: |  |  |  |
| Debt | 1,070 | 1,672 | 192 |
| Other | 376 | 370 | 210 |
| Total | 1,446 | 2,042 | 402 |
| Other securities related* | 1,000 | 1,327 | 265 |
| Residual | 1,056 | 1,065 | 229 |
| Total revenues | $8,357 | $5,646 | $2,702 |
| Pre-tax profit margins† | 6.9% | 15.4% | 11.5% |
| Pre-tax returns to equity capital‡ | 24.0% | 54.3% | 37.5% |

*Includes merger and takeover service revenues.

†Ratio of pre-tax income (income after partners' compensation but before taxes) to total revenues.

‡Pre-tax income as a percent of average of four quarters of ownership equity capital.

SOURCE: SEC, *The Securities Industry in 1981* (Washington, D.C.: 1982), Table III–1 and Appendix C–1, 2, 4.

ties commissions as they did from underwriting. And, along with margin interest revenues, underwriting profits constituted one of the smaller components of total revenues (about 6 percent). By far the largest single source of revenue was trading gains, especially from debt issues (including U.S. government securities); revenues from such services as mergers and takeovers came in second. Indeed, the large investment houses did better on trading account than full-line firms (whose assets are larger), although the latter are involved in more retail-oriented trading situations. That retail orientation, finally, is also reflected in the full-line firms' relatively large earnings from margin interest.

Considering the relationship of these earnings (pre-tax) either to total revenues or to equity capital, the large investment banking houses show up particularly well. First, their profit margins were better than twice those of full-line firms and about half again as good as those of NYSE regionals. In terms of profitability, returns to equity were of the same order of multiplication (about 3.5 times) to profit margins as were those of the other two sets of firms. Finally, these 1981 results for investment banking houses were the same as the 1980 results, a consistency record not achieved by the other two sets of firms.[3]

Taking revenue data a step further, the SEC has separated out the distribution of trading gains from debt issues and from market-making activities in OTC equities. As Table 2–3 indicates, better than four fifths of the industry's debt gains came from the two major sets of firms, with the large investment bankers counting for about half of the industry's total.

On the other hand, about half of market-making gains from OTC equity securities—a much more labor-intensive activity—were earned by full-line firms (using about an equal proportion of the industry's employees), with investment bankers providing about one tenth of the total industry, based on a comparable employee share. (See Table 2–4.)

---

[3] Pre-tax margins and returns to equity (in percent) for 1980:

|  | Full Line | Investment Banking Houses | NYSE Regionals |
|---|---|---|---|
| Pre-tax margins | 10.8% | 17.6% | 15.0% |
| Returns to equity | 43.1 | 52.9 | 52.7 |

**TABLE 2-3**

Distribution of Trading Gains in Debt Securities among Carrying
Firms in 1981

|  | Number of Firms | Percent of Gains | |
|---|---|---|---|
| Large investment banking houses | 10 | 49.4% | } 81% |
| National full-line firms | 11 | 31.6 | |
| Non-NYSE regional firms | 315 | 7.8 | |
| NYSE regional firms | 126 | 5.7 | |
| Other carrying firms | 598 | 5.5 | |
| All carrying firms doing a public business in 1980, 1981 | 1,060 | 100.0% | |

SOURCE: SEC, *The Securities Industry in 1981* (Washington, D.C.: 1982).

**TABLE 2-4**

Distribution of Gains from Market Making in OTC Equity Securities
among Carrying Firms in 1981

|  | Number of Employees | | Percent of Gains | |
|---|---|---|---|---|
|  | In Thousands | Percent | | |
| National full-line firms | 96 | 47.8% | 46.7% | } 56.7% |
| Large investment banking houses | 18 | 9.2 | 10.0 | |
| NYSE regional firms | 29 | 14.4 | 22.5 | |
| Non-NYSE securities dealers | 8 | 4.0 | 11.9 | |
| Other carrying firms | 49 | 24.6 | 8.9 | |
| All carrying firms doing a public business in 1980, 1981 | 200 | 100.0% | 100.0% | |

SOURCE: U.S. Securities and Exchange Commission, FOCUS report, prepared by Directorate of Economic and Policy Analysis.

The NYSE-member regional firms contribute the second most important OTC earnings share (better than a fifth) with only one seventh the number of employees. Finally, all the other carrying firms (598), employing about one fifth of the personnel, produced less than one tenth the gains of the industry's OTC market making. The foregoing suggests the conclusion that even in a labor-intensive output like OTC market making, there may be significant differences in productivity (and/or scale economies) as well as other factors.

The large investment banking houses were the major earners of other securities-related income, which includes earnings from merger and takeover fees. These 10 firms garnered better than one third of the industry's income, with the 11 full-line firms making up another third. The more than 99 percent of all other firms together produced only about the last third of such service earnings.

## More Recent Revenue Data

Data covering *all* NYSE members for 1983 and 1984 (the only data presently available) show that the relative proportion of major income items has not changed dramatically since 1981.[4] As indicated in Table 2–5, underwriting income in 1983 and 1984 remains at about 10 percent of total revenues, while trading and investments and securities commissions each come to about one fourth of total revenues for each of those years. Finally, other forms of security income (mainly from mergers and acquisitions) average out to about one fifth for the two years. (Recall that these data cover *all* NYSE members but that the large investment banking firms earn the lion's share, as before.)

## INDUSTRY STRUCTURE AND SERVICE OUTPUTS

Large firms in the national full-line and large investment banking groups are by far the most important firms and, in fact, currently provide the major asset and output components of broker-dealer firms. Accordingly, these 21 firms are generally representative of the investment banking industry even though some major regional firms also had substantial market influence and power in 1981 and individual firms may emphasize different service outputs. Chapter 3 brings the data up to 1984 by looking at two representative investment banking firms, one full line (Hutton), and one large investment banking house (First Boston). That discussion will serve another useful purpose, namely, to develop a healthy skepticism about

---

[4]Table 2–1 indicates that the assets for the 21 full-line and investment banking firms constitute better than three fourths of all NYSE member firm assets. It is unlikely that enormous increases in asset productivity of the smaller NYSE firms could significantly change revenue proportions in 1983 and 1984.

**TABLE 2–5**

Income Statement for NYSE Member Firms

| Sources of Gross Income ($ millions) | 1983 | | 1984 | |
|---|---|---|---|---|
| | Amount | Percent | Amount | Percent |
| Securities commissions | $ 8,348 | 28.3% | $ 7,082 | 22.7% |
| Trading and investments | 7,571 | 25.6 | 8,253 | 26.5 |
| Interest on customers' debit balances | 2,130 | 7.2 | 2,811 | 9.0 |
| Underwriting | 3,530 | 11.9 | 2,706 | 8.7 |
| Mutual fund sales | 953 | 3.2 | 751 | 2.4 |
| Commodity revenues | 832 | 2.8 | 736 | 2.4 |
| Other income: Related to securities business* | 4,969 | 16.8 | 7,024 | 22.6 |
| Unrelated to securities business | 1,209 | 4.1 | 1,785 | 5.7 |
| Gross income | $29,542 | 100.0% | $31,148 | 100.0% |

*Fees for investment advice and counsel, service charges and custodian fees, dividends and interest on term investments, and miscellaneous other income.

SOURCE: *Fact Book, 1985*, New York Stock Exchange, 1986.

industry data. Not only can these firms change policies rapidly since they deal in efficient markets, but they may also change (or continue to carry) significantly different reporting policies.

## APPENDIX TO CHAPTER 2

### Classified NYSE Carrying Firms to Be Used in the 1981 Staff Report

National full-line firms:

Bache Halsey Stuart Shields, Inc.

Becker (A. G.), Incorporated

Drexel Burnham Lambert, Incorporated

Edwards (A. G.) & Sons, Inc.

Hutton, (E. F.) & Company Inc.

Merrill Lynch, Pierce, Fenner & Smith, Inc.

Paine, Webber, Jackson & Curtis, Inc.

Shearson/American Express, Inc.

Smith Barney, Harris Upham & Co., Incorporated
Thomson McKinnon Securities Inc.
Dean Witter Reynolds Inc.

Large investment banking houses:
Bear, Stearns & Co. Inc.
Dillon, Read & Co. Inc.
First Boston Corporation (The)
Goldman, Sachs & Co.
Kidder, Peabody & Co., Incorporated
Lazard Frères & Co.
Lehman Brothers Kuhn Loeb, Inc.
Morgan Stanley & Co., Incorporated
Salomon Brothers Inc.
Wertheim & Co., Inc.

# 3

# The Investment Banking Industry: Mid-1980s

SEC surveys of the industry ceased in 1981, the last year of a congressional mandate. Under the Security Act Amendments of 1975, the SEC was required to follow the fate of the broker-dealer industry to assess the damage, if any, caused by the fully negotiated trading commissions instituted on May 1, 1975. Since the industry did not disappear following that mandated competition—as some had feared—the surveys were stopped. This leaves the analyst with a complicated chore: trying to replace a uniform reporting system (one hopes) that included financial statements of corporations *and* partnerships.

## SOME ACCOUNTING PRELIMINARIES

The industry numbers the SEC derived from FOCUS accounts prior to 1981 appear comparable and consistent. With the development of many financial innovations since that time, however, coverage and comparability may be somewhat doubtful.

Consider further that the financial environment of rapid deregulation and more intense competition not only tended to

26

erase previously established market boundaries and market structures but also produced an expansion of activities of, say, investment banking firms into a much broader range of financial services. Fitting the data for new activities into the same definitions of financial activities would require arbitrary decisions by the reporting employees attempting to squeeze new security products into the old definitions of activity. Accordingly, in the first section below, I set some orders of magnitude for the major firms engaged in the investment banking business.

## FINANCIAL STATEMENT ANALYSIS?

The question mark in the heading suggests that analyzing data for financial-services firms can become very complicated. Furthermore, various financial innovations may involve off balance sheet transactions (e.g., interest-rate swaps).

Outside observers are as disadvantaged as federal regulators or even internal management. Consider the level of understanding of real-time numbers necessary for management to assess the firm's own rates of return for various activities. Such analysis would require, first, an unequivocal statement of the denominator of the ratio, namely, the size and the structure of the firm's capital. Further, in 1975, the SEC (1) adopted a uniform net capital rule, (2) established minimum net capital requirements as well as debt/equity guidelines, and (3) set criteria for debt subordination agreements and the requirements relating to consolidation of subsidiaries.

Taking the last point first, previously free-standing firms began to combine with other institutions to make, by merger or takeover, a smaller number of very large financial-services institutions. Financial conglomerates such as American Express or nationwide retailers such as Sears or large insurance firms such as Prudential have become parent organizations of investment banking firms.[1] This further complicates attempts at comparing the remaining free-standing firms with composite firms, even using the broadest definition of the investment banking industry. Finally, and most importantly, because

---

[1] Prudential/Bache; Sears/Dean Witter; Shearson, Lehman Brothers,/ American Express.

many major firms still maintain the partnership type of organization (see data on Goldman, Sachs below), they publish only partial data and only on those dates for which partial balance sheet information is required. For better or worse, the following data represent the best possible estimate of the industry's capital for year-end 1984.[2]

As shown in Table 3–1 the total equity share of capital backing the broker-dealer operations of the major firms shown came to about $7 billion at year-end 1984.[3] For the industry, this amount slightly exceeds the 1984 market value of Citicorp's equity or the combined equity market values of J. P. Morgan & Co. ($4.3 billion) and Bankers Trust Co. ($2.4 billion). The current equity valuation of the industry's major firms is still the equivalent of the largest (or of two large) money center banks.

To see how diverse are the asset and liability structures of the various major firms, consider the impact of resale-repurchase agreements on total assets/liabilities (see Table 3–2).

For Salomon Brothers, for example, total assets are boosted to $48 billion by nearly $17 billion from resale agreements. Liabilities are similarly swollen by repurchase agreements. On the other hand, for Merrill Lynch, the fact that ML government securities are *not* consolidated (unlike Salomon's statements) omits $7.4 billion from resale agreements. This discussion not only points out differences in accounting procedures but also emphasizes that different major firms engage in vastly different proportions of the same activities. As a result of both factors, Merrill's assets in the statement shown appear to be one quarter the size of Salomon's! (Compare these data with figures on capital in Table 3–1.)

Further differences in the meaning of balance sheet data may occur in spite of the availability of the AICPA's draft audit guide for broker-dealers. For example, First Boston uses trade-date accounting (as opposed to settlement date); according to First Boston's management, a shift to settlement-day accounting would lower balance sheet asset and liability totals by about 40 percent while leaving income statement data unaf-

---

[2] These data are based on an analysis written by Samuel G. Liss of Salomon Brothers entitled: "Security Brokers: A Glimpse at the Topic of Capital," May 13, 1985.

[3] This compares with total equity capital for 1981 of *all* full-line and large investment banks of $4.5 billion.

**TABLE 3–1**
Security Brokers—Capital Rankings, December 1984 (dollars in millions)

| | Consolidated | | | Broker-Dealer | | | Regulatory | | Number of Employees* |
|---|---|---|---|---|---|---|---|---|---|
| | Total Capital | Total Equity | Long-Term Debt | Total Capital | Total Equity | Subordinated Liabilities | Net Capital | Excess Capital | |
| Merrill Lynch & Co. Inc. | $4,242 | $2,079 | $2,163 | $1,488 | $1,026 | $462 | $611 | $490 | 42,232 |
| Phibro Salomon Brothers Inc. | 3,057 | 2,406 | 651 | 1,577 | 1,383 | 194 | 615 | 455 | 3,293 |
| Shearson Lehman Brothers | 1,915 | 1,029 | 886 | — | — | — | 368 | 317 | 15,293 |
| Dean Witter Financial Services | 1,162 | 937 | 225 | 758 | 608 | 150 | 171 | 134 | 18,840 |
| E. F. Hutton Group Inc. | 1,020 | 638 | 382 | 612 | 463 | 149 | 166 | 126 | 16,842 |
| Goldman, Sachs & Co.† | — | — | — | 859 | 585 | 274 | 587 | 568 | 3,903 |
| The First Boston Corporation | 659 | 463 | 196 | 527 | 380 | 147 | 318 | 302 | 2,709 |
| Prudential-Bache Sec. Inc. | — | — | — | 618 | 394 | 224 | 154 | 108 | 12,870 |
| Paine Webber Group Inc. | 568 | 325 | 243 | 426 | 324 | 102 | 131‡ | 29‡ | 10,978 |
| Drexel Burnham Lambert Gr. | — | — | — | 504 | 372 | 132 | 133 | 118 | 6,543 |
| Bear, Stearns & Co. | — | — | — | 463 | 325 | 138 | 353 | 318 | 3,920 |
| Morgan Stanley & Co. Inc. | — | — | — | 355 | 275 | 80 | 94 | 87 | 3,084 |

*Institutional Investor magazine.
†As of November 30, 1984.
‡Paine Webber required by debt covenants to maintain net capital of not less than 7 percent of aggregate debit items.
SOURCE: Company filings.

**TABLE 3-2**
Year-End 1984 Broker-Dealer Balance Sheets (dollars in millions)

| Assets | Merrill Lynch, Pierce Fenner & Smith Inc. | Shearson Lehman Brothers Inc. | Dean Witter, Reynolds Inc. | E. F. Hutton & Co., Inc. | Prudential Bache Secur. Inc. | Paine Webber Inc. | Salomon Brothers Inc. | Goldman, Sachs & Co. | The First Boston Corporation | Drexel Burnham Lambert Inc. | Bear, Stearns & Co. | Morgan Stanley & Co. |
|---|---|---|---|---|---|---|---|---|---|---|---|---|
| Cash | $ 118 | $ 761 | $ 79 | $ 36 | $ 181 | $ 41 | $ 37 | $ 10 | $ 9 | $ 103 | $ 9 | $ 26 |
| Cash segregated under regulations | 33 | 290 | 123 | 141 | 97 | 69 | 12 | 26 | 398 | 69 | 61 | — |
| Securities owned (at market): | | | | | | | | | | | | |
| U.S. gov. & fed. agencies | 667 | 4,367 | 815 | 1,282 | 1,807 | 955 | 20,978 | 6,526 | 4,275 | 440 | 2,658 | 859 |
| Municipal debt | 915 | — | 281 | 1,148 | 567 | 200 | 564 | 103 | 562 | 192 | 95 | — |
| BAs, CDs, commercial paper | 45 | 2,424 | 998 | 768 | 383 | 697 | 3,570 | 922 | 3,335 | 1,146 | 1,293 | 1,275 |
| Corporate debt | 1,846 | 818 | 139 | 1,092 | 858 | 243 | 3,494 | 2,067 | 1,339 | 826 | — | 1,083 |
| Equities | — | 471 | 127 | — | — | 596 | 445 | — | — | — | — | — |
| Exchangeable securities | — | — | — | — | — | — | 18 | — | — | — | — | 95* |
| Total securities owned | 3,472 | 8,151 | 2,361 | 4,290 | 2,615 | 2,472 | 29,068 | 9,618 | 9,511 | 2,605 | 4,045 | 3,313 |
| Resale agreements | 136† | 4,913 | 7,127 | 6,778 | 6,531 | 2,879 | 16,866 | 4,939 | 13,832 | 2,720 | 8,899 | 7,222 |
| Receivable from clients | 5,578 | 2,314 | 1,651 | 2,277 | 1,924 | 1,348 | 801 | 5,047 | 1,027 | 659 | 1,443 | 259 |
| Receivable from brokers-dealers | 548 | 2,200 | 603 | 1,516 | 1,182 | 793 | 1,497 | 983 | 243 | 953 | 1,372 | 1,024 |
| Fixed assets | 506 | 221 | 111 | 154 | — | 75 | 70 | — | 66 | — | 37 | 44 |
| Other | 1,750 | 11,396 | 265 | 262 | 643 | 467 | 24 | 442 | 239 | 147 | 74 | 26 |
| Goodwill | — | 368 | 231 | — | — | — | 188 | — | — | — | — | — |
| Total assets | $12,142 | $22,509 | $12,552 | $15,455 | $13,173 | $8,144 | $48,563 | $21,065 | $25,325 | $7,256 | $15,943 | $12,027 |

## Liabilities

| | | | | | | | | | | | | |
|---|---|---|---|---|---|---|---|---|---|---|---|---|
| Bank loans | $ 131 | $ 3,442 | $ 745 | $ 832 | $ 1,938 | $ 831 | — | — | $ 1,848 | $1,083 | $ 623 | $ 904§ |
| Repurchase agreements | 503† | 7,798 | 6,234 | 7,746 | 7,328 | 3,015 | 35,499‡ | 12,798‡ | 17,034 | 2,878 | 6,611 | 7,726 |
| Drafts and checks payable | 4,605 | — | 596 | 405 | 277 | — | — | — | — | 164 | 59 | — |
| Securities sold (at market): | | | | | | | | | | | | |
| U.S. gov. & agencies | 161 | 2,434 | 2,233 | 1,707 | — | 1,331 | 7,620 | — | — | 123 | 4,823 | 797 |
| Municipal | 80 | — | 11 | 86 | — | 32 | 4 | — | — | — | 15 | — |
| Corporate | 668 | 123 | 29 | 513 | — | 47 | 709 | — | — | 75 | — | 500 |
| Equities | — | 196 | 111 | — | — | 506 | 208 | — | — | 316 | — | 258* |
| Exchangeable securities | — | — | — | — | — | — | 17 | — | — | — | — | — |
| Total securities sold (at market) | 909 | 2,998 | 2,384 | 2,306 | 221 | 1,907 | 8,557 | 5,347 | 4,178 | 514 | 5,336 | 1,555 |
| Payable to clients | 2,758 | 1,098 | 733 | 1,462 | 996 | 444 | 725 | 1,278 | 721 | 430 | 1,230 | 355 |
| Payable to brokers and dealers | 400 | 2,075 | 646 | 908 | 1,447 | 853 | 1,401 | 171 | 475 | 828 | 1,324 | 773 |
| Other | 852 | 2,713 | 352 | 174 | 349 | 320 | 804 | 403 | 267 | 857 | 248 | 354 |
| Accrued comp. | 496 | — | 76 | 137 | — | 112 | — | — | — | — | 49 | — |
| Dividends and interest payable | — | — | — | 86 | — | 87 | — | — | 149 | — | — | — |
| Income taxes payable | — | — | — | 26 | — | 41 | — | — | 106 | — | — | — |
| Payable to parent | — | 1,005 | 28 | 763 | — | 108 | — | — | 20 | — | — | — |
| Subordinated liabilities | 462 | 867 | 150 | 149 | 224 | 102 | 194 | 274 | 147 | 132 | 138 | 80 |
| Stockholders' equity | 1,026 | 1,029 | 608 | 463 | 394 | 324 | 1,383 | 585‖ | 380# | 372 | 325 | 275 |
| Total liabilities and stockholders' equity | $12,142 | $22,509 | $12,552 | $15,455 | $13,173 | $8,144 | $48,563 | $21,065 | $25,325 | $7,256 | $15,943 | $12,027 |

*Commodities.

†Merrill Lynch Government Securities Inc. is not consolidated in the broker-dealer category. Resale and repurchase agreements totaled $7.4 billion and $9.7 billion, respectively, at year-end 1984.

‡Includes bank loans.

§All short-term borrowings.

‖Excludes reserve for partners' income taxes of $209 million, all data as of November 30, 1984.

#Excludes any recognition of Financiere Credit Suisse–First Boston.

fected. And finally, as noted earlier, the accounting treatment for new financial vehicles (for example, interest rate swaps) is far from uniform. Any rates of return for the same firm through time, or between brokers at any one time, must be carefully reviewed with respect to reporting comparability.

## OUTPUT CATEGORIES

Assessing gross revenues causes still other problems. Take the example of NYSE share volume and the presumptive revenues generated by secondary trade commissions.

As NYSE stock trading becomes more institutionalized, unit revenues to brokers will decline since institutional commissions in 1984 came to about 5 to 10 cents per share, whereas retail commissions brought in from 20 to 25 cents per share. In 1980 about one third of trades were in units of 10,000 or larger share lots, but in 1984–85 that proportion had risen to about 50 percent. Looked at slightly differently, in 1980 a 60-million-share day would have brought all broker-dealers the following income composition:

*1980*

| | | |
|---|---|---|
| Institutional share | = ⅓, or 20 million shares at 10 cents | = $ 2.0 million |
| Retail share | = ⅔, or <u>40</u> million shares at 25 cents | = <u>$10.0</u> million |
| | 60 million | $12.0 million |

*1984*

| | | |
|---|---|---|
| Institutional share | = ½, or 30 million shares at 10 cents | = $ 3.0 million |
| Retail share | = ½, or <u>30</u> million shares at 25 cents | = <u>$ 7.5</u> million |
| | 60 million | $10.5 million |

Or, to put the same relationships in a different light, the commission dollars that broker-dealers could earn in 1980 from a 60-million-share-day would now require a volume of about 70 million shares. These structural changes make commission income less predictable, especially for firms doing a primarily institutional business or even for firms doing the (changing) market average mix of retail/institutional trades.

### Interest Income

Broker-dealers who understand cash management principles can create a powerful source of income, especially from retail transactions in a stock rally. That leverage works best for firms that do not depend on bank loans and, instead, use fixed and convertible debt and commercial paper to fund their call loans to customers. Again, reporting styles vary. For some, statements may report gross interest income and expenses and may exclude income from resale agreements, client accounts, and portfolio positions. Likewise, on the expense side, statements may exclude interest costs related to repurchase agreements, commercial paper, bank loans, and other types of debt.[4] Since activity and profit cycles may produce different levels of interest revenues and expenses, as well as significant differences in spread between income and expense, even a historically consistent treatment by each firm will generate different results in any comparison between them. Especially for some of the largest firms, interest income represents a major (if not an overwhelmingly important) source of income. For Merrill Lynch, for example, interest income in the first nine months of 1984 was more than four times greater than the firm's total pre-tax income for the same period (see Table 3–3). In three of the five preceding years, moreover, interest income represented virtually all of Merrill's pre-tax income. Similar results are obtained for E. F. Hutton and Paine Webber, whereas for First Boston, an institutional firm, interest income represents a lower but nonetheless significant share of pre-tax income for all of the periods shown.

## HOW DO ANALYSTS VALUE INVESTMENT BANKING OR BROKER-DEALER FIRMS?

As these firms increasingly turn to the corporate form of organization and away from the partnership form, how can their stock price be evaluated? Or in the broader context, how do potential corporate clients select the investment firm they will use to float their new issue(s) or to negotiate an acquisition or a divestiture? To take the last point first, investment banking firms purchase tombstone lineage in major newspapers to boost name recognition. Publications such as *Institutional Investor* publish quarterly scores on underwriting performance that are calculated in the same old way even though

---

[4]E. F. Hutton, for example, *includes* lease financing flows on income and expense statements, while other firms do not.

**TABLE 3–3**

Security Brokers—Interest Income Summary, 1979–1984 (dollars in billions)

|  | 1984 | 1983 | 1982 | 1981 | 1980 | 1979 |
|---|---|---|---|---|---|---|
| **E. F. Hutton:** | | | | | | |
| Net interest income* | $136 | $117 | $94 | $117 | $96 | $50 |
| As a percentage of | | | | | | |
| pre-tax income | NM† | 64% | 70% | 94% | 62% | 72% |
| Net income | $53 | $111 | $81 | $79 | $83 | $37 |
| **First Boston:** | | | | | | |
| Net interest income | $57 | $43 | $55 | $23 | $5 | — |
| As a percentage of | | | | | | |
| pre-tax income‡ | 49% | 40% | 36% | 30% | 10% | — |
| Net income | $64 | $65 | $81 | $40 | $28 | $17 |
| **Merrill Lynch & Co.:** | | | | | | |
| Net interest income | $343 | $357 | $337 | $324 | $252 | $177 |
| As a percentage of | | | | | | |
| pre-tax income | NM† | 91% | 61% | 97% | 70% | 92% |
| Net income | $95 | $226 | $309 | $203 | $201 | $117 |
| **Paine Webber:** | | | | | | |
| Net interest income | $86 | $91 | $95 | $111 | $27 | $35 |
| As a percentage of | | | | | | |
| pre-tax income | NM† | 51% | 139% | 257% | NM† | 127% |
| Net income | $13 | $91 | $36 | $24 | $1 | $16 |
| **Shearson Lehman:** | | | | | | |
| Net interest income | $79 | $121 | $136 | $165 | $111 | NA |
| As a percentage of | | | | | | |
| pre-tax income | 47% | 34% | 60% | 76% | 96% | NA |
| Net income | $105 | $174 | $124 | $112 | $66 | NA |
| **A. G. Edwards:** | | | | | | |
| Net interest income | $37 | $35 | $34 | $42 | $33 | $20 |
| As a percentage of | | | | | | |
| pre-tax income | 80% | 67% | 55% | 96% | 75% | 69% |
| Net income | $27 | $29 | $34 | $25 | $24 | $16 |

*Includes lease and credit activities, but excludes investment tax credits.

†Exceeds 100 percent.

‡Computation excludes Financiere Credit Suisse-First Boston.

NA = Not available.

NM = Not meaningful.

the 415 rule has diminished the importance of the selling group's share of syndicate operations. Further, announcements are bought regarding merger, takeover, and divestiture activities and consultations—all, perhaps, because this type of marketing is expected to produce more direct results for the investment banker. And, as noted, financial statement data are somewhat ambiguous. As Samuel G. Liss of Salomon Brothers notes, a close reading of each firm's proxies, tenders, and prospectuses may be a more fertile and useful ground for real data regarding investment banking-type earnings from, say, merger and acquisition-type services than the firm's advertising or even its published financial statements.

## MAJOR SOURCES OF INCOME AND EXPENSE

The following data illustrate the two different types of firms—institutional and retail—into which the industry tends to organize itself (although other categories are found).

First Boston, an institutional firm, is a by-product of the Glass-Steagall Act; it was formed in 1934 out of the security affiliates of the First National Bank of Boston (hence the name) and Chase Harris Forbes (an affiliate of Chase National Bank). In 1946 Mellon Securities Corporation was merged into First Boston. (See Table 3–4 for First Boston's operating record.)

First Boston has become an important factor in two investment banking areas: (1) mergers and acquisitions and (2) Eurobond (international) financing.

Table 3–5 indicates some of First Boston's major merger/takeover deals in 1984. Fees and revenues from those deals came to about $40 million (nearly 20 percent) of total investment banking revenues and were produced by 75 professionals.

First Boston's powerful presence in the international bond markets is based on a partnership started in 1978 with Credit Suisse, one of Switzerland's big-three banks. Credit Suisse had previously been associated with White Weld until that firm was acquired by Merrill Lynch. The venture with First Boston is called Financiere Credit Suisse-First Boston (FCS-FB); it operates a London-based merchant bank that has been the largest underwriter of Eurodollar issues. By emphasizing the floating-rate note market and "bought deals," FCS-FB's

TABLE 3-4
The First Boston Corporation—Operating Record, 1980-85 (dollars in millions)

|  | 1984 | 1983 | 1982 | 1981 | 1980 |
|---|---|---|---|---|---|
| Total interest revenue | $1,506 | $1,010 | $951 | $578 | $368 |
| Total interest expense | $1,449 | $ 967 | $896 | $555 | $363 |
| Net interest income | $ 57 | $ 43 | $ 55 | $ 23 | $ 5 |
| Percentage of net interest to pre-tax income | 49% | 40% | 36% | 30% | 10% |
| Other pre-tax earnings | $ 59 | $ 65 | $ 99 | $ 53 | $ 46 |
| Percentage of other earnings to pre-tax income | 51% | 60% | 64% | 70% | 90% |
| Pre-tax income | $ 116 | $ 108 | $154 | $ 76 | $ 51 |
| Tax | $ 52 | $ 43 | $ 73 | $ 36 | $ 23 |
| Net income | $ 80 | $ 80 | $ 93 | $ 46 | $ 34 |

TABLE 3-5
First Boston's Major Merger/Takeover Deals, 1984

Texaco/Getty
Broken Hill Proprietary/Utah International
P.A.C.E./City Investing
American General/Petrolane
Texas Eastern/Petrolane
American Medical International/Lifemark
Nestle/Carnation (1985 transaction)
American Express/IDS
Bank of Montreal/Harris Bancorp
Unimar/Enstar

share in lead-managed underwriting abroad was raised from about 5 percent to 20 percent in five years. As Table 3-6 indicates, First Boston's 1979 and 1980 U.S. flotations and its international taxable issues were about equal in size, but since then the volume of international flotations has been about double that of domestic. The statements of income and expense shown (Table 3-7) suggest that investment banking revenues and income from principal transactions are, by far, the major sources of income while, on the expense side, compensation and benefits constitute about two thirds of the

**TABLE 3–6**
The First Boston Corporation and Subsidiaries—Underwriting and
Placement Summary, 1979–83 (dollars in billions*)

|  | 1983 | 1982 | 1981 | 1980 | 1979 |
|---|---|---|---|---|---|
| Taxable public issues managed or co-managed: |  |  |  |  |  |
| U.S. corporate (negotiated) | $17 | $14 | $ 9 | $10 | $ 4 |
| U.S. corporate (sealed bidding) | 1 | 2 | 2 | 2 | 3 |
| International† | 34 | 35 | 16 | 9 | 9 |
| Total taxable public issues | 52 | 51 | 27 | 21 | 16 |
| Direct placements‡ | 6 | 2 | 1 | 2 | 4 |
| Total taxable issues | $58 | $53 | $28 | $23 | $20 |
| Tax-exempt issues managed:§ |  |  |  |  |  |
| Negotiated ‖ | $13 | $14 | $ 9 | $ 8 | $ 6 |
| Competitive | 10 | 10 | 10 | 10 | 9 |
| Total tax-exempt issues | $23 | $24 | $19 | $18 | $15 |
| Total offerings | $81 | $77 | $47 | $41 | $35 |
| Total number of issues | 768 | 753 | 505 | 503 | 468 |

*Except number of issues.
†Includes Yankee bonds.
‡Includes PROJECT CLUB LOAN℠ transactions and Title XI placements.
§Includes short-term note issues.
‖Includes direct placements.

total. It is interesting to compare these figures to those for a large retail broker, E. F. Hutton.

Hutton, formed in 1904, is one of the oldest and largest brokerage firms in the United States. Like other firms with investment banking capacity, it has also diversified into other types of financial activity—primarily life insurance and leasing/credit operations. The contributions made to pre-tax income by all of these activities over the recent past are shown in Table 3–8. As the table suggests, investment services produce a major share of income in good times, but the insurance sector, in particular, adds a degree of stability to the totals over the years.

Table 3–9 shows that Hutton's income and expenses reflect the volatility of the retail business as well as the disadvantages of relating some major personnel expense factors such as commission sharing to volatile commission income. On the other hand, the firm's balance sheet appears to be quite liquid, with relatively little bank debt. (A relatively volatile income structure should require more liquidity on the balance sheet).

**TABLE 3-7**

## THE FIRST BOSTON CORPORATION
### Statement of Consolidated Income and Retained Earnings,
### For the Years 1980–1985E
#### (dollars in millions)

| | 1985E | Percent Change | 1984 | Percent Change | 1983 | Percent Change | 1982 | Percent Change | 1981 | Percent Change | 1980 | Percent Change |
|---|---|---|---|---|---|---|---|---|---|---|---|---|
| **Revenues:** | | | | | | | | | | | | |
| Principal transactions...... | $255 | 30% | $196 | 11.1% | $177 | (24.8)% | $235 | 112.1% | $111 | 11.8% | $99 | 59.0% |
| Investment banking ........ | 255 | 16 | 220 | 11.1 | 198 | 31.7 | 150 | 26.0 | 119 | 81.7 | 66 | 29.3 |
| Commissions............. | 100 | 33 | 75 | 5.2 | 72 | 51.1 | 47 | 36.9 | 35 | 7.3 | 32 | 57.3 |
| Interest and dividend income (net) ......... | 50 | (15) | 59 | 35.1 | 43 | (22.0) | 56 | NM | 23 | NM | 5 | NM |
| Other revenues .......... | 20 | 25 | 16 | (39.6) | 26 | NM | 11 | NM | 4 | NM | 12 | 52.1 |
| Total revenues ........ | 680 | 20 | 566 | 9.8 | 515 | 29.9 | 499 | 71.2 | 292 | 36.1 | 214 | 52.7 |
| **Expenses:** | | | | | | | | | | | | |
| Emp. comp. and benefits .... | 340 | 14 | 298 | 5.0 | 283 | 13.7 | 249 | 66.8 | 149 | 36.8 | 109 | 52.3% |
| Occup. and equip. rental .... | 63 | 35 | 47 | 36.1 | 34 | 23.1 | 28 | 83.7 | 15 | 8.2 | 14 | 35.2 |
| Brokerage, clearing, and exch. fees............. | 35 | 25 | 28 | 17.8 | 24 | 54.4 | 16 | 27.0 | 12 | 17.4 | 10 | 47.6 |
| Communications........... | 21 | 25 | 17 | 30.6 | 13 | 29.0 | 10 | 23.2 | 8 | 17.1 | 7 | 5.3 |
| Other oper. expense ........ | 67 | 15 | 58 | 11.7 | 52 | 23.6 | 42 | 38.7 | 30 | 34.8 | 23 | 23.6 |
| Total expenses ........ | 527 | 18 | 448 | 10.1 | 407 | 18.0 | 345 | 60.1 | 216 | 32.0 | 163 | 43.1 |

| | | | | | | | | | | | | |
|---|---|---|---|---|---|---|---|---|---|---|---|---|
| Income before income taxes and equity in earnings of affiliates | 153 | 31 | 117 | 8.5 | 108 | (29.7) | 154 | 102.8 | 76 | 49.5 | 51 | 95.0 |
| Income taxes | 72 | — | 53 | — | 42 | — | 73 | — | 36 | — | 23 | — |
| Effective tax rate | 47.0% | | 45.3% | | 39.2% | | 47.3% | | 47.9% | | 45.1% | |
| Income before equity in earnings of affiliates | 81 | 27 | 64 | (2.4) | 66 | (18.9) | 81 | 105.1 | 40 | 43.8 | 28 | 91.7 |
| Equity in earnings of affiliates, net of deferred taxes | 18 | 20 | 15 | 7.2 | 14 | 20.8 | 12 | 76.9 | 7 | 5.5 | 6 | 111.6 |
| Net income | $99 | 24% | $80 | (0.7)% | $80 | (13.8)% | $93 | 101.0% | $46 | 36.6% | $34 | 95.1% |
| Shares outstanding† | 14.2 | — | 14.2 | — | 13.8 | — | 13.0 | — | 11.5 | — | 9.9 | — |
| Earnings per share† | $7.00 | 21.1% | $5.87 | (4.1)% | $6.12 | (15.0)% | $7.20 | 76.0% | $4.09 | 34.5% | $3.04 | 92.4% |
| Total assets | $26 | — | $26 | — | $22 | 27.0% | $17 | 68.0% | $10 | 71.3% | $6 | 23.0% |
| Stockholders' equity | 513 | 11 | 462 | 19.7 | 386 | 42.7 | 271 | 36.5 | 199 | 28.5 | 154 | 20.5 |

*Except total assets, which is in billions, and per-share amounts.

†Fully diluted.

E = Estimate.

N = Not meaningful.

TABLE 3–8

E. F. Hutton Group, Inc.—Operating Record, 1980–85 (dollars in millions)

| | 1984 | 1983 | 1982 | 1981 | 1980 |
|---|---|---|---|---|---|
| Interest revenue: | | | | | |
| Resale agreements | $459 | $302 | $223 | $276 | $166 |
| Client accounts | 162 | 121 | 114 | 177 | 133 |
| Firm positions | 191 | 106 | 65 | 71 | 74 |
| Lease financing* | 60 | 52 | 44 | 30 | — |
| Other | 102 | 52 | 44 | 25 | 8 |
| Total interest revenue | $974 | $632 | $490 | $580 | $380 |
| Interest expense: | | | | | |
| Repurchase agreements | $549 | $344 | $246 | $320 | $211 |
| Commercial paper | 124 | 58 | 52 | 31 | — |
| Notes payable | 39 | 28 | 23 | 14 | 1 |
| Bank loans | 33 | 21 | 9 | 32 | 27 |
| Subordinated liabilities | 12 | 14 | 15 | 19 | 8 |
| Debentures | 4 | 3 | 9 | 9 | 2 |
| Other | 77 | 46 | 42 | 37 | 35 |
| Total interest expense | $838 | $515 | $396 | $463 | $284 |
| Net interest income | $136 | $117 | $ 94 | $117 | $ 96 |
| Percentage of net interest income to pre-tax income | — | 64% | 70% | 94% | 62% |
| Other pre-tax earnings | $(111) | $ 67 | $ 41 | $ 7 | $ 60 |
| Percentage of other earnings to pre-tax income | — | 36% | 30% | 6% | 38% |
| Pre-tax income | $ 25 | $184 | $135 | $124 | $156 |
| Tax | $ (27) | $ 73 | $ 54 | $ 45 | $ 73 |
| Net income | $ 53 | $111 | $ 81 | $ 79 | $ 83 |

*Excludes investment tax credits.

†Data are being restated for sale of credit operation.

A few conclusions may be drawn from the foregoing summary.

1. Each investment banking firm has built a structure of particular activities for itself.
2. That structure is subject to change over time.
3. No two firms will do exactly the same things in the same proportions.
4. Although all financial statements may start from similar reporting and analytical principles, they are not always comparable.
5. An identifiable industry does exist, and some major activities are common to all.

**TABLE 3–9**

## THE E. F. HUTTON GROUP, INC., AND SUBSIDIARIES
### Consolidated Balance Sheet
### For the Years 1982–1984
(dollars in millions)

| | 1984 | | | 31 December 1983 | 31 December 1982 |
|---|---|---|---|---|---|
| | 31 December | 30 September | 30 June | | |
| **Assets** | | | | | |
| Cash subject to immediate withdrawal | $67 | $67 | $34 | $42 | $33 |
| Amounts segregated under federal commodity and other regulations: | | | | | |
| Cash | 119 | 109 | 74 | 112 | 127 |
| Securities at market value | 22 | 21 | 22 | 23 | 27 |
| Securities purchased under agreements to resell | 6,778 | 6,118 | 6,311 | 5,496 | 2,040 |
| Securities at market value: | | | | | |
| U.S. government | 1,307 | 1,222 | 984 | 1,553 | 1,033 |
| Certificates of deposit | 801 | 851 | 682 | 557 | 480 |
| State and municipal | 1,148 | 231 | 188 | 608 | 265 |
| Corporate | 1,099 | 878 | 595 | 589 | 343 |
| Receivable from clients | 2,277 | 1,776 | 1,709 | 1,851 | 1,153 |
| Investments of insurance subsidiaries | 1,174 | 944 | 828 | 421 | 634 |
| Receivable from brokers or dealers | 1,525 | 895 | 822 | 637 | 456 |
| Net finance receivables | 739 | 647 | 609 | 580 | 290 |
| Other investments | 100 | 76 | 70 | 95 | 84 |
| Deferred insurance policy acquisition costs | 120 | 85 | 78 | 66 | 46 |
| Equipment, leasehold improvements and property at cost | 209 | 186 | — | 142 | 113 |
| Other assets | 669 | 437 | 423 | 393 | 199 |
| Total assets | $18,153 | $14,544 | $13,602 | $13,164 | $7,321 |

**TABLE 3-9** *(concluded)*

## Consolidated Balance Sheet
### For the Years 1982–1984

| Liabilities and Stockholders' Equity | 1984 | | | 31 December 1984 | 31 December 1982 |
|---|---|---|---|---|---|
| | 31 December | 30 September | 30 June | | |
| Bank loans | $847 | $186 | $145 | $585 | $96 |
| Commercial paper | 1,272 | 1,257 | 1,134 | 1,048 | 623 |
| Drafts and checks payable | 413 | 236 | 205 | 446 | 186 |
| Notes payable | 271 | 259 | 266 | 246 | 174 |
| Securities sold under agreements to repurchase | 7,746 | 6,381 | 5,534 | 5,551 | 2,249 |
| Market value of securities sold but not yet purchased: | | | | | |
| U.S. government | 1,707 | 1,592 | 2,115 | 1,631 | 1,071 |
| State and municipal | 86 | 25 | 43 | 53 | 24 |
| Corporate | 513 | 491 | 344 | 313 | 279 |
| Payable to brokers or dealers | 908 | 873 | 835 | 619 | 793 |
| Future insurance policy benefits | 1,161 | 912 | 802 | 368 | 591 |
| Payable to clients | 1,462 | 844 | 714 | 959 | 289 |
| Accrued compensation | 148 | 101 | 82 | 155 | 97 |
| Floating-rate notes due 1994 | 200 | 200 | 100 | — | 30 |
| Sinking-fund debentures, 12% due 2005 | 30 | 30 | 30 | 30 | 60 |
| Subordinated liabilities of subsidiaries | 152 | 146 | 140 | 129 | 103 |
| Other liabilities | 600 | 396 | 521 | 445 | 241 |
| Total liabilities | 17,514 | 13,929 | 13,008 | 12,577 | 6,906 |
| Stockholders' equity: | | | | | |
| Common stock | $26 | $26 | $26 | $25 | $18 |
| Additional paid-in capital | 140 | 136 | 132 | 120 | 46 |
| Retained earnings | 477 | 458 | 440 | 445 | 353 |
| Cumulative translation | (5) | (4) | (3) | (3) | (2) |
| Total stockholders' equity | 638 | 616 | 594 | 587 | 415 |
| Total liabilities and stockholders' equity | $18,152 | $14,545 | $13,602 | $13,164 | $7,321 |

## DREXEL BURNHAM LAMBERT

Since 1983, the operations and policies of the firm of Drexel Burnham Lambert illustrate the conclusions indicated on page 40: it has leveraged its preeminent position in high-interest (or junk) bonds into a force for peer recognition. The example is most appropriate to its time; the use of junk bonds was triggered, and continues to be stimulated, by the megabuck takeover and merger waves of the mid 1980s (see Chapters 7 and 8). Beyond its underwriting of junk bonds, Drexel Burnham further built up its niche by a strenuous market-making effort in these same junk bonds (for discussion of market making see Chapter 4). The megabuck revenues thus earned have financed the acquisition of capital and personnel that have permitted Drexel Burnham to broaden its market-making services into more conventional areas of investment banking.

## MORGAN STANLEY & CO., INC.

As this book went to press, one of the last major firms still organized as a partnership, *Morgan Stanley,* moved to a corporate form of organization. As the prospectus cover in Figure 3–1 indicates, Morgan Stanley sold about 4½ million shares, or 20 percent of its authorized common stock that, at the offering price of 56½ per share, raised about a quarter of a billion dollars. The firm's management (managing directors and principals) own the remaining 81 percent of the common as well as all of the convertible preferred stock.

As in any other public offering, and in particular the stock of an investment banker who is also the lead underwriter of the syndicate selling the stock, the pricing of the new issue would carry certain conflicts of interest for that underwriter. In addition, as we indicated earlier, the complex mix of activities and revenues and the cyclical nature of the risks of the investment banking business make the valuation of that type of firm especially tricky. Under the provisions of Schedule E to the bylaws of the National Association of Securities Dealers, to which all broker-dealers (such as Morgan Stanley) belong, the offering price "can be no higher than that recommended by a 'qualified independent underwriter' meeting certain standards."[5] The "qualified independent underwriter(s)" used

---

[5]Citation is from Morgan Stanley prospectus, p. 55.

**FIGURE 3–1** _____

---

*PROSPECTUS*

## 4,500,000 Shares

# Morgan Stanley Group Inc.

### COMMON STOCK

All 4,500,000 Shares of Common Stock are being sold by the Company. Of such Shares, 2,900,000 Shares are being underwritten by U.S. Underwriters, and 1,600,000 Shares are being underwritten by International Underwriters. See "Underwriters". Prior to this offering, there has been no public market for the Common Stock. The initial public offering price has been determined by agreement between the Company and the Underwriters in accordance with the recommendation of "qualified independent underwriters", as required by the by-laws of the National Association of Securities Dealers, Inc. See "Underwriters" for a discussion of the factors considered in determining the offering price. The Company's Common Stock has been approved for listing on the New York Stock Exchange.

THESE SECURITIES HAVE NOT BEEN APPROVED OR DISAPPROVED BY THE SECURITIES AND EXCHANGE COMMISSION NOR HAS THE COMMISSION PASSED UPON THE ACCURACY OR ADEQUACY OF THIS PROSPECTUS.  ANY REPRESENTATION TO THE CONTRARY IS A CRIMINAL OFFENSE.

### PRICE $56½ A SHARE

| | Price to Public(1) | Underwriting Discounts and Commissions(1) | Proceeds to Company(2)(3) |
|---|---|---|---|
| Per Share ....................................... | $56.50 | $2.95 | $53.55 |
| Total (4) ....................................... | $252,922,500 | $11,947,500 | $240,975,000 |

(1) Up to 450,000 Shares are being reserved for sale to employees of the Company and their families at the initial public offering price less underwriting discounts and commissions.  In determining total price to public and underwriting discounts and commissions, it is assumed that all of such reserved Shares will be sold to such persons. See "Underwriters".

(2) Before deduction of expenses payable by the Company estimated at $1,940,000.

(3) Morgan Stanley & Co. Incorporated and Morgan Stanley International, wholly owned subsidiaries of the Company, have committed to purchase, as a U.S. Underwriter and an International Underwriter, respectively, an aggregate of 10.4% of the Shares on the same basis and at the same price as all other U.S. Underwriters and International Underwriters.  To the extent that part or all of such Shares are not resold by them at the initial public offering price, the funds derived by the Company from the offering will be reduced. See "Underwriters".

(4) The Company has granted to the U.S. Underwriters an option, exercisable within 30 days of the date hereof, to purchase up to 675,000 additional Shares at the price to public less underwriting discounts and commissions for the purpose of covering over-allotments, if any.  If the U.S. Underwriters exercise such option in full, the total price to public, underwriting discounts and commissions and proceeds to Company will be $291,060,000, $13,938,750 and $277,121,250, respectively. See "Underwriters".

The Shares are offered, subject to prior sale, when, as and if accepted by the U.S. Underwriters named herein and the International Underwriters and subject to approval of certain legal matters by Davis Polk & Wardwell, counsel for the U.S. Underwriters.  It is expected that the delivery of the certificates for the Shares will be made on or about March 31, 1986, at the offices of Morgan Stanley & Co. Incorporated, 55 Water Street, New York, New York, against payment therefor in New York funds.

**MORGAN STANLEY & CO.**
  *Incorporated*
  **BEAR, STEARNS & CO. INC.**

  **THE FIRST BOSTON CORPORATION**

  **GOLDMAN, SACHS & CO.**

   **MERRILL LYNCH CAPITAL MARKETS**

    **SALOMON BROTHERS INC**

     **SHEARSON LEHMAN BROTHERS INC.**

March 21, 1986

# FIGURE 3-2

## SELECTED CONSOLIDATED FINANCIAL DATA

The following selected consolidated financial data of the Company for the five years ended December 31, 1985 are derived from the Company's consolidated financial statements that have been examined by Arthur Young & Company, certified public accountants. The information set forth below should be read in conjunction with the Consolidated Financial Statements, related notes and other financial information included elsewhere in this Prospectus.

| | 1981 | 1982 | 1983 | 1984 | 1985 |
|---|---|---|---|---|---|
| | | | | Year Ended December 31, | |
| | | (In thousands of dollars, except per share amounts) | | | |
| **Income Statement:** | | | | | |
| Revenues: | | | | | |
| Investment banking | $ 159,284 | $ 172,863 | $ 212,247 | $ 266,870 | $ 423,515 |
| Principal transactions | 45,485 | 75,091 | 78,385 | 121,703 | 243,040 |
| Commissions | 76,662 | 95,994 | 131,133 | 130,129 | 154,360 |
| Interest and dividends | 345,248 | 362,647 | 415,005 | 794,858 | 937,995 |
| Asset management | 8,939 | 16,342 | 21,315 | 25,241 | 34,825 |
| Other | 1,396 | 2,481 | 1,466 | 1,683 | 1,167 |
| Total revenues | 637,014 | 725,418. | 859,551 | 1,340,484 | 1,794,902 |
| Expenses: | | | | | |
| Interest | 323,156 | 335,510 | 390,867 | 747,957 | 900,216 |
| Employee compensation and benefits | 145,857 | 191,442 | 253,747 | 304,504 | 421,473 |
| Occupancy and equipment rental | 24,040 | 32,619 | 38,177 | 51,658 | 79,092 |
| Brokerage, clearing and exchange fees | 10,222 | 13,874 | 22,818 | 31,472 | 45,480 |
| Communications | 12,000 | 15,860 | 20,146 | 28,815 | 39,159 |
| Business development | 11,074 | 12,434 | 17,756 | 25,452 | 35,725 |
| Professional services | 9,136 | 9,828 | 10,247 | 14,499 | 29,529 |
| Other | 11,993 | 21,126 | 19,634 | 30,393 | 60,938 |
| Total expenses | 547,478 | 632,693 | 773,392 | 1,234,750 | 1,611,612 |
| Income before income taxes | 89,536 | 92,725 | 86,159 | 105,734 | 183,290 |
| Income taxes | 41,642 | 42,072 | 35,003 | 44,526 | 77,440 |
| Net income | $ 47,894 | $ 50,653 | $ 51,156 | $ 61,208 | $ 105,850 |
| Pro forma net income per share(1) | 2.38 | 2.52 | 2.55 | 3.06 | 5.32 |
| **Balance Sheet:** | | | | | |
| Total assets | $3,184,261 | $4,868,863 | $7,442,043 | $13,053,504 | $15,794,107 |
| Total long-term debt(2) | 57,113 | 76,217 | 83,610 | 135,763 | 172,495 |
| Total liabilities(3) | 3,055,121 | 4,698,086 | 7,235,364 | 12,815,397 | 15,480,126 |
| Stockholders' equity | 129,140 | 170,777 | 206,679 | 238,107 | 313,981 |

(1) Pro forma net income per share in each year is calculated based on the number of shares of Common Stock outstanding at December 31, 1985 and after giving effect to the recapitalization. See Note 9 of Notes to Consolidated Financial Statements.

(2) Excludes current portion of long-term debt.

(3) Does not include commitments and contingencies. For a description of such commitments and contingencies at December 31, 1985, see Note 7 of Notes to Consolidated Financial Statements.

were those (other than Morgan Stanley) listed on the prospectus' cover page.

Since all of the major investment banking firms were involved in pricing the new issue, the price should have been close to the market. What happened, however, was an egregious example of "underpricing": on the first day of trading (March 21, 1986), the stock moved to 70 a share, rising as high as 74¼ during the day and closing at 71¼ a share, up 14¾, or better than 26 percent higher than the offering price!

This performance raises a number of questions:

a. Is it especially difficult to price an investment banking issue? (Perhaps)
b. Is it possible that the six firms who were "qualified underwriters" purposely priced on the low side? (Unlikely)
c. Is it difficult to price any new issue? (Very)
d. Are all new issues of investment bankers underpriced? (Not by 26 percent)

Morgan Stanley's major financial data are given in Figure 3–2 (taken from p. 11 of its prospectus). The structure of income and expense components shown there are similar to those of the industry generally (compare with Table 2–2). What may have made the stock particularly attractive to potential buyers is the ratio of pretax income to (book-value) equity: for 1985, for example, the book-value equity rate of return came to about 58 percent! This same information, of course, was available to the investment bankers who priced the stock. The jump in Morgan's new-issue price illustrates both the difficulty in valuing any investment banking firm and in pricing any new issue. The latter point will be discussed at length in Chapters 9 and 10.

# 4

## Investment Banking as Market Making in the Real World

Over the past decade academic research in finance has resulted in concepts that help explain market performance and, going deeper, the actions of market makers. To understand market functioning, it is necessary to understand how a security's price is influenced by the market process.

The efficient-market hypothesis is now widely accepted. While security markets are essential to permit trading between sellers and buyers, the security price information produced by the markets permits analysts to assess how new company information influences price formation. That by-product of securities markets, namely, price information, has recently been studied in some depth. Scholars doing research on price formation have examined how a market maker in a structured market—be he (or she) a floor trader, a specialist, a banker in a call market, and so on—is interposed between buyer and seller. If the market for each security does not clear automatically at one price, the market maker can supply securities out of his inventory or add the market's excess to his inventory. He adds a service (for a fee) to provide liquidity—or market pricing continuity. That fee makes the buy/sell market prices different from each other and different from a single equilibrium price.

The nature of the service(s) offered, their pricing, and the industrial organization of that service industry are discussed under such terms as *auction markets, specialist systems, call markets, banking systems,* and *investment banking.* Put differently, an examination of market making helps in understanding the structure of real-world pricing as opposed to assumptions of perfect competition and a single equilibrium price.

In its most general sense, a market permits investors to adjust portfolios efficiently to meet changing objectives.[1] Some traders want to change portfolios because they believe that new information has changed the relative value of one security (information traders). Since neither the initial trading incentive nor the trade parameters of any buy/sell pair of transactions are necessarily the same, the existence of market makers provides continuity of trading with presumably smaller price swings. These services are often subsumed under the term *market liquidity.* In the U.S. secondary markets for stocks, such as the New York Stock Exchange, specialists behave as "passive stabilizers." That is, they do not gear their decisions to anticipated price changes but to actual price changes. They buy when there is excess supply (net sell orders) and sell on "upticks," (incremental price increases). Because such behavior occurs in over 90 percent of all transactions, the NYSE concluded that the system provides a "fair and orderly market."[2]

These specialist market makers have a privileged position in that they observe customer limit orders in their "book"— their schedule of buy or sell orders at specified prices that have yet to be filled.[3] This added information suggests that market makers can protect themselves against accumulating excess inventory by lowering the bid price after a purchase. It has been argued that what is called price stabilization by the NYSE and others is a by-product of profit maximization by

---

[1] The following is based on an article by H. R. Stoll, "Alternative Views of Market Making" (Working paper no. 84–113, Vanderbilt University, 1984).

[2] NYSE, "The Quality of the New York Stock Exchange Market Place in 1979," March 6, 1980 (Report of Quality Markets Committee, NYSE).

[3] This is the practical equivalent of supply-and-demand schedules.

dealers since unregulated NASDAQ market makers behave the same way as regulated NYSE specialists.[4] Because of the large volume of trades and the large number of traders, most observers believe that specialists cannot move "equilibrium" market price up or down and that their function is to narrow price variances over time rather than pushing prices in one direction or another. (Block trading is covered in a later chapter.)

Market-making arrangements thus provide a service called immediacy or liquidity to all asset holders. Immediate purchase or sale capacity, even in size and at little price variance, represents a service for traders who can view the cost of this service as a share of the bid/ask spread. And the seller does not deal directly with the buyer even in a single round-lot transaction, nor does he receive the price paid by the buyer.

## A NOTE ON TECHNOLOGICAL CHANGE

Although the institutional processes described here have been called by the same names for many years, data processing technology has revolutionized securities trading. For example, the great shift of equity trading from an emphasis on individual trading in the 1960s to institutional transactions in the 1980s required, first, instant communication, and, second, the capacity to execute large-scale trades just as quickly. In turn, market makers needed the capacity to accept offers, hit bids, and do it in size. It follows that market makers for institutions must have substantial capital resources to participate, and, since this is where the action is, smaller market makers are likely to have a more difficult time.

Another by-product of the electronics revolution is the fact that the market can exist wherever a market maker has a terminal or CRT. Even though the NYSE will record (or "print") the outcome of each completed trade in registered stock, the actual transaction may have occurred away from the NYSE floor ("upstairs").

In addition, large-scale market makers must be able to

---

[4]H. R. Stoll, "Dealer Inventory Behavior: An Empirical Investigation of NASDAQ Stocks," *Journal of Financial and Quantitative Analysis,* September 1976, pp. 359–80.

manage large-scale portfolios that represent the unsold counterpart of institutional trades, to lay off the associated risks, to
provide the services to clients that will generate fees, and to
avoid major losses on unhedged positions. Because information on large-scale trades is available instantaneously, trading
departments of investment banking firms have acquired more
personnel, absorbed more capital, and gained in relative
importance.

Some large-scale trades are automatically "crossed" (purchase and sales price are the same) within a firm or on the
exchange floor. Since both seller and buyer pay commission,
the trades—after transaction costs—are not made at the same
effective prices even though the tape will indicate a trade done
at identical prices.

## TYPES OF MARKET MAKING

Three different market structures have been developed to trade
securities, and they can be adapted to the trading of any
security type. In order of declining familiarity, these are:

1. Brokered trading.
2. Dealer trading.
3. Market making.

### Brokered Trading

This approach to securities trading involves a buyer's agent
and a seller's agent, both typically trading on an exchange.
Brokered markets are supported by a bureaucracy of floor
personnel in charge of (1) transacting securities, (2) recording
and publishing price and volume information, and (3) recon-
ciling cash flows and other transaction-related mechanics.
(See Figure 4–1A.) All of these activities are regulated by the
exchanges and other units called self-regulatory organizations
(SROs). The exchanges and all securities brokers and dealers
must belong to an umbrella organization called the National
Association of Securities Dealers (NASD). Because the SEC
has delegated many of its regulatory powers to the NASD and
the exchanges, these units are called self-regulatory organizations.

**FIGURE 4-1** _____
Security Transaction Processes
_____

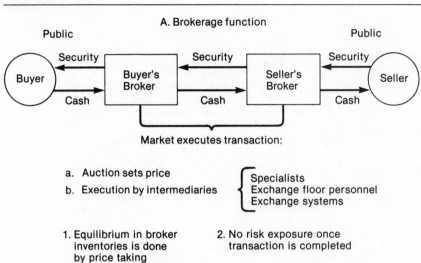

A. Brokerage function

a. Auction sets price
b. Execution by intermediaries

Specialists
Exchange floor personnel
Exchange systems

1. Equilibrium in broker inventories is done by price taking

2. No risk exposure once transaction is completed

A professional trading *as an agent* is a price taker, and all broker inventories in the market will be set by the same price-taking decision as those of other investors. Brokers incur no inventory risks for the completed agency transactions.

**Dealer Markets**

When acting as a *dealer,* the market participant sets a bid-and-ask price for each security he offers to trade: He is the price maker. When his bid is hit, he buys a security from the seller (a broker, an institution, and so forth) with cash. His asset position is now less liquid (more securities, less cash) and riskier. He may want to readjust the entire bid/ask structure of his assets to lighten the security inventory (or reduce his risks); that is, he lowers ask and bid prices.

If, on the other hand, the dealer lays off systematic or market risks in satellite markets, such as financial futures markets, the risk-reducing downward shifts in inventory pricing may not take place. On the income side, however, a fee has been charged to lay off the risk implicit in the larger securities inventory. (See Figure 4–1B.)

**FIGURE 4–1** *(continued)* _____

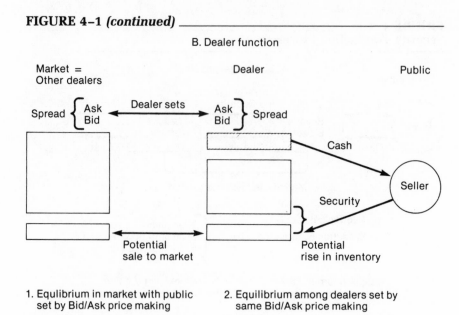

B. Dealer function

1. Equlibrium in market with public set by Bid/Ask price making

2. Equilibrium among dealers set by same Bid/Ask price making

## Market Making

Many underwriters in initial public offerings act as market makers for some time after the issue is sold to the public and after the closing of the underwriting. In fact, the position of market maker represents the entire market structure on the other side of any trade by a seller of the security or by most buyers. Even when more than one market maker is active in the same security, it takes time for the market to acquire sufficient depth before price-making policies shift toward price taking as the major market process. A deep and wide market is required, one that carries the entire panoply of floor traders, specialists, and so on to facilitate routine agency trading on a price-taking basis. (See Figure 4–1C.)

Even in broad and deep markets such as the NYSE, certain large transactions can overwhelm the process. Very large sell offers require the arrangement of an "upstairs deal" by a trading unit acting as a dealer. Once completed, the block trade (as it is called) is recorded by the NYSE floor bureaucracy and prints on the tape. Yet the pricing and transacting of a block trade are done on a dealer basis, with the block trader often winding up the deal—like any other dealer—with a

**FIGURE 4–1** *(concluded)*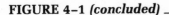

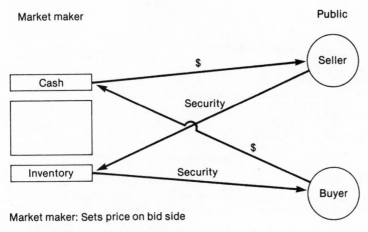

C. Market-making function

Market maker: Sets price on bid side

Market maker: Sets price on ask side

Net result of transactions produces changes in risk
of market maker's portfolio until there are:

   a. More than one market maker, which leads to
      professional trading by dealer (see A above) or

   b. Registration on exchange (see B above)

larger inventory than before. (The NYSE defines a block trade
as a transaction consisting of a minimum of 10,000 shares.)

    Figure 4–2 illustrates the preceding analysis. The shaded
area represents the brokered trading that takes place on exchange floors. The market maker trading as a follow-up to an
initial public offering—usually in small units per trade—is
usually an investment banker. In the brokered trading markets, investment bankers and brokers perform essentially the
same functions, with the exception of the block trades noted
above.

    Dealer trading is what is often called over-the-counter
trading. In the OTC stock markets, the improvements in communications processes and recent (1984) regulatory changes
have produced a mechanism that may approach the brokered
trading process (at least in its mechanical aspects). The bond
markets, on the other hand, imply over-the-counter market

**FIGURE 4-2** _____
Comparative Market Structures
_____

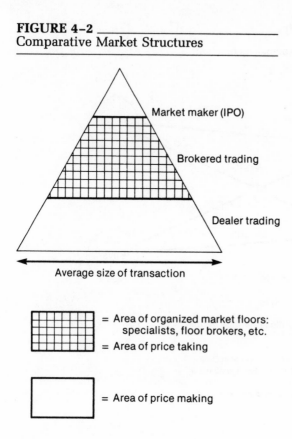

Average size of transaction

= Area of organized market floors:
    specialists, floor brokers, etc.
= Area of price taking

= Area of price making

making on a large scale with large amounts of risky inventories being positioned by dealers such as investment bankers and commercial banks—but not usually by brokers.

In Figure 4-2, therefore, institutionally oriented firms are active (although to a lesser extent) at the top and most active at the bottom of the pyramid, while retail-oriented firms are most active at the top and in the middle (compare with Chapter 3). This classification is not exclusive, but it does suggest that emphasis of trading practices can be used to distinguish retail-oriented from institutional-type firms.

## SOME CONCLUSIONS

The purpose of the several different trading systems may be the same: (1) to earn a rate of return acceptable to the trading firm, (2) to perform a service for clients, (3) to develop a continuous information set that assists the investment banker or broker-dealer firm in pricing any security at new issue or at other times, and (4) to establish trading relationships with institutional-sized buyers and sellers. Volume dealing is a major factor that distinguishes dealers from brokers. This trading capacity, however, goes beyond mere size.

# 5

# Market Making by
# Financial Innovation

In their trading activities, particularly as dealers, underwriters, and market makers, as well as in managing inventory, investment bankers acquire continuous information with respect to market pricing (information on trades) and demand (the portfolio needs of their clients). By analyzing client requirements, they may discover issues that will better meet current portfolio requirements of the institutional money manager. At the same time, these new types of issues might provide the issuer with a lower cost of capital just because the innovative characteristics of the new issue can more directly meet the buyer's portfolio needs and hence can be sold at a premium.

## MORTGAGE PASS-THROUGHS AS INNOVATIVE FINANCE

Originally, the successful effort in using the Government National Mortgage Association's (Ginnie Mae) guarantees helped to improve the liquidity of residential mortgage portfolios by the development of pass-through securities. In retrospect, that development was a conceptual breakthrough to financial innovation. Starting in the early 1970s, an entirely new approach to financing residential mortgages shifted the process away from financial intermediation and into the securities markets. The guarantees provided by the Government National Mortgage Association (GNMA) helped to generate about $300 billion of pooled residential loans. GNMA pass-throughs provided investors with attractive returns, and, when rates rose sharply at the end of the decade, they assisted potentially troubled savings and loans in outplacing mortgages (that is, selling assets) to a far greater extent than would have been feasible in the secondary mortgage market. The GNMA program has been supplemented by similar programs sponsored by the Federal Home Loan Mortgage Corporation and the Federal National Mortgage Association.[1] In the 1980s pass-throughs have been backed not only by less risky seasoned mortgages but by newly originated mortgages to such an extent that one estimate places the 1983 volume of residential mortgages so financed at 40 percent.[2] This compares with estimates of about 10–20 percent of such financing in the years 1979–82. Prior to the GNMA process, the financing of residential mortgages was based nearly entirely on the volume of deposits (or share capital) that savings institutions could attract. And, until the early 1980s, that type of financial intermediation was constrained by Regulation Q.

Finally, with the mortgage pass-through program well established, changes in the structure of the standard (in 1983) pass-through format could be made. For example, the maturity terms of some pass-through issues were shortened from 30 to 15 years. Beyond this, some issuers sold mortgage-backed bonds—that is, liabilities—as secured debt instruments, as opposed to the earlier sale of assets, to develop pass-throughs. The *variety* of mortgage-backed bonds developed in 1983 was truly amazing. The intent was to provide to those holders that wished it a cash flow similar to that generated by government or corporate bonds, with semiannual interest payments and repayment of principal at maturity. Other holders were pro-

---

[1] For a discussion of technical differences among these programs, see J. C. Hu, "The Revolution in Securitizing Residential Mortgages," *Real Estate Review*, Summer 1984, pp. 42–50.

[2] Ibid., p. 46.

vided with a "self-liquidating" feature implicit in the underlying collateral (namely, level-pay residential mortgages). Among the latter were:

1. Serial zero coupon bonds.
2. GNMA collateralized bonds.
3. Collateralized mortgage obligations (CMOs) of FHLMC.
4. GNMA-type CMOs issued by subsidiaries of investment bankers, mortgage bankers, and home builders.

The first of these (serial zeros) represents a conversion of mortgage flows (from collateral first mortgages) by the issuer to single, scheduled annual payments that reflect, in part, the issuer's reinvestment of the cash flows of well-seasoned older mortgages that carry below-market rates (and, therefore, very low risk.[3] The payment structure innovation of the serial zeros is specifically designed to appeal to the investor's preferences.

The second type is designed, instead, to assist mortgage lenders to finance home buyers. The packaging of mortgage-backed securities to secure a bond issue sold by the finance affiliates of home builders permits these builders to make new mortgage loans on newly built structures. By selling debt with conventional cash flows, more funds can be raised (at less cost) than by trying to place the new mortgages in the secondary market.

By the mid-1980's the major issuers of CMOs were FHLMC (Freddie Mac), investment bankers, homebuilders, and thrifts.[4]

The major purchasers of these bonds were:

1. For *shorter-term* issues,
   Thrifts.
   Commercial-bank portfolios.
   Money-market funds.
   Corporate treasurers.
2. For *intermediate-term* and *longer-term* issues,
   Insurance companies.
   Pension funds.

---

[3] Serial zeros were first issued by the financing unit of a real estate subsidiary of Prudential Insurance Company.

[4] For further discussion see Janet Spratlin and Paul Vianna, *An Investor's Guide to CMOs*, Salomon Brothers, May 1986.

Bank trust departments.
Investment advisors.
International investors.

Accessibility of new sources of finance for mortgage lending by restructuring financial arrangement or instruments provides a substitute for the savings-and-loan type of deposit intermediation. The latter approach became inappropriate when interest rates turned much more volatile and when the yield structure rose and became negatively sloped.[5] Financial innovation provided new sources of funds for financial intermediaries by permitting the latter to sell assets (mortgages) as a way to rebuild liquidity. Further, by shifting new mortgage financing away from intermediaries and into the capital market, the structure of residential financing could adapt to higher rates and greater volatility. By providing this service, investment bankers became strategically involved in facilitating the shift to capital market based financing of residential mortgages. They also learned that excess returns can be generated through innovative services.

## DEEP-DISCOUNT BONDS AND OTHER VARIANTS

When interest rates rose very sharply after 1979, nearly the entire supply of outstanding debt began to sell at a discount. At that time a number of analysts and some corporate officials questioned the feasibility of selling new-issue bonds at a substantial discount (from par). Among some issues sold in 1981 were bonds with 30 percent to 40 percent discounts below par and with coupons significantly below current yields to maturity; for bondholders, the rate of return came in part from the rise in the value of the bond based on the accrual of "noncash" interest. Firms such as IBM, Alcoa, ITT, and J. C. Penney issued this type of debt. In June 1981 an issue of 10-year notes sold by GMAC went all the way to a zero coupon, where the bondholder's income would come totally from accruals of

---

[5] Often the same problem is put in terms of the maturity mismatch between S&L liabilities (short-term variable rate deposits) and assets (long-term fixed-rate mortgages). See further discussion regarding interest rate swaps.

interest on the original purchase price until, at maturity in 1991, the GMAC bonds would be paid off at par.

This type of issue was partly supported by preferential tax treatment for the borrower and not (as some early commentators mistakenly supposed) from preferential capital-gains tax treatment of the incremental value to the lenders. Such tax treatment was never granted. The best way to explain the borrower's tax treatment is by the example shown below.

## A Zero Coupon Prototype

The implicit rate of return on an issue price of $252.50 per 10-year bond is 14.8 percent; this is, of course, another way of indicating that the present value of $1,000 in 10 years, discounted at 14.8 percent, is equal to $252.50.[6] The lender's position can be evaluated as follows:

In the first year, the bonds appreciate by 14.8 percent; their value (per bond) increases by .148 × $252.50 = $37.30; at the end of the first year, the bond will be worth $252.50 + $37.30 = $289.80. In the second year, the value goes up by .148 × $289.80, or $42.80; and so on (see Table 5–1).

The aggregate change in future value (FV) ($747.50) is added to purchase price ($252.50) to get par, or $1,000.

In 1981 the IRS took the position that even though GMAC would have no cash interest outflow until year 10, it nevertheless was accruing obligations to make such payments; accordingly, interest deductions for tax purposes could be taken. The amount then permitted for tax deduction was the total sum of interest to be paid ($747.50) divided by 10, or $74.75 per note per year. A comparison of columns 2 and 3 of Table 5–1 indicates that the accrual of interest falls short of allowable tax write-offs for the first six years of a note's maturity, while the last four years show the reverse (deductions lower than accruals). All else the same, the present value of the borrower's tax deductions (net accruals) are clearly maximized in that process, thereby further lowering the after-tax cost of capital to the borrower.

---

[6]The value using 14 percent as a discount factor (D.F.) is equal to $269.70; using 15 percent as a D.F., the value equals $247.20. Interpolation will not be precise because accruals are semiannual.

**TABLE 5–1**
Zero Coupon Bond Cash Flows, 10-Year Issue

| Year | Lender's Position Present Value at Start of Year | Change in Future Value during Year | Borrower's Position (Allowable Annual Tax Write-Off = 10% of Interest Total) |
|------|------|------|------|
| 1 | $252.50 | $ 37.30 | $ 74.75 |
| 2 | 289.80 | 42.80 | 74.75 |
| 3 | 332.50 | 49.10 | 74.75 |
| 4 | 381.60 | 56.30 | 74.75 |
| 5 | 437.90 | 64.60 | 74.75 |
| 6 | 502.50 | 74.10 | 74.75 |
| 7 | 576.60 | 85.10 | 74.75 |
| 8 | 661.70 | 97.60 | 74.75 |
| 9 | 759.40 | 112.00 | 74.75 |
| 10 | 871.40 | 128.60 | 74.75 |
| Total | | $747.50 | $747.50 |

This type of present value "tax loss" should be offset to some extent by tax collections from lenders (note holders). It quickly became apparent, however, that those institutional investors who were in low (or zero) tax brackets were the major buyers of these issues. Further, investors quickly became aware that zeros were the only securities available that carried *assured* reinvestment rates for interest earnings, thereby guaranteeing yields for the life of the security. In an environment of volatile rates and, worse, volatile short/long rate relationships, that assurance was especially valuable to institutional investors seeking to meet contractual cash flows in the future (for example, pension funds). The fact that these very same investors carried no current tax liabilities made the acquisition of these issues all the more attractive. Finally, the development of individual IRAs and the liberalization of Keogh plans further added to the demand for zero coupon bonds.

**Synthetic Zeros: Conversions of Government Securities**

Beginning in August 1982, Salomon Brothers and, subsequently, other investment bankers began to issue certificates of accrual on Treasury securities (CATS), which represented the

**TABLE 5-2** _____
Stripping a 10 Percent, $200 Million Issue
with 15 Years Maturity (in millions of dollars)

|  | Period |  |  |
|---|---|---|---|
| Interest date | 1 | (3 months hence) | $10 |
|  | 2 | (9 months hence) | $10 |
|  | 3 | (15 months hence) | $10 |
|  | • |  | • |
|  | • |  | • |
|  | • |  | • |
|  | 30 | (15 years hence) | $10 |
| Maturity date |  | (15 years hence) | $200 |

repackaging of coupon-bearing U.S. Treasury issues into a more tradable form. This was done by "stripping" the Treasury securities of their coupons, with each dated semiannual coupon and the principal of the security held by Morgan Guaranty Trust Company of New York as the custodian on behalf of the owners of the CATS.

Suppose that Salomon "stripped" $200 million of a 10 percent issue of securities that had a 15-year maturity (see Table 5-2). This means that for each six-month interest date, $10 million of CATS could be sold.

Current interest rates in the capital market may show 90-day Treasury bill yields (the equivalent of the first CATS in the table) to be different from 10 percent; the same may be true for all the maturities up to 15 years. Nevertheless, the discount factor applied to the rate of return from the several issues of CATS will reflect the market yields for the relevant maturity. Of course, the two yields—that on CATS and the yield to maturity (YTM) of a Treasury issue of equivalent maturity—will not be the same. This is because the yield to maturity of a Treasury issue, which is based on the current price, implies an assumed reinvestment of interest cash flows equal to the YTM rate. On the other hand, the reinvestment rate of each issue of CATS beyond the first year implies an assured rate of reinvestment since each issue of CATS—that is, each set of stripped coupons of a given date and the principal as well—has now been converted to the equivalent of a zero coupon bond. In that sense, from the packager's point of view, CATS represent a more marketable set of securities. These securities, in turn, are more marketable because some buyers will pay an additional premium for tax and other advantages conferred by the equivalent of a zero coupon issue.

## The Next Step: STRIPS

In 1985 the U.S. Treasury got into the act by introducing the Separate Trading of Registered Interest and Principal of Securities, or STRIPS. Under that program "selected Treasury securities may be maintained in the book-entry system operated by the Federal Reserve banks in a manner that permits separate trading and ownership of interest and principal payments."[7] The only difference between this program and the physical "stripping" of existing Treasury issues by investment bankers is that those bondholders who have access to a book-entry account at any Federal Reserve bank may, for the designated issues, ask the Fed to "strip" interest components from the issue; the Fed does not charge for that service.

The Treasury set a unit size of $1,000 for a set of STRIPS. Further, to originate STRIPS, a bondholder must have enough bonds to obtain $1,000 units. For example, if interest rates are at 10 percent and interest is paid semiannually, at least $20,000 of bonds are needed to produce the minimum unit of $1,000 per interest date.

At the inception of the program, a number of 10-year notes (maturing in 1995) were made eligible for the origination of STRIPS. The interesting aspect of this process is that a successful innovation may induce a borrower (here the U.S. government) to further facilitate the process, presumably because the cost of capital may be reduced and because a new technology (a computerized book-entry system at the Fed) makes it easy to trade.

## INTEREST-RATE SWAPS

Asset swaps have been a familiar part of the finance landscape as long as large-scale bond trades have taken place. In a typical asset swap a financial institution trades in one set of bonds

---

[7] From offering circular of the U.S. Treasury.

with a bond dealer in exchange for another set and then pays or receives from the dealer the difference in the two agreed-on value totals. This constitutes a swap of assets.

Interest-rate swaps, on the other hand, are a partial misnomer because no swap of title takes place. And even though they deal with the cash flows of liabilities (or debts) rather than assets, the actual indebtedness obligations of the two sets of borrowers *does not change*. The only things that are swapped are the debt-service obligations that the two borrowers must continue to make to their lenders in order to remain in good standing.

At first blush this sounds like a strange kind of arrangement. Why is it done? The simplest answer is that one borrower (A) has a comparative advantage in raising funds in the one market in which the swap partner (B) would like to borrow but cannot do so at acceptable rates. Suppose borrower A raises, at a fixed rate, the equivalent of seven-year bond money. Meanwhile, B would like to borrow seven-year money but cannot get rates anywhere near as low as A is able to.

Suppose further that A is a commercial bank and B is an S&L. The latter swaps its variable-rate liability costs (that is, money-market equivalent rates paid to its savers on money market deposit liabilities, or MMDL) for the fixed-rate interest payments on the seven-year bond raised by the bank. Suppose the bank's bond rate is 11 percent, while the S&L's fixed-rate mortgage portfolio yields 13 percent. By concluding the swap, the S&L gets out of the present maturity mismatch by the dollar amount of the swap. This means that long-term average revenue (based on the mortgage portfolio) will be larger than the fixed cost of financing liabilities. As a result, the S&L not only immunizes itself from possible costly increases in marginal cost (MMDL rising above 13 percent) but, in addition, locks in a net return of 2 percent, neglecting taxes.

The section below examines a swap described by the Philadelphia Fed.[8]

---

[8]Jan G. Loeys, "Interest Rate Swaps: A New Tool for Managing Risks," *Business Review,* Federal Reserve Bank of Philadelphia, May–June 1985, pp. 17–25.

## Swap Mechanics

The upper panel of Figure 5–1 shows the parties to the swap, going from left to right:

    a. The bank, with a seven-year 11 percent liability (fixed) and expectations of acquiring short-term, variable-rate assets.

    b. The intermediary, or swap arranger, namely, an investment banker who collects a fee for his trouble.

    c. The S&L, with assets in the form of a fixed-rate mortgage portfolio averaging 13 percent net return and variable-rate liabilities (based on T bill rate).

The intermediary, or arranger, is charged with calculating the costs to each of the swappers. For the fixed-rate payer, for example, cost may include not only the coupon rate of the

**FIGURE 5–1** _____
How the Swap Works

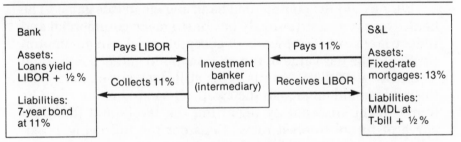

*Net Payment Flows*

| (1) Date | (2) LIBOR | (4) Floating-Rate Payment* | (5) Fixed-Rate Payment | (7) Net Payment: Bank to S&L (4 > 5) | (8) Net Payment: S&L to Bank (5 > 4) |
|---|---|---|---|---|---|
| May 1983 | 8.98% | $4,540,000 | $5,500,000 | 0 | $ 960,000 |
| Nov 1983 | 8.43 | 4,215,000 | 5,500,000 | 0 | 1,285,000 |
| May 1984 | 11.54 | 5,770,000 | 5,500,000 | $27,000 | |
| Nov 1984 | 9.92 | 4,960,000 | 5,500,000 | 0 | 540,000 |
| Nov 1985 | 8.44 | 4,220,000 | 5,500,000 | 0 | 1,280,000 |

*LIBOR at six-month rate (LIBOR × $50 million).

Note: LIBOR is London Interbank offer rate, or the cost at which banks lend funds to each other in the London money market.

bond but the annualized (over seven years) new-issue costs of issuing the bond and whatever other costs are required to produce an "all-in" rate acceptable to the long-term borrower. For the counterparty, all of these fees must, of course, be acceptable before the swap is consummated; that last point may include, for example, a short-term rate higher than (or lower than) LIBOR. For the sake of simplicity, the swap is set at $100 million net; the fixed rate is set at 11 percent paid semiannually; and the floating rate is set at the monthly average of LIBOR during the two semiannual payment months.

In the period shown, which saw a general decline in interest rates as inflationary pressures receded, the fixed-rate payer made just a single payment to the floating-rate payer, while the floating-rate payer made four payments. Lest this arrangement be considered unfair to the S&L, recall that the S&L has locked in a $2 million per year gross return over and above the implied 11 percent fixed rate while at the same time largely covering its own risk exposure regarding the spread between short-term and long-term rates.

Why would the commercial bank engage in this game? The bank expects to continuously be able to make commercial and industrial (short-term) loans of acceptable risks in an amount similar to the par value of the original bond and at a rate equal to LIBOR + 50 basis points. This still does not explain why the bank would engage in the swap. The explanation must be found in the uncertainty regarding the levels and the yield curve of future interest rates. Consider the following possibilities:

Figure 5–2 illustrates two possible rate scenarios for future short-term rates. The first, (LIBOR I) assumes that for the next 7 years, short-term rates will generally be below the 11 percent (fixed) 7-year rate. These lower short rates, given their significant variance, will, at times, approach the 11 percent long-term cost of the original 7-year bond. Because the cash raised by the bond issue can be loaned at LIBOR + 50 basis points, the bank in effect locks in that return spread after the swap, no matter what the current cost of funds may be. If rates drop in the future, relending the bond funds by the bank implies a net *negative* spread for the life of the bond.

The LIBOR II scenario assumes LIBOR rates above 11 percent for the entire period. Since the bank still makes its 50

**FIGURE 5-2**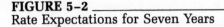
Rate Expectations for Seven Years

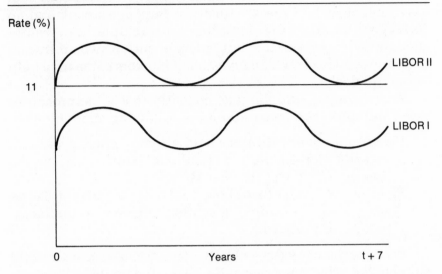

basis point spread, the benefits to the bank, *post-swap*, fall short of not having done the swap only if forecasts of the next 7 years suggest that future short rates will be 50 basis points better *on average* than the 11 percent bond rate. This may occur, but it is clearly impossible to forecast with as high a probability as a LIBOR spread. From the point of view of the bank, then, a liability swap is done for the same costs and benefits involved in any other risk-reducing financial transaction (for example, a covered versus a naked foreign exchange transaction).

The benefits to the S&L (the fixed-rate payer) are much more direct:

**1.** Fixed cost rates make sense as long as a positive spread remains between the amount of the bond issue and a fixed-rate mortgage portfolio of equal (or larger) size, whatever happens to short rates.

**2.** If short rates should fall sharply and remain low, condition 1 might no longer hold because too many high-rate mortgages are prepaid. This would require that a cancellation (or roll-up) of the swap be written into the swap contract or that the S&L's fixed-rate mortgage prepayment penalties be set high enough.

For the S&L as for the bank, the swap permits offsetting risks implicit in the liability/asset maturity mismatches that may impact each of these industries. Suppose a bank and an S&L agree on all of the preceding on principle, how would they actually agree on the particulars of such a swap if it were done today? This is where investment bankers come in to help value the deal.[9]

The Salomon study argues cogently that an approach to swap valuation can be based on the following simulation:

Fixed-rate payer (S&L) has sold a hypothetical fixed-rate security (for example a synthetic bond issue) to the floating rate payer (the bank).

Floating rate payer (bank) has sold a hypothetical floating rate note (for example, a synthetic floater) to the fixed-rate payer (the S&L).

Because the par values of both synthetic issues are exactly equal to the principal value of the swap, the netting of the sale price of the two synthetic issues (when the swap begins, at settlement) and of repayments at maturity produces no net cash flows of principal. At the same time, by considering these synthetic securities as if they did exist, each may be valued separately. And because, at the initial point of swap (that is, the settlement date) the floater is always valued at par, the only question is whether the synthetic bond's yield to maturity is above or below its contract rate. The valuation approach can then focus on the present value of the synthetic bond, adjusted for all required flotation costs. Expressing the latter as an interest rate gives the swap's all-in cost of capital. An example of the clean, or generic, swap is shown in Table 5–3.[10]

---

[9]The following discussion borrows liberally from R. Kopprasch, J. Macfarlane, D. R. Ross, and J. Showers, *The Interest Rate Swap Market*, Salomon Brothers, June 1985, especially pp. 4–11.

[10]The swap is clean because no adjustments are needed at the beginning or during its life since: (1) the floating payment is the index flat; (2) the floating rate is based on Reuters; (3) the payment and reset frequencies of the floating payment are equal to the term of the index; (4) there are no day-count discrepancies between payments and their standards; (5) the initial floating coupon is a current rate; (6) there is no premium or discount; (7) the swap settles "corporate"; (8) there are no short or long first coupon payments; and (9) the swap is priced on the trade date.

**TABLE 5–3** _____
The Generic Swap—A Base Case Example

| | |
|---|---|
| Notional principal amount | $10,000,000 |
| Maturity | May 15, 1992 |
| Trade date | May 8, 1985 |
| Effective date | May 15, 1985 |
| Settlement date | Effective date |

*Fixed Payment*

| | |
|---|---|
| Fixed coupon | 12.50% |
| Payment frequency | Semiannual |
| Day count | 30/360 |
| Pricing date | Trade date |

*Floating Payment*

| | |
|---|---|
| Floating index | Six-month LIBOR |
| Spread | None |
| Determination source | Reuter monitor money rates Service |
| Payment frequency | Semiannual |
| Day count | Actual/360 |
| Reset frequency | Semiannual |
| First coupon | Six-month LIBOR quoted for value as of the settlement date |
| Premium or discount | None |
| All-in cost | 12.50% (semiannual) versus six-month LIBOR flat |

SOURCE: R. Kopprasch, J. Macfarland, D. R. Ross, and J. Showers,
*The Interest Rate Swap Market* (Salomon Brothers Inc., June 1985).

Table 5–3 indicates that, by swapping liabilities, two types
of financial institutions can continue to ensure a return spread
while occupying a preferred habitat with respect to asset
(maturity) selection. Such arrangements are increasingly popular; as two major market participants state, "interest rate
swap(s) may be the fastest growing financial instrument in the
world."[11]

_____

[11] P. J. Dunlavy and T. W. Jasper, "The Interest Rate Swap Gains a
Following," *American Banker*, February 12, 1985, p. 16. The authors are,
respectively, managing director and vice president, Salomon Brothers Inc.
They estimate in that article that some $85 billion of such swaps were
outstanding. This section borrows heavily from the article.

The authors go on to state: "In less than three years this instrument has been transformed from a heavily negotiated private placement transaction into a tradable commitment. Swaps that two years ago involved two to three weeks of negotiation are now consummated on the wire."[12] The increased simplicity in setting up has even moved to the capacity to trade swaps. Transactors, by viewing such an arrangement like a trade, now have the same capacity to change liability portfolios by the acquisition of any financial asset such as a Treasury or corporate security. Indeed, the authors argue that the continued growth of the market requires exactly that capacity to trade a liability swap. The present discussion covers that secondary market aspect.

### How to Change: Reversal

At first attempts were made to create puttable or callable swaps; that procedure did not work. The next best approach turned out to be a "reversal"—namely, a refinancing (or a prepayment of a synthetic security) that would neutralize one side of the swap arrangement. One reason for such a change might be a prepayment of the S&L's fixed-rate assets so that a fixed-rate liability is no longer needed to be matched against it on the liability side. One way of producing the equivalent of the status quo ante for the S&L would be to find a third party willing to accept LIBOR as payment by the S&L for paying the S&L ½ percent per year for the residual period of the original swap. On a gross basis, the S&L still earns a net spread between the two fixed rates at which it swapped and—deswapped—its (variable) liabilities. This game works best if rates have risen between the original swap and its reversal because it implies a gain for the S&L.[13] The analysis makes clear, however, that such a reversal involves the S&L in *two* swaps; as a result, risk rises because there is now a doubled credit exposure and operational management.[14] In addition, a new document must be negotiated at some loss of time and

---

[12] Ibid.

[13] By the same token, a drop in rates from the swap to its reversal results in a loss.

[14] Dunlavy and Jasper, "Interest Rate Swaps."

expense, and finally, even if a positive spread exists between the two swap flows, its present value may be reduced if the benefits must be collected over time.

### Swap Sale

From the point of view of the institution seeking a reversal of the swap, there should be a better way—one less risky or cumbersome as well as less expensive. In short, a demand arose for a secondary market in swaps. Such a sale involves another institution "taking on" the obligation of the seller by "stepping into" the seller's place in the swap. One way of doing this is for the third institution in the above reversal simply to pay the S&L the present value of stepping into the earlier swap contract after rates rose. Or if rates had fallen, the S&L pays the new entrant into the swap the present value of its gain (which equals the entrant's loss). Of course, if the S&L thinks the price is not right, it does not sell the swap. In either case (gain or loss), a sale gets the S&L out of the swap clean.

The foregoing assumes that the original (and remaining) party to the swap finds the new partner an acceptable credit risk and that the new partner likewise finds the remaining partner acceptable. It further supposes that the old swap arrangement remains acceptable as written to both partners. And the fee structure (to old partners) must be found to make the sale acceptable to all.

### ASSET-BACKED SECURITY ISSUES

This chapter began with a discussion of a financial innovation designed to provide a tradable instrument—a mortgage pass-through—to represent a pool of mortgages. This type of "envelope security" was needed because any mortgage in the pool would have been very difficult to place in a secondary market. Other financial innovations similarly have converted one security—a U.S. Treasury bond—into a series of zero coupon issues thereby establishing a vehicle that provides investors with guaranteed rates for reinvestment of interest income. Finally, interest-rate swaps give two different portfolio managers a kind of liability arbitrage that moved the cost of capital for both closer to an optimal level.

The most recent (mid-1980s) innovations are attempts to raise the scale of such financial rearrangements. They represent a more general willingness to reorganize and restructure the corporate sector on the part of the managements involved (for further discussion of financial reorganization see Chapters 7 and 8).

The recent interest in refinancing a large volume of the financial assets of financial intermediaries is, from a conceptual point of view, not really different from a mortgage pass-through. The difference comes in the *scale* of the potential market. By the end of 1985 more than a decade of such pass-throughs have refinanced less than 10 percent of the nearly $4 trillion of mortgages outstanding.

Considering the entire spectrum of financial assets held by, say, typical financial intermediaries such as commercial banks or savings and loan associations, there are probably trillions of financial assets that could provide new sources of raising funds or mechanisms to improve current income.

Such intermediaries as commercial banks (commercial and industrial loans) and savings and loan associations carry portfolios whose maturities—to take only one dimension into account—carry a potentially risky mismatch relative to their liability structures. Accordingly, a number of investment banking firms have proposed to these large-scale asset holders that they refinance these assets in a somewhat less risky manner; i.e., that they repackage these issues into what are now called *asset-backed securities*. The financial institution could: (1) sell these assets to an investor-owned trust and pledge the cash flows from the assets under an indenture for the payment of the new debt obligations or (2) sell the assets directly to another investor.

By engaging in this type of asset divestiture, the financial intermediary could improve its financial position as follows:

1. Eliminate interest rate and maturity risk on assets sold or pledged.
2. Raise new money. One assumes the new funds are reinvested in a less risky way.
3. Create additional fee income from servicing of sold or pledged assets.

4. Improve the firm's financial measurements:
   a. The sale of financial assets could permit a dollar-for-dollar reduction in liabilities. By itself, this could raise a number of financial ratios such as:
      (1) Return on equity and/or assets.
      (2) Coverage ratios (liabilities).
      (3) Capitalization ratios.
   b. Collection of servicing income would further enhance all of the above.

The form taken by the new asset-based issues would be either:

a. Pass-through securities for certain pools of securities.
b. Collateralized notes.
c. Whole-asset sales.

The actual types of assets recently refinanced include automobile loans and computer leases, but many investment bankers are planning to refinance just about every relatively homogeneous and identifiable financial asset (e.g., commercial and industrial loans).

The pools of assets would carry wide geographical diversification and overcollateralization to minimize risk including unlimited recourse to high-quality paper by good-quality issuers to enhance pool quality. In addition, with the use of letters of credit and surety bonds from third parties, AAA or AA ratings should be obtained whatever the quality rating of the asset-seller corporation. As a result, the cost of capital for the asset-based debt issues can be held down below the rates that a bond issue of the asset seller himself would have to carry.[15]

## Further Reflections on Asset Sales

Capital costs may not fall as much as expected, however, for the following reasons. The bank has placed its least risky

---

[15] It has been argued that such pieces of debt would bring down the bank's cost of capital even further because the new debt does not require an expensive equity component to be added to the capital structure. The argument is not quite so simple, however. See further discussion below.

assets into a trust for refinancing (and has overcollateralized that portfolio into the bargain). Necessarily, the residual portfolio of the bank would then carry a higher risk classification than before because the least risky share of the bank's assets has been segregated into the trust. If the market for bank stocks is efficient, that cost of capital will rise. Whether the bank's overall cost of capital will go up or down thus becomes an empirical question that should be evaluated on a case-by-case basis. And the use of the proceeds raised by asset sales, including the riskiness of the new investments made, will have an important bearing on each bank's stock valuation and, by extension, on its cost of capital.

From the point of view of the regulators of financial intermediaries, this incremental trading and financing loop superimposed on operations of typical financial intermediation would be interpreted as another step in the direction of do-it-yourself deregulation. Whether the regulators are comfortable with these changes and with the potential implication on the regulators' insurance liabilities or lender-of-last-resort functions also remains to be seen.

## INNOVATION AS EXPERIMENT: WHO ASKS THE GUINEA PIG?

Any novel financing scheme, after its design is developed, must be tested. And the test must be taken by an issuer. Before the test is taken, corporate management must understand how the new type of security will lower the firm's cost of capital below a more conventional alternative. At the same time, potential investors in the new security should be informed about its benefits—if they don't buy, even the most ingenious innovation won't raise funds as expected.

A story detailing Morgan Guaranty Bank's success in developing new security types, clearly states how reluctant potential borrowers may be to innovate.[16] Morgan Guaranty proposed a bond to be sold in 1982 in the Eurodollar bond market

---

[16] S. Wittebort, "Inside the Morgan Machine," *Institutional Investor*, July 1985, pp. 170–78.

that also carried long-term warrants with a call option.[17] Potential borrowers resisted the idea of warrants since warrants would commit them to sell more bonds later at the same low prices as prevailed in that year's high-rate environment. Protection against this event was offered by the call option. It took a while to sell the idea, and after the Development Bank of Singapore sold out a $75 million issue with these characteristics, other firms quickly asked Morgan Guaranty (and not other investment banks) to do similar deals for them.[18] In discussions with investment bankers, I found out that it had been difficult to sell the idea of zero coupon bonds to potential borrowers because no one wanted to be the first.

## SUMMARY AND CONCLUSION ON MARKET MAKING

Innovation is a by-product of the information processing revolution and continues to be stimulated by the aftereffects of increased competition and negotiated trading commissions. Competitors' capacities to imitate as well as innovate have driven the management of each investment banking firm to do both. Accordingly, the half-life of excess returns to innovations has shortened, and the rate of innovation has accelerated.

Seen from a different perspective, the trading departments of broker-dealer firms now perceive that they can generate a higher rate of return than minimal commissions by innovative repackaging of securities in the firm's or someone else's portfolio and by innovations in new-issue characteristics. All of this involves the trading of financial assets.

Financial intermediation can also take place by facilitating transactions among streams of liabilities, that is, interest-rate swaps. The capacity to transact, or trade, on a large scale is fundamental to these activities and innovations. As a result trading departments in the investment banking firms have

---

[17] Commercial banks, like Morgan Guaranty, are *not* constrained by the Glass-Steagall Act in international bond markets such as Eurodollar bonds.

[18] Wittebort's article details another issue called a bumblebee because it had so many features that no one thought it could fly. And, in fact, it did not fly. Wittebort, "Inside the Morgan Machine," pp. 176–77.

accumulated more power and personnel—as well as larger bonuses.

Finally, innovations in repackaging securities have now become important among the largest financial institutions as well, namely, the commercial banks. Morgan Guaranty was mentioned above; in an article on Bankers Trust,[19] the author cogently argued that Bankers Trust could succeed by the packaging innovations discussed: "A key part of [Bankers] . . . strategy is to convert all the bank's corporate loans into the equivalent of interest-bearing bonds that can be sold to investors." To the extent that Bankers Trust follows through on this strategy, it may develop the following financial structure: It can accept deposits on the liabilities side. On the asset side, deposit proceeds would first appear as bank loans that are subsequently converted into tradable securities. That portfolio would then be traded like any other dealer portfolio, and the other dealer-type security activities and fee-based actions such as mergers and acquisitions would logically follow.

In short, financial intermediation can be converted into a transaction-type market as opposed to a private placement type of intermediary institution. And, in that sense, the paths of commercial banks and of investment bankers are converging even faster than in the conventional, and more over-argued, areas of Glass-Steagall conflicts regarding new issues.

The preceding chapters are by no means an exhaustive description of innovative market making. New products appear almost weekly (see Figure 5–3). The foregoing is a partial history of the creative response to demands for more efficient financing vehicles. The term *efficiency* may imply less risk not exclusively in the classic portfolio sense of lower standard deviations of a set of returns (even with lending and borrowing). Instead, market makers offer *value added by hedging techniques*. The use of interest-rate swaps deals directly with that particular problem.

The other techniques discussed, such as zero coupons and the stripping of interest coupons from the bond corpus, likewise attempt to provide greater assurance regarding the certainty of future rates of return. In that sense, the innovation is an attempt to satisfy what one is tempted to call "actuarial

---

[19]R. A. Bennett, "Sanford's New Banking Vision," *The New York Times*, March 13, 1985.

**FIGURE 5–3**
Financial Innovations in 1985*

| Instruments | Description |
| --- | --- |
| **International Markets** | |
| Floating-rate coupon securities: | |
| • Capped | Upper limit on coupon reset rate. |
| • Mini/max | Upper and lower bounds set. |
| • Mismatched | Coupon reset and coupon payment occur at different frequencies. |
| • Partly paid | After initial payment for first part of an issue, purchaser must subscribe to future parts of the issue. |
| Nondollar FRNs | Introduction of deutschemark- and yen-denominated FRNs. |
| Nondollar zero-coupon bonds | Introduction of deutschemark-, Swiss franc-, and Japanese yen-denominated issues. |
| Shoguns | U.S. dollar bonds issued in Japan. |
| Sushis | Eurobonds issued by Japanese entities that do not count against limits on holdings of foreign securities. |
| Yen-denominated yankees | Yen bonds issued in U.S. market. |
| ECU-denominated securities | Increased utilization in U.S. markets; introduction of issues in Dutch and Japanese markets. |
| Dual-currency yen bonds | Interest paid in yen; principal paid in other currency at a specified exchange rate. |
| "Down-under" bonds | Increased utilization of Euro-Australian dollar and Euro-New Zealand dollar bond issues. |
| **Domestic Markets** | |
| Variable-duration notes | At coupon payment date, holder elects either to receive coupon or an additional note with identical terms. |

**FIGURE 5-3** *(continued)* _____

| Instruments | Description |
|---|---|
| **Domestic Markets** *(cont.)* | |
| Zero-coupon convertible | Zero-coupon bond with option to convert to common stock. |
| Collateralized securities: | |
| • Multifamily pass-through | Pass-throughs collateralized by multifamily mortgages. |
| • Lease backed | Collateralized by leases on plant and equipment. |
| • Automobile backed | Collateralized by automobile loans. |
| • Revenue indexed | Mortgage-backed security in which interest payments are augmented by a percentage of issuer's gross earnings. |
| Commercial real estate: | |
| • Finite-life real estate investment trust | Portfolio of real estate equities with a specific date by which the portfolio must be liquidated. |
| • Commercial mortgage pass-throughs | Pass-throughs collateralized by commercial mortgages. |
| • Cross-collateralized pooled financing | Pooled securities allowing recourse to other mortgages in the pool. |
| • Rated, pooled nonrecourse commercial mortgage | Publicly rated nonrecourse real estate-backed bonds. |
| Tax-exempt securities: | |
| • Daily adjustable tax-exempt securities | Puttable long-maturity bonds with coupon rate adjusted daily. |
| • Zero coupon | Zero-coupon tax-exempts. |
| • Capital appreciation bonds | Zero-coupon bonds sold at par or better. |
| • Stepped tax-exempt appreciation on income-realization securities | Zero-coupon bonds for an initial period, after which they are converted to interest-bearing securities. |
| • Municipal option put securities | Puttable bonds with detachable puts. |
| • Periodically adjustable rate trust securities | Participant certificates based on tax-exempt commercial mortgage loans. |

**FIGURE 5–3** *(concluded)*

| Instruments | Description |
| --- | --- |
| **Futures and Options** | |
| Municipal bond contract | Introduction of futures contract to tax-exempt market. |
| Options on Eurodollar futures | Introduction of exchange-traded options on futures to the short end of yield curve. |
| Options on treasury note futures | Introduction of exchange-traded options on futures to intermediate section of yield curve. |
| Japanese government yen bond futures | Introduction of Japanese financial futures contracts. |
| ECU warrants | Introduction in Europe of publicly offered and listed options on ECU. |
| European-style options | Introduction in United States of options that can only be exercised at expiration. In addition, currency strike prices are in European rather than American terms. |
| Range forward contract | A forward exchange contract that specifies a range of exchange rates for which currencies are exchanged on the expiration date. |
| U.S. dollar index | Introduction of a futures contract on the dollar's trade-weighted value. |
| Options on cash 5-year treasury notes | Introduction of options to this sector of the yield curve. |

*Instruments that were either introduced or became widely used during 1985.
SOURCE: Salomon Brothers.

efficiency." This is done by the reduction of uncertainty regarding future cash flows by specifying in advance the reinvestment rates of return to income flows generated by long-term assets.

Finally, the provision of the envelope security for financial assets represents an aspect of *operational efficiency*. At this writing, the most important share of that market is the repackaging of residential mortgages.

Prior to the development of pass-through issues, the secondary mortgage market was but a fraction of what the pass-through market was to become. The growth in transactions volume was based both on reduction in transactions costs and risks and on market liquidity of pass-through issues. The residential mortgage market based on the old-style S&L financial intermediation process was on the rocks in the 1970s and early 1980s so financial innovation and the associated operational efficiency also had some real investment effects in terms of added construction output. This is not to gainsay that investment banking revenues did not benefit from the process—but then, one proxy measure of improved efficiency may be the excess returns to the innovator-packager.

# 6

# The Venture Capitalist

The new-issue flotation process is a subset of the general market-making activities discussed in the preceding chapters. In an operational sense, every underwriter for a new issue is involved in the secondary market as a matter of course. This is true of both bond markets and stock markets.

A first step into the realm of new-issue flotations and, more specifically, initial public offerings (IPOs) of equity issues is the venture-capital process. Moreover, this process is very important in financing the high-tech and entrepreneurial development process. Venture capital investment leading to an initial public offering is the market-making counterpart to the progression of laboratory science into industrial output.

## THE VENTURE CAPITAL PROCESS

The term *venture capital* is an ancient one in finance, suggesting such state-of-the-art investments as the financing of the New England whaling fleet in the 19th century or the voyages of Captain Drake and other privateers in the 17th century. Even today the term implies risk, uncertainty, and hopes of a bonanza.

Venture capital investment is a useful institutional prereq-

**TABLE 6–1**

Source of Funding for Venture Funds (independent private firms only)

| | Total Capital Committed (millions) | | | Percent of Total Capital Committed | | |
|---|---|---|---|---|---|---|
| | 1981 | 1982 | 1983 | 1981 | 1982 | 1983 |
| Pension funds | $200 | $ 474 | $1,054 | 23% | 33% | 31% |
| Individuals and families | 201 | 290 | 714 | 23 | 21 | 21 |
| Foreign | 90 | 188 | 544 | 10 | 13 | 16 |
| Insurance companies | 132 | 200 | 408 | 15 | 14 | 12 |
| Corporations | 142 | 175 | 408 | 17 | 12 | 12 |
| Endowments and foundations | 102 | 96 | 272 | 12 | 7 | 8 |
| Total | $867 | $1,423 | $3,400 | 100% | 100% | 100% |

SOURCE: Venture Economics, Inc.

uisite to a new public offering. In addition, the process illustrates a peculiarly American phenomenon of the 1980s—a surge in private financial support for academic or scientific entrepreneurs. Venture capital financing has increased fourfold over a three-year period in the early 1980s. In the high-tech environment of, for example, genetic engineering or information-processing technology, a financing problem must be solved before a laboratory-volume activity can be moved into commercial production.

### The Organization of Venture Capital Funds

Given the high risk of unpredictable cash flows, each venture is set up as a separate unit, subject to the vagaries of its own development. Until the public offering appears, there is no marketplace where any part of the investment can be sold or bought. The investors/organizers of each venture set themselves up as a freestanding partnership (or corporation). Such partnerships are run by the (active) general partner(s); the investors (as opposed to managers) are limited partners. (A few venture funds are organized as publicly traded corporations.) This type of organization provides management continuity even if some limited partners decide to sell to other partners during the venture. Capital funds can thus be looked on as mutual organizations that reduce risks by diversification into multiple free-standing ventures. This is an important factor since some studies show that 40 percent of venture investments don't pay off. General partners usually receive about 20 percent of the fund's gains as income. They also share in the losses of the fund. Similarly, limited partners share gains and losses to the tune of about 80 percent.

Funds must make distributions annually to allow partners to cover taxes. In addition, the general partner (manager) may make other distributions—typically securities transferred to limited partners rather than in cash proceeds from security sales. Such distributions do not generally produce taxable income for partners or the partnership; they are only internal redistributions of assets. Tax liability follows only when such assets are sold to outsiders.

## VENTURE CAPITAL FINANCING OF A NEW FIRM: BIOENGINEERING

In the 1970s and 80s, the scientific basis for a new industry was evolving in major university departments of biochemistry and biomedical engineering. The industry was based on scientific developments derived from the analysis of DNA, improvements in the understanding of the body's genetic makeup and immune system, and the development of products used to diagnose and treat a number of severe diseases. The overall name for this application of research is genetic engineering.

Genetic engineering is not a new industry. In agriculture, hybrid corn, rice, and livestock are half a century old. Bacteria are now used in sanitary engineering and mining. What is new is the *monoclonal antibody* technique, among others, that permits the reorganization of specific bacterial materials to perform a particular function; some call this development designer genes. A number of formidable technical and, subsequently, business problems are inherent in these schemes because bacteria mutate quickly. A perfectly designed gene for a particular task may change its characteristics in a week. And yet large-scale production is necessary for clinical testing and pilot production. Such large-scale requirements quickly forced scientists and technologists to realize that the volume of production needed even for medical research exceeded the capacity of university laboratories.[1] They also recognized the possibility for substantial wealth by moving out of the laboratory and into an industry setting.[2]

## MOVING INTO THE WORLD OF FINANCE

The scientist-engineer moving out of the sheltered environment of the university or corporate laboratory is usually far removed from the stereotypical professor portrayed in the movies. Many have climbed career ladders as slippery and competitive as those found in the industrial world. Some have served on corporate boards of directors or in university administration. Others are academic entrepreneurs experienced in managing a group of highly trained and highly strung academics.

In the production start-up, some use their own financial resources (or those of friends and other investors); others have contacts with interested corporations or commercial banks. In the following discussion, these sources are listed in order of potentially increasing conflict of interest with the scientist-entrepreneur.

### Venture Capital

An entrepreneur's concern over losing scientific (or patent or process) control to the financial collaborator/potential competitor opens the door to the venture capitalist. The venture capitalist may present a conflict over corporate control some time down the road. But this problem is not obvious at the initial organizing step when the entrepreneur is facing a daily struggle to develop a costly production process without any inflows of funds from sales or any immediate prospects for such sales.

---

[1] All of this assumes that the host communities fear no major environmental problems. In some cases of DNA recombinant research and development, litigation has resulted in delays and constraints.

[2] A similar scenario has developed in such areas as artificial intelligence and industrial development of computer hardware and software. For a more specific description, see Tracy Kidder, *The Soul of a New Machine* (Boston: Little, Brown, 1981).

**Seed Financing.**   Seed financing is provided to the entrepreneur to establish the feasibility of the concept; no marketing is done at this stage. The next step is *start-up financing.*

**Start-up Financing.**   This stage involves financing for product development and the initial marketing. At this stage a company may be formally organized or operating for less than one year. Although no product is yet sold commercially, in contemplation of such sales, the following are organized:

1. Key management group.
2. Business plan.
3. Marketing studies.

The end of the beginning comes with *first-stage financing.*

**First-Stage Financing.**   At this point the firm has just about exhausted its initial capital; has developed a prototype that appears workable and salable; and is now ready to begin manufacturing and selling. In fact, the firm now begins its growth through *second-stage financing.*

**Second-Stage Financing.**   Such funds provide working capital to finance goods in process, inventories, shipping, and accounts receivable. The firm needs enough funds to carry its net investment in current assets until the collection from receivables begins to reduce that aggregate investment substantially. The company is now much larger. Its output may be growing rapidly even though its rate of return may still be negative. However, hopes for profitable business development are reflected in progressively lower loss rates per unit of output. This development process leads directly to *third-stage financing.*

**Third-Stage Financing.**   In this stage funds are provided for major expansion of the firm when its sales volume begins to take off and its income statement is near the break-even point or developing some positive (if modest) profits per unit. The financing helps to expand plant and equipment, broaden the marketing effort, and, if necessary, finance more working capital or product improvement.

Table 6–2 shows a schematic for High-Flying Technology

**TABLE 6-2**
High-Flying Technology Corporation—Financing History

| | | | Stage of Development | | | |
|---|---|---|---|---|---|---|
| | Seed | Start-up | First Round | Second Round | Mezzanine | IPO |
| Date | September 1980 | January 1981 | March 1982 | September 1982 | January 1983 | June 1983 |
| Money raised | Office space, living expenses | $3,000 | $1,500,000 | $5,000,000 | $20,000,000 | $100,000,000 |
| Total valuation of company | — | $3,000 | $1,750,000 | $10,000,000 | $80,000,000 | $500,000,000 |
| Security | — | Common stock | Series A convertible preferred | Series B convertible preferred | Series C convertible preferred | Common stock |
| Price per share | — | $0.005 | $1.00 | $4.00 | $10.00 | $15.00 |
| Number of investors | — | Founders | 3 + founders | 10 + founders + employees | 25 + founders + employees | General public |

Corporation. Note that it took about three years before the company could go public with a common stock offering.

The company's founders provided $3,000 of seed and start-up financing and acquired the common stock of the firm at 0.5 cents per share. The first round financing adds $1.5 million convertible preferred (Series A), while the second round adds another $5 million, once again through convertible preferred (Series B).

### Brief Digression on Convertible Preferred

Why convertible preference stock to finance first and second round (and subsequent rounds) of financing? As in many other problems in finance, the answer is taxes. Consider, for example, the tax problems of holders of common (rather than of convertible preferred) stock at $5 per share. If the original owners' and employees' 0.5 cents per share common is now valued at $5—without an easy market for the shares, more-over—they may face a devastating tax bill. They may have to make an election under Section 83(b) of the Internal Revenue Code or risk recognition of an even larger "bargain stock" later under Section 83 as their stock vests.[3] Further, since the founders and venture capitalists are the only stockholders, there is no way to sell the shares without losing control of a potential bonanza. Worse yet, any distress sale to meet tax obligations will only drop the price (and price expectations) of the shares in a high-risk, high potential gain situation.

Preferred stock also gives venture capitalists a preferred position in the event of liquidation (that is, failure). In the event of success, on the other hand, the legal provisions associated with senior securities (such as preferred) lies in the protection that may be written into the "term sheet" under which the new securities are sold. That protection involves provisions against dilution and for votes for the board of directors.[4] Finally, the specific terms of the several issues of

---

[3]The preceding discussion is taken from M. J. Halloran, L. F. Benton, and J. R. Lovejoy, *Venture Capital and Public Offering Negotiation* (New York: Harcourt Brace Jovanovich, 1983), Supplement, pp. 253–54.

[4]Specifically, the number of shares of common issuable at conversion of preferred is adjusted upward by some formula if there are issuances by the firm of additional common at a price below the conversion price.

**FIGURE 6-1**
Venture Capital Financing

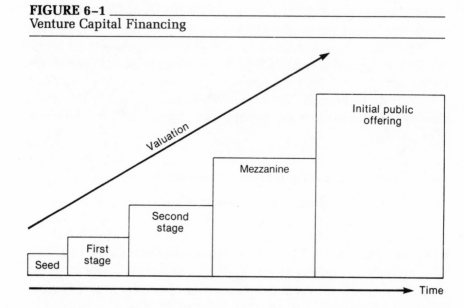

preferred regarding rights to interest or cumulation of dividends or rights of repayment of investment frequently become an area of contention among the venture capitalists. As long as only one issue of preference stock is outstanding (Series A), no conflicts arise. However, features such as noncumulative dividends, proceeds at liquidation equal to investment, no mandatory redemption, voting rights equal to common stock, and no restrictive covenants must be made acceptable to the two (or more) sets of investors. Conversion to common will take place only when agreed-on financial targets are met.

When Series B preferred is issued (or if nonconvertible debt is issued with warrants), a third party enters the contest.[5] Frequently, the terms required then become substantially more constraining, and the higher the price, the more constraining the terms. Figure 6-1 shows the venture financing strata necessary to build the firm's financial foundation *even prior to* the IPO.

---

[5] If nonconvertible debt is sold with warrants, the lenders are given the option to uncouple the potential for capital gain from the repayment of the loan.

The valuation levels shown for the firm represent proxies for market values. These values are derived by calculating the equity values as if each tranche of financing had been converted at the amount that will ultimately obtain just as the issue goes effective with an IPO.

This means that among the sellers of stock at the IPO will be the (prior) venture capitalists who may wish to reinvest their substantial gains in other ventures or in less risky opportunities. Of course, all of them will have a powerful interest in the pricing of the IPO because each incremental price improvement, no matter how small, represents (at least for some investors) a multiplicand over the original purchase price of each share of stock. If the venture capital department of the investment banking firm was one of the investors, it, likewise, will attempt to push the firm's syndicate department to price the new stock as richly as possible. Thus what might have appeared as a potential conflict of interest to the issuing firm may turn out to be a benefit in the pricing.

## THE IPO: THE END OF ANOTHER BEGINNING

The culmination of the venture capital process is the initial public offering and, most specifically, the IPO price per share. For many limited partners this is the payoff for years of waiting—the time to decide whether to undertake a conversion to cash or to common stock. Those investors who sell out accept the new-issue price as the acceptable conversion price to cash for the preferred. Those investors who accept the exchange into common stock hope to gain more from holding the common than by selling off at the IPO and reinvesting the proceeds.

Consider the attitude toward new-issue pricing (or more specifically, *underpricing*) of the two sets of investors. Only the seller at the IPO would be immediately concerned about the new-issue price even though:

1. He is not concerned about new-issue reception in a fixed-price offering.
2. He is not concerned about the firm's cost of capital for new money.

In fact, if he believes that his funds should now be reinvested in other types of investments, he may accept a lesser new-issue price (as a fee for liquidity) to switch out more rapidly.

By contrast, the continuous investor in the new firm's common stock, having converted from the preferred held as a venture capitalist, may be persuaded that (a temporary?) dip in price at new issue may be his "acceptability fee" to access the market at a propitious time. He understands that the implicit rise in the firm's cost of capital (equal to per-share underpricing) implies lesser future gains as well as some dilution of control. And yet sophisticated investors accept these costs.

## The Investment Banking Function

The venture capital process is market making; it is the financing that must occur before a market can be made for the securities in an initial public offering. Nevertheless, as noted above, these premarket financings are marketed in the form of venture capital partnerships or, in some instances, through a publicly traded venture capital fund. A few investment banking firms are active in this area (for example, L. F. Rothschild, Unterberg, Towbin). Venture capital financing is an important function that should be observed if only to assess how an embryonic corporate structure must be nurtured. That nurture, if successful, will then permit the issue of new common stock that brings the firm its independent life.

# 7

# Mergers and Acquisitions I: Market Making as a Circus

When investment banking activities move from the business pages to the front pages of the newspaper and when the same merger gives rise to at least three trade books full of insider details,[1] show biz and the merger business share more than the same nomenclature. Today publicity campaigns and image making are an integral part of the information maneuvering of giant corporations and the megabucks risked to finance mergers and takeovers. This chapter goes a bit deeper than the headlines—back to the business pages of the paper and to the not necessarily quieter environment of the professional literature.

The total volume of mergers and takeovers since 1980 has been unprecedented. The size of the largest mergers and takeovers keeps on increasing, and multibillion dollar acquisitions are now commonplace (See Table 7–1.)

The concepts "mergers," "takeovers," and "acquisitions" all involve the absorption of one firm (the target firm) by another (the acquiring firm). *Merger* generally implies a less-

---

[1] See A. Sloan, *Three Plus One Equals Billions* (Arbor House); H. Lampert, *Till Death Us Part* (New York: Harcourt Brace Jovanovich, 1983); and P. Hartz, *Merger* (Morrow, 1985).

**TABLE 7-1**
Five Recent Mergers/Acquisitions (in billions of dollars, by size)

| Acquirer/Acquired | Year | Value | Type of Transaction |
|---|---|---|---|
| Chevron/Gulf | 1984 | $13.3 | Acquisition (cash) |
| Texaco/Getty | 1984 | 10.1 | Acquisition (cash and notes) |
| Du Pont/Conoco | 1981 | 7.2 | Acquisition (cash and notes) |
| U.S. Steel/Marathon | 1982 | 6.0 | Acquisition (cash and notes) |
| ELF Acquitaine/Texas Gulf | 1981 | 4.3 | Acquisition (cash) |

reluctant attitude on the part of the target firm; *takeover* usually implies an unfriendly bid for the target firm. Either approach, if successful, means disappearance of the target firm.

Curiously, financial analysts have no agreed-on theory to explain merger activity.[2] Mergers (or takeovers) are undertaken by the acquiring firm in the expectation of significant gains. What is the nature of these gains?

## DEFINING ECONOMIC COSTS AND GAINS[3]

If the acquiring firm A believes there is a net gain to be made by combining with firm B to make firm AB, that gain can be stated in present value terms (PV) as follows:

$$\text{GAIN} = PV_{AB} - (PV_A + PV_B)$$

[2] The word most often used to explain the urge to merge is *synergy*— the new math of 2 + 2 = 5. Synergy implies that the combined two (or more) firms are worth more than their separate values due to (1) operating economies (of scale); (2) financial economies (or a lower cost of capital); (3) differential efficiency (target firm's management is inefficient); (4) increased market power. The last item is illegal under the Sherman and Clayton antitrust statutes, but some mergers *not* challenged by the U.S. government nevertheless have increased market-share effects. All the other rationales may be socially desirable, and so may be the proposition that the acquisition of assets by merger may be cheaper than new construction (this appears to be the efficiency argument in another guise). Yet each one of these propositions is subject to controversy, first, in the academic literature and, second, in the implementation of actual decisions.

[3] The following is based on Richard Brealey and Stewart Myers, *Principles of Corporate Finance*, 2nd ed., (New York: McGraw-Hill, 1984), chap. 31.

Only if GAIN were positive, so that the present value of $PV_{AB} > PV_A + PV_B$, would a merger make sense. If it makes sense, B must still be acquired, and that acquisition will carry a price. Let's call that price (from A's point of view) COST. Assume, only for the sake of simplicity, that A buys B with cash rather than a package of securities. In that case the *cost* to A is as follows:

$$COST = CASH - PV_B$$

where CASH includes all the outlays (including transaction costs, legal fees, and so forth) needed to place $PV_B$ within the combined firm. In the end, the merger makes sense only if the following post-merger, $NPV_M$, is *positive*:

$$NPV_M = GAIN - COST = PV_{AB} - (PV_A + PV_B) - (CASH - PV_B)$$

All the values in the preceding equations must be estimated by the acquiring firm in advance of any merger. On the assumption that markets can efficiently place values on securities, each of the variables also has to be estimated on a post-merger *announcement* basis for the target firm, as does the forecast of the present value of the (as yet unknown) cash flows of the combined enterprise. And finally, the acquiring firm must have enough faith in such forecasts to risk a substantial amount of funds.

Only on that basis can the acquiring firm's management be satisfied that some positive GAIN will follow. If the decision turns out to be a mistake, the acquiring firm's management not only loses prestige but may be dismissed by its board of directors and/or the stockholders and the now financially vulnerable acquiring firm may even become a takeover target itself.[4] As partial protection from the errors of excessive optimism, plain bad luck, or both, the managements of acquiring firms almost always retain an investment banking firm to estimate the relevant variables for the target firm and for itself. Investment bankers active in the merger game have a great deal of experience in making such estimates and enough expertise in trading blocks to assess both strategic as well as

---

[4] See the discussion of the Bendix-Martin Marietta merger fight below.

tactical price changes expected to take place in both the acquiring and the target firms' stock prices.

The prior equation is a clear statement of not only the GAIN that makes the deal possible but COST, which is primarily the premium payment to target firm B. Since firm A has retained an investment banker to help bring about a positive result for it, the management of firm B will do the same to maximize its stockholders' wealth. In fact, the presentation is based purposely on the separation of two questions:

1. The analysis of GAIN establishes prima facie rationale for A of whether merger should even be considered and of how much to bid.
2. The analysis of COST sets the division of GAIN between the target firm and the acquiring firm. Suppose that the estimate of pre-merger GAIN is positive. Suppose, further, that COST = GAIN; then all of the benefits of the merger go to the *target* firm.

To clarify, suppose the following relationships hold, premerger:

$$PV_A = \$2,000,000$$
$$PV_B = \$200,000$$
$$GAIN = +\$120,000$$

Separately, the values of firms A and B are $2 million and $200,000, so the sum of their separate values equals $2.2 million. A believes that by combining with B the joint firm (because of synergy, economies of scale, magic, and so on) would be worth *not* $2.2 million but $2,320,000. This gives the merger a present value (or a GAIN) of $120,000.

Suppose now that A buys B for $250,000 cash. Immediately, B's stockholders enjoy a 25 percent rise in the value of their former holdings—let's call this B's premium. If A's estimate of the merger is right, its stockholders, too, are ahead of the game:

$$
\begin{aligned}
NPV_M &= \text{Value with merger} - \text{Value pre-merger} \\
&= (PV_{AB} - CASH) - PV_A \\
&= (\$2,320,000 - \$250,000) - \$2,000,000 \\
&= +\$70,000 = \$120,000 - \$50,000 \\
&= GAIN - \text{B's premium}
\end{aligned}
$$

Remember, however, that B's premium is *fact*, whereas GAIN is entirely a function of A's ability to accurately forecast the present value of an uncertain future. (A's stockholders must make a similar forecast.)

## TWO BIG MERGER CASES

In February 1984 Getty Oil, the 14th largest U.S. oil firm, was acquired by Texaco, the 4th largest, at a total price exceeding $10 billion. Prior to the merger, the descendants (and principal owners) of J. Paul Getty (the founder) were restless with their own management because Getty shares were selling at about $65 per share. First, the trustees of the Sarah C. Getty trust, together with Pennzoil Co., announced a plan to take the firm private through an offer to buy shares not yet controlled at a price of $112.50 per share. Texaco subsequently raised the ante with an offer of $125 per share. Getty's heirs clearly got a good deal.

Whether Texaco made a good decision remains to be seen, although the purchase doubled its domestic oil and gas reserves and Texaco acquired more retail outlets (the Getty gas stations). Since Texaco already had ample refining capacity, the merger was deemed a good fit—and yet, in view of the declining price of crude since the merger, the return on the price paid for Getty's reserves may or may not turn out to be profitable. (The suit won by Pennzoil against Texaco is, of course, another negative; see further discussion in Chapter 8.)

A seeming diversion that arose at the end of the merger— namely, the Bass Brothers' acquisition of about $1 billion of Texaco stock—caused some concern among Texaco's management that the Basses were attempting a takeover of Texaco. To avoid that risk, Texaco bought back that stock at a 20 percent premium. A number of Texaco stockholders charged that that payment amounted to "greenmail" (that is, that stockholders' money was used to safeguard the jobs of Texaco's executives).

A number of empirical studies find that one unequivocal result of mergers is that stockholders of the *target* firm clearly benefit.[5] In the above example, Getty stockholders doubled

---

[5] See, for example, P. Asquith, "Merger Bids, Uncertainty, and Stockholder Returns," *Journal of Financial Economics*, April 1983, pp. 51–83.

their money because of the merger. For Texaco, on the other hand, not only did the merger's benefits (GAIN) become subject to the vagaries of subsequent oil prices, but the firm was hostage to the market pressures associated with the mechanics of the merger itself.

By contrast, in another megamerger, that of Conoco in 1981, the stockholders in the target firm appeared to have chosen the less attractive alternative. Moreover, that takeover was hostile; Conoco's managers preferred that the firm remain a freestanding unit.

In 1981 Conoco had $11 billion of assets (book value) and was the 14th largest U.S. firm in terms of sales. It became a target for (1) Mobil (another oil company and the second largest U.S. firm), (2) Du Pont (the 15th largest U.S. firm), and (3) Seagram (a large Canadian firm). In size, the merger, that was eventually consummated was as large as *total* merger activity in any prior year.

Prior to the bidding, Conoco's price was about $50 per share; Conoco's coal, oil, and gas reserves plus its plant and equipment were thought to far exceed their market or book values. Not surprisingly, in the bidding for Conoco, its stock price rose above $100 per share.

In the struggle for Conoco, the U.S. Department of Justice indicated that it would fight a merger with Mobil (a horizontal, or market-share, merger) but *not* a merger with Du Pont or Seagram. Thus, although Mobil made the highest bid ($115 per share), stockholders chose a Du Pont offer of about $95 per share. They made that decision because a Department of Justice objection to the Mobil merger might have stopped the process and dropped the Conoco price below Du Pont's $95 offer.

For Du Pont, the need to borrow to finance the takeover more than quadrupled its $1.6 billion debt, thereby causing it to lose its AAA bond rating—evidence that benefits to the acquiring firm are less than certain or may even be equivocal at best. Why, then, do the acquiring firms do it?

## MERGER CALCULATIONS

Both of the previous case studies indicate that the target firm is the beneficiary of a share of the merger's GAIN. Following

Brealey and Myers's approach again, and if the following relationships hold (with firm A the acquiring and firm B the target), suppose that the market values B firm differently before and after, the *announcement* of the merger.[6]

| Outcome | Value of B's Stock |
|---|---|
| 1. No merger | $PV_B$: Value per share of B as a separate unit |
| 2. Merger occurs | $PV_B$: *Plus* some part of the GAIN from merger |

Suppose the following numbers hold for outcome 1 above.

|  | Firm A | Firm B |
|---|---|---|
| Market price per share | $75 | $15 |
| Number of shares | 100,000 | 60,000 |
| Market value of firm | $7,500,000 | $900,000 |

Assume that firm A expects to pay a $300,000 premium, or a total of $1.2 million cash, for B. A's COST would be:

$$A's\ COST = (CASH - MV_B) + (MV_B - PV_B)$$
$$= \$300,000 + 0 = \$300,000$$

Now suppose that, instead of paying cash, A offers B's stockholders 16,000 shares of its own stock. Then A's estimated cost would be (less $PV_B$) as follows:

$$Estimated\ COST = 16,000 \times \$75 - \$900,000 = \$300,000$$

But there are three reasons why this might *not* be so:

1. B's value (as a separate unit) may not be $900,000.
2. A's value (as a separate unit) may not be $7,500,000.
3. Since, after the merger, B's stockholders now own a share of A, they also own a share of A's merger GAIN over and above their own GAIN.

The proportionate share of A owned by B's old stockholders (call this X) after the merger will be as follows even if the stock price estimates of the two firms turn out to be correct:

---

[6]Brealey & Myers, *Principles of Corporate Finance*, pp. 711–13.

$$X = \frac{16,000}{100,000 + 16,000} = 0.138$$

Now assume that A's total GAIN from the merger is $400,000; then:

$$
\begin{aligned}
PV_{AB} &= PV_A + PV_B + GAIN \\
&= \$7,500,000 + \$900,000 + \$400,000 \\
&= \$8.8 \text{ million}
\end{aligned}
$$

It follows that

$$
\begin{aligned}
A\text{'s FINAL COST} &= X(PV_{AB} - PV_B) \\
&= 0.138(\$8.8 \text{ million}) - \$900,000 \\
&= \$314,000
\end{aligned}
$$

In effect, if the total GAIN is $400,000, then firm A, which began the whole game, receives for its stockholders only: $400,000 - $314,000 = $86,000. Again, the target firm receives by far the largest value of the GAIN, and relative to pre-merger value, B's stockholders enjoy a more than one-third capital gain, while A's stockholders get a bit more than a 10th.

The benefits accruing to the acquiring firm, which are long term in nature, are clearly much more difficult to calculate than those for the acquired firm. For that reason, while the market's view of A's present value may remain fairly stable, it may now represent a stable averaging of a much wider set of expectations than that which held prior to the merger.


## ROLE OF INVESTMENT BANKERS

The specific case studies and examples noted above did not consider such problems for the *bidding firm* as:

1. Forecasting GAIN for some time in the future.
2. Planning and transactions costs associated with a tender proposal (friendly or unfriendly) or a merger. This also requires the preparation of legal and financial documents.
3. Estimate of probability (and/or cost) of potential for antitrust action by the Department of Justice or another relevant government agency (FTC, FCC, SEC, 50 states).

4. Estimates of prices per share of the target firm following the announcement of the takeover, merger, and so forth. This has a strategic impact on COST.
5. Estimates of prices per share of the bidding firm following the announcement. From the bidding firm's view, this will affect GAIN.
6. Estimates of types and amount of additional financing needed to execute the deal (recall Du Pont's downgrading of debt quality).

The target firm will seek investment banking advice especially if the merger or takeover is neither sought nor wanted.[7] Defenses by unwilling firms often involve battles in which heavyweight corporations, as well as heavyweight investment bankers, engage in mutually taxing fights over financial and corporate control. One such example is the bizarre four-way fight in 1982 that began with an attempt by Bendix Corporation to take over Martin Marietta Corp.[8] At one stage it looked as if, in a so-called Pac-Man defense, Bendix might own 70 percent of Martin Marietta, while Martin Marietta (perhaps with the aid of United Technologies) might own 50 percent of Bendix. If that fight had gone to the finish, the outcome would have depended on who could vote whose shares first—a tangle that the courts would have spent some time to unravel. To avoid a stalemate, Allied Corporation was brought in as a white knight, entered a bid for Bendix, and acquired that firm for $1.8 billion, while Bendix and Martin Marietta swapped their holdings of each other's stock on the basis of market value. Further residual (and major) financial readjustments required further investment banking actions. The originator of the whole struggle, Bendix, disappeared,[9] while Martin Marietta maintained its independent status, albeit with almost

---

[7] This brings up another role for investment bankers—finding a "white knight" for the target firm. A white knight is another corporation with which the target firm prefers to merge for many reasons (for example, better fit, hence better terms).

[8] For a complete discussion, see Hope Lampert, *Till Death Do Us Part* (New York: Harcourt Brace Jovanovich, 1983).

[9] The former president of Bendix, William M. Agee, first accepted a senior, but not the top, position with Allied Corporation, a position he resigned in less than a year. When he left Allied, (including membership on its board) he received a golden parachute worth $4.1 million.

$900 million of new debt raised to buy Bendix stock in its Pac-Man defense. In addition, Martin Marietta had to issue almost $350 million of new stock to buy back the shares that Allied had acquired during the struggle. (Chapter 15 on block trading discusses Allied's disposal of a block of RCA shares previously owned by Bendix.)

The foregoing is a much-condensed version of a complex, if not Byzantine, struggle. Each transaction in the secondary markets required quick and effective execution of the equivalent of large-scale blocks. Bids and offers involved nearly hourly consultations with investment bankers on all sides regarding current pricing of present values of enormously large future cash flows.[10] Investment bankers can serve as important consultants prior to and in the process of decisions that may mean the survival or the disappearance of multibillion dollar firms.

Finally, the merger and acquisition departments of major investment bankers can execute deals, provide continuous consultations, offer tactical and strategic advice regarding proxy fights, antitrust implications, and last—but not least—the new-money financing required during and after the battle. But before moving into that part of the operational activities of investment banking firms and their clients, an important issue must be resolved, namely, the valuation to merging firms of mergers, acquisitions, and tender offers. This is not a simple task.

## MEASURING BENEFITS TO THE BIDDING FIRM

Modern studies of the benefits to acquirers and acquired firms use the same currency—price per share of the firm's stock. Nearly all studies of benefits to the bidding firms suggest that such benefits are much more difficult to perceive than those of

---

[10]For the record, the following firms and investment bankers were involved:

| Firm | Investment Bankers |
|------|--------------------|
| Bendix | Salomon Brothers, First Boston |
| Martin Marietta | Kidder, Peabody |
| United Technologies | Lazard Frères |
| Allied Corp. | Lehman Brothers |

the acquired firms. Rather than repeat these results, shown in many academic studies,[11] note the following analysis of GAIN and its distribution between the bidding firm and the acquired firm.

Consider, first, the impact on the acquirer's GAIN produced by mere difference in *size* between the two firms involved. On average, the acquiring firm is about five times the size of the acquired firm. Suppose, then, that a $5 billion firm seeks to acquire a $1 billion firm. The expected GAIN from the merger is $500 million, or a hefty 50 percent premium for the acquired firm, of which the acquiring firm originally expects to capture one half (or $250 million). Table 7–2 indicates in part I the pre-merger and in part II the *expected* post-merger situation for firm A, the acquiring firm. In fact, it is the expectations set forth in part II that induce firm A to begin the merger process.

But now suppose that, in the process of putting together the merger and its transaction and financing costs, the split of the GAIN becomes less favorable to the acquiring firm. Since it is difficult to stop any megabuck-sized process, the final distribution of the GAIN tends to shift further in favor of the acquired firm, leaving the results as shown in part III of the table.

Firm A winds up with a stock price about 3 percent higher than pre-merger, while firm B's stock price, at the merger's consummation, yields its stockholders a GAIN of nearly 38 percent. Because there is likely to be a good deal of random noise regarding the level of stock A's price, especially in the neighborhood of a merger owing to, say, the unwinding of arbitrage positions (see the next chapter), some small price variance could be accounted for on purely technical grounds. The combined relative size effect and transaction factors could make it much more difficult to show a positive GAIN for the acquiring firm than for the acquired firm. And all of the above hold even without any assumption of greenmail, which affects only the GAIN of the acquiring (or surviving) firm.

Finally, the preceding valuation of the acquiring firm's

---

[11] The following discussion owes a good deal to a paper by Baruch Lev, "Observations on the Merger Phenomenon and a Review of the Evidence," *Midland Corporate Finance Journal* 1, no. 4 (1983).

**TABLE 7–2**

Calculation of GAIN and Its Distribution between Acquiring and Acquired Firms

| | | | Share Price |
|---|---|---|---|
| **I. Pre-merger** | | | |
| 1. Acquiring firm, $PV_A$ | = | $5 billion | $50 |
| 2. To be acquired firm, $PV_B$ | = | $1 billion | $50 |
| **II. Expected post-merger (GAIN** | = | **$500 million)** | |
| 1. $PV_A$ – $5 billion + .5 ($500 million) | = | $5.25 billion | $52½ |
| 2. $PV_B$ – $1 billion + .5 ($500 million) | = | $1.25 billion | $62½ |
| **III. Actual post-merger** | | | |
| 1. $PV_A$ – $5 billion + .25 ($500 million) | = | $5.125 billion | $51¼ |
| 2. $PV_B$ – $1 billion + .75 ($500 million) | = | $1.375 billion | $68¾ |

price per share assumed away the effect on the stock price of raising the funds to finance the acquisition. Suppose that the acquisition had been financed by new borrowing, for that clearly has been the recent funding of choice for cash acquisitions. The consequent rise in the acquiring firm's debt/equity ratio could certainly explain at least some part of that firm's short-term slack performance in the stock market. Indeed, the closer the volume of new debt comes to the size of the acquisition, the more likely a rise in the combined firm's debt/asset ratio. In the short run, then, the bidding firm's stock price should show a relatively low GAIN, if any.

# 8

# Mergers and Acquisitions II:
# Risk Arbitrage and Merger Market
# Making as Insurance

In the process of participating in the merger game as a market maker, investment bankers perform many roles, most obviously as advisers to the target and bidding firms. Yet even when they are participating indirectly—that is, when they are *not* acting as advisers to either side in the transaction—their role can still be sizable and profitable. And when they act as arbitrageurs, they help make the market more efficient with respect to the merger process itself.

## RISK ARBITRAGE

Arbitrageurs take a position in the firms involved in a merger or a takeover. They are interested in the *AB deal* not in becoming stockholders in A or B. In order to commit funds to the deal, they must be sure that the deal will go through.[1]

The assessment made by the "arb" may be based on security analysis of the two firms' financial statements and on reports in Moody's and Standard & Poor's—all designed to

---

[1] The following is based in part on G. P. Wyser-Pratte, *Risk Arbitrage II* (Monograph 1982–3/4, Salomon Brothers Center, Graduate School of Business Administration, New York University, 1982).

evaluate the economic logic behind the combination. (This is the equivalent of an independent evaluation of what was called GAIN above). The arb may also attempt to get more information from the two firms. In Wyser-Pratte's words, "It is at this point that the curtain rises on one of the great comic operas of Wall Street. . . the [acquired firm] is normally totally cooperative, realizing that the arbitrageur can, by purchasing [its] stock, accumulate votes which will naturally be cast in favor of the merger. . . . The [acquiring] firm is an entirely different matter. He will not be pleased that [his]. . . stock may become the subject of constant short selling by arbitrageurs; he is thus often elusive in his responses."[2]

Arbs go long on the target firm and short on the acquiring firm. That way, the arb's hedged position is not at the mercy of the market (and its changing prices) but is at risk only with respect to the consummation of the deal (hence the term, risk arbitrage). At the consummation of the merger, the arb tenders his long stock in B, the acquired firm, like every other B stockholder, and with the proceeds (or the new shares received from the merger) covers his short in A. If the market falls during these negotiations, and even if his proceeds from B are less, he makes money on the short position. If the market rises, he makes on the long what he loses on his short. In the end, if the arb is not nimble enough to unwind his position should the merger unravel, he becomes an unwilling investor with a possible problem position in his short. The following example examines this process more closely.

## THE RISK-ARBITRAGE DEAL[3]

Suppose a merger is being contemplated by company A with company B. The bidder (A) expects to acquire the target (B) through a one-for-one exchange of stock: one share of A for one share of B. Prior to the announcement of A's intent, A's price is $30 per share, while B is trading at $20 per share. B's price had risen to $25 per share prior to the announcement of A's intent (and the associated, customary, and temporary sus-

---

[2] Ibid., pp. 8–9.

[3] This discussion is based on Ivan F. Boesky, *Merger Mania* (New York: Holt, Rinehart & Winston, 1985), chap. 2.

THE RISK-ARBITRAGE DEAL / **105**

pension of trading in B's stock). Because, ultimately, the arbitrageur can acquire a share of A (price $30) with a share of B (pre-merger), he counts the $5 difference between B's price and A's as his potential gross profit. That $5 spread exists because B cannot be converted into A immediately; the arbitrageur's problem is to ensure that the spread is maintained until the merger is consummated. But the spread may narrow and/or disappear entirely:

1. As the merger becomes more likely.
2. As the time prior to merger shortens.
3. As market prices of A and B change owing to the market's vagaries.

Taking the latter point first, if A's price should fall toward $25, the spread could narrow and even vanish. Thus, as a first step, the arbitrageur sells short the number of shares he wants to acquire of A at $30 per share. As protection against the open-ended risk that A could rise sharply, the arbitrageur also buys the same number of shares of B long, thereby indirectly acquiring A at the merger price.[4]

Two possible sets of price changes might affect the relative values of A and B at the time of the merger's closing. Company A's price could drop prior to merger, or it could rise. Suppose A drops in price to $27 at the closing; in a share-for-share merger, B would then be worth $27 as well. By selling A short (at $30) and holding B at $25, the arbitrageur maintains his $5 spread as follows:

1. Sells B at $27 per share:

Per share profit = $27 – $25 = $2

2. Buys A at $27 per share; covers $30 short at $27:

Per share profit = $30 – $27 = $3
Per share total profit = $5

If, on the other hand, A's price rises to, say, $34 per share, so will the price of B rise to $34 per share at closing. The capital

---

[4]A short sale involves borrowing the number of shares sold short (from a broker or an investment manager) and then returning those shares to the lender when the short sale is reversed.

gain from B (per share) will be $34 − $25 = $9. If that gain is subtracted from the loss of $4 per share on the short sale of A at $30 ($34 − $30 = 4), the gross spread of $5 still holds.

Even if the actual exchange of securities is more complicated than a one-for-one stock deal (as it usually is), the principle in structuring the arbitrage spread is the same: the target firm's securities are held long; the bidding firm's securities are sold short.

## CALCULATING THE RATE OF RETURN FROM RISK ARBITRAGE[5]

Continue the assumption that B is merging into A and each share of B will get a share of A in an even exchange of stock. B is now selling at $25 per share while A is selling at $30 per share, and neither company is expected to pay a dividend prior to consummation.[6] Consummation will take place in four months, an important variable in the calculation of the annualized rate of return to the deal (see following calculations).

The arb's first analysis of the rate of return works as follows, at an annual rate:

Gross return on deal multiplied by annualized rates:[7]

$$\frac{\$30 - \$25}{\$25} \times 3 = 60 \text{ percent}$$

The short sale of A is necessarily part of this approach since new (post-merger) shares (call these $A_n$) are "created" by buying B long. This makes sense since the arb shorts the old $30 A stock and buys long the equivalent of $A_n$ at $25 (that is, holds B long). Here is one of the technical problems of arbitrageurs. If there is a struggle for controlling the shares in a merger or a takeover, the arb may have trouble borrowing enough stock for a short position to set up the hedge counterpart of the arbitrage position he wants to achieve. On the other side of the deal, competitive forces tend to drive up the premium on B, thereby lowering the gross return on the deal.

---

[5] The example is adapted from Wyser-Pratte, *Risk Arbitrage II*, pp. 18–19.

[6] This is only a simplifying assumption.

[7] There are three periods of four months per year.

Entirely apart from hedging the position with respect to changes in market-price levels, shorting the acquiring firm makes sense because, if the arb did not do so, an exchange of B stock for A, post-merger, might concentrate too many shares of the surviving firm in unwilling arb hands. In turn, the arb's interest in selling out that position might depress A's price following the merger's closing, not only cutting the acquiring firm's GAIN further but also (and from arb's point of view, more importantly) cutting into the profit from the position. Finally and not unexpectedly, the short sale helps to establish some tax benefits for the arb. The short sale may provide possible short-term losses to offset short-term gains.[8]

Setting up and unwinding of arbitrage positions tends to produce positive price effects on B, which is held long until closing; in that sense, arbitrage supports the acquired firm's GAIN. Conversely, for the acquiring firm, the establishment of a short position, and its subsequent unwinding, generates a great deal of noise/signal price information especially at the time of consummation. The arb's disparate treatment of the two firms tends to support the price of the acquired firm, while generating a high ratio of noise/signal price information for the acquiring firm, especially at the time of closing. The more contested the merger, the greater the size of the noise/signal ratio. As Stewart Myers pointed out, "in mergers, the ratio of 'noise' to 'signal' is very high."[9]

Who are these arbs? According to Wyser-Pratte they are members of the best-known investment banking firms "who commit house capital . . . in the various forms of arbitrage. The list includes such outstanding firms as Lehman Brothers (in an earlier incarnation), Goldman Sachs, L. F. Rothschild, Morgan Stanley, and Salomon Brothers.[10] He is too modest to mention his own firm, Prudential Bache, and in another context he also mentions Ivan Boesky, who heads the largest free-standing firm of arbs; Wyser-Pratte also indicates that Morgan Stanley and Merrill Lynch are important players in risk arbitrage.

---

[8] See Wyser-Pratte, *Risk Arbitrage II*, especially pp. 22–24.

[9] Stewart Myers, "The Evaluation of an Acquisition Target," *Midland Corporate Finance Journal* 1, no. 4, p. 39.

[10] Wyser-Pratte, *Risk Arbitrage II*, p. 4.

Also, because most arbitrage transactions are deal oriented rather than market oriented, other broker-dealer firms as well as individuals deemed to be "fringe players" try to participate in some deals. Nevertheless, Wyser-Pratte and others have argued that market shocks and problem deals tend to send the fringe players to the showers early. After all, the pros can afford to lose on some deals what they previously made on others. The occasional player will not be as effectively diversified in a cross-section of deals.

Finally, nonprofessional traders are at a substantial rate-of-return disadvantage relative to the pros. First, the amount of funds (nonborrowed) needed by NYSE member firms to participate in a deal is far less (haircut on long position plus modest capital/liabilities ratio) compared to a 50 percent capital margin rule for individuals.[11] Further, for member firms there is no capital requirement on short positions, while the same (Regulation T) margin rule applies to all credit transactions of individuals. Whatever returns are earned are thus applied for individuals against a much larger capital position than for member firms; in addition, the out-of-pocket transaction costs to the member firms are probably significantly less. Wyser-Pratte argues that the risk-adjusted return advantage of professionals over individuals is about 8.5 times.[12] Even if it were only half as great, it would, at best, make nonprofessionals a minor element in mergers.

## INVESTMENT BANKERS: OTHER ACTIVITIES IN CORPORATE RESTRUCTURING[13]

Investment bankers are substantially involved with client consultations on both sides of acquisitions and mergers, finding a white knight, and so forth. They also participate in risk arbitrage on their own. Only a few additional functions remain to

---

[11] Wyser-Pratte's data refer to an 80 percent margin rule (Fed. Regulation T).

[12] Wyser-Pratte, *Risk Arbitrage II*, pp. 30–31.

[13] This section is based in part on K. Schipper, "The Evidence on Divestitures, Going-Private Proposals and Spin-Offs," *Midland Corporate Finance Journal* 1, no. 4, pp. 51–55; and C. Ferenbach, "Leveraged Buyouts: A New Capital Market," *Midland Corporate Finance Journal* 1, no. 4, pp. 56–63.

be discussed: divestitures, going private, leveraged buyouts, and spin-offs. The first and last of these are, once again, examples of the new math: 5 − 1 = 5, or more.

A divestiture is, pure and simple, a sale of assets for cash, where presumably the sale and its attendant improvement in balance-sheet liquidity make the firm more valuable than holding the (now sold) assets. In other words, the substitution of *cash* in the asset portfolio called the firm for the *assets* sold raises the firm's value.

All the other corporate restructuring policies mentioned imply no change in the value of the assets but claim a benefit from a restructuring of the right side of the balance sheet. For example, "going private" means the repurchase of shares from the market—not on a piecemeal basis but the entire outstanding stock issue—so that ownership is no longer public but is concentrated in a small private group typically centered on management. A spin-off is an internalized divestiture where a subsidiary is set up with its own separate shares that are then issued to the original stockholders. These stockholders may then decide on their own portfolio (or liquidity ratio) policies by selling the shares for cash or holding them in portfolio.

The going-private type of reorganization of the firm's capital structure is done to improve monitoring incentives for management by eliminating the separation of ownership and management. In other words, agency costs are eliminated by collapsing a public corporation into private ownership.

Leveraged buyouts are what they say they are: the new owners (that is, *the lenders*) buy out the current stockholders. A firm that might have had a ratio of equity/debt of 9/1 turns that ratio upside down. Management may take a more significant position in the much reduced equity, while lenders may benefit from higher rates on the larger debt. Many of these deals were made during the high-interest-rate periods of the early 1980s. Such decisions were made easier for many lenders because of (1) long-standing credit relationships and (2) the substitution of a 14 percent buyout issue for a 9 percent bond.[14] On the risk analysis side, as long as a lender's portfolio remained effectively diversified among credit ratings as well

---

[14] To the extent that these same lenders were concerned about marking to market some 9 percent bonds selling below par, that same decision appeared even more sensible.

as among industries, the higher coupons as well as the elimination of below-par bonds made the risks appear acceptable. Besides, many banks (and other lenders) became packagers of leveraged buyouts and actively sold such deals as agents, happily collecting the fees involved. Why would they demonstrate their lack of faith in the product by not investing in it? Investment banking firms proper also invested in such deals as well as working as packagers.

It is interesting to examine the quantitative importance of all of the above on common stock retirements. Mergers, acquisitions, going private, and leveraged buyouts all necessarily involve a gross reduction in some equity issues. The next to last line of Table 8-1 indicates that, beginning with the first half of 1984, stocks as a source of corporate funding turned negative. In other words, the total volume of outstanding equity declined by:

$41.5 billion in the first half of 1984.
$34.5 billion in the second half of 1984.
$18.9 billion (estimated) in the first half of 1985.

A comparison with capital requirements by the total non-financial corporate sector (upper half of Table 8-1) shows that 1983 capital requirements (when equity sources of funds were a positive number) were not significantly different from the needs for capital funds in 1984 or 1985. From this it follows that the switch of equity sourcing to a net negative number was based on the excess of stock retirements over gross new issues.

### Investment Banker Fees Once Again

All of these stock retirements and the issuing of new paper to finance acquisitions involve investment bankers not only as advisers to each of the parties involved but also as experts in pricing either the new securities or in setting a fair price on securities to be retired. Setting a price on a stock for a firm in a leveraged buyout or in going private is, in most respects, an analog to pricing a secondary or block trade.

This point regarding fee income was restated as follows in an article in The Wall Street Journal (August 12, 1985, p. 13):

**TABLE 8–1**

Sources and Uses of Corporate Funds* (annual income, expenditures, and net increases in amounts outstanding, dollars in billions)

| | 1983 | | 1984 | | 1985† |
|---|---|---|---|---|---|
| | First Half | Second Half | First Half | Second Half | First Half |
| **Requirements:** | | | | | |
| Total physical investment | $115.2 | $145.2 | $176.4 | $187.8 | $180.1 |
| Plus net receivables | 16.4 | – 2.8 | 20.3 | – 0.2 | 17.4 |
| Less internal cash generation | 117.5 | 153.7 | 152.6 | 168.5 | 155.5 |
| Capital requirement | 14.0 | – 11.3 | 44.2 | 19.1 | 42.0 |
| Plus requirement for financial assets | 27.7 | 66.6 | 7.4 | 46.9 | 2.3 |
| Less foreign equity investment | 5.5 | 4.5 | 9.1 | 7.6 | 10.2 |
| Total external requirements | $36.3 | $50.8 | $42.6 | $58.4 | $34.1 |
| **Sources:** | | | | | |
| Mortgages | $1.9 | $1.1 | $0.5 | $ – 0.1 | $ – 0.4 |
| Bank loans | – 3.2 | 22.1 | 44.1 | 31.1 | 9.7 |
| Finance company loans | 3.9 | 9.8 | 10.1 | 9.3 | 8.2 |
| U.S. government loans | 0.3 | – 0.7 | 0.1 | 2.4 | 2.4 |
| Net sales of open market paper | – 0.5 | – 0.3 | 17.9 | 4.9 | 13.0 |
| Tax-exempt bonds | 5.3 | 4.1 | 4.2 | 14.3 | 4.3 |
| Taxable corporate bonds‡ | 9.4 | 5.8 | 5.8 | 25.7 | 11.6 |
| Eurobonds (for domestic uses)‡ | 1.4 | 1.1 | 1.4 | 5.3 | 4.2 |
| Stocks‡ | 17.7 | 7.9 | – 41.5 | – 34.5 | – 18.9 |
| Total external sources | $36.3 | $50.8 | $42.6 | $58.4 | $34.1 |

*Nonfarm, nonfinancial corporations.

†Partly estimated.

‡Salomon Brothers Inc. estimates. All other data from Federal Reserve Board of Governors.

The current rush to restructure offers investment bankers lots of ways to make money. For example, Morgan Stanley & Co. could earn more than $10.4 million for helping CBS buy back its stock, $1.5 million for financial advice, $1.9 million for placing preferred stock with institutional investors, and $3 million if Morgan Stanley can fend off unwanted suitors for another year. Morgan Stanley could earn additional fees if it helps CBS sell the $300 million in assets the company plans to shed.

The market-making skills performed by investment bankers in their routine activities can be transferred to mergers, acquisitions, divestitures, reorganizations, and risk arbitrage. One of the underappreciated examples of synergism in mergers and acquisitions is the pricing and operating skills investment bankers develop at their trading desks and put at the service of their merger clients.

## THE MERGER FEE AS AN INSURANCE PREMIUM

Early in 1985, in a suit involving the Trans-Union Corporation's directors, a Delaware court found that the latter had failed to "exercise informed business judgment" in selling the company. The directors agreed to a settlement in which shareholders were paid $23.5 million in damages. Insurance, the acquiring firm, *and the directors themselves* paid for the damage award. Later that same year, a Texas court rendered a $10.53 billion judgment for Pennzoil and against Texaco, following the Getty merger, thereby starting a clock on interest costs that could run Texaco an additional $1 billion per year. Partly in response to a flurry of stockholder suits, insurance companies have raised the premiums on corporate directors' liability coverage to "astronomical" levels—if they make it available at all. And finally, outside corporate directors are resigning, even while many directors' slots remain vacant.

This set of phenomena should be kept in mind when reviewing the large size of advisors' fees (for lawyers, investment bankers, and so forth) in recent megamergers, takeovers, leveraged buyouts. The fairness opinions and other services purchased by corporate managers and directors from investment bankers, big-eight accounting firms, and merger lawyers should themselves be looked on as insurance premiums. Board members and managers buy that additional insurance because they believe it will protect them from legal attack from any parties to the deal (even if the attacks are ultimately unsuccessful). This demand for insurance has also been expanded because the "business-judgment rule" can no longer be assumed to provide an automatic or procedural legal defense. Every day brings news of expensive liability insurance settlements and still more costly increases in directors' liability insurance coverage.[15]

These developments have been in the making for some time and are reflected in the large fees paid to the major investment banking firms in merger and takeover cases. Managements and the boards of directors are buying insurance for themselves from the investment banking firms. The best way to see this is to separate the demand side from the supply side of these phenomena.

## Demand for Advice

**A. Attitudes.** Suppose a firm's board members and management find they are the target of an unwanted and unanticipated takeover bid. The first shock has worn off, the panic, anger, and other emotional reactions have been talked out. The next policy step is to evaluate an appropriate response policy with board and management participants who have had prior experience with such events. In most cases, and especially if a board member happens to be an investment banker, there will be a call for experts in the following areas:

1. Defense: poison pill, crown jewel sale, and so forth.
2. Implementation of defense and/or other strategies that are designed to lead to higher premiums on the target firm's stock.
3. Alternative reorganization: leveraged buyout and so forth.

---

[15]The settlements referred to involved, among others, Chase Manhattan Corp. in a suit against its own officers who were connected with the purchase of loans from Penn Square Bank in Oklahoma. The same source cited more than tenfold increases in the direct cost of coverage for directors' liability as well as a fourfold jump in deductibles and an "insertion of a dozen new exclusions" in the policies. (Source: L. Sloane, "Insurer-Management Rift Seen Growing," *The New York Times*, December 19, 1985.)

For most of these activities, outside consultants will probably be brought in and *not necessarily because* board members
have not had similar experience before.

Board members have an attitude that can be described in its
simplest terms as a "negative agency" approach. Consider the
following:

a. In the past, directors may have been insured against
   liability suits, but that insurance was never unlimited
   and is becoming less available.
b. Decisions that are made regarding the price of assets to
   be sold or the pricing of securities to be issued in an
   atmosphere of conflict and contested policies are not
   going to be easy. Nor are these pricing decisions necessarily related to currently published price data.
c. A good decision will be rewarded by the renewal of a
   director's contract at a decent (but not exorbitantly attractive) rate of return. A bad decision (in the perception of some litigious stockholder) may result in ruin-
   ous legal costs even if the board's decision is ultimately
   upheld.

Because, in the absence of experts, board members are
exposed to a risk of substantially greater losses than of potential gain, board members and management may opt for a call to
lawyers and investment bankers. This attitude aspect of the
demand side is reinforced by the second major element,
namely, funny money.

**B. Funny Money.**  In megamergers, target firms have been
able to leverage enormous sums out of the bidding firms as
premiums paid to stockholders. Moreover, the fact that the
bidding firm is likely to have its investment bankers and
lawyers as active participants in the negotiations will reinforce the demand side for similar services by the target firm.
And finally, for the board members of the target firm, the
payment of a $100 million fee out of a $1 billion (or larger)
premium can be rationalized as representing a transaction cost
of some 10 percentage points. From point of view of the
bidding firm, the fact that the funds are raised by borrowing or
other "cheap" sources can be rationalized by the same type of
argument.

**C. The Supply Side.** It might be argued that investment bankers charge the large fees they do because they take on the risks of stockholder suits transferred to them by the boards that hire them. This is true in a general way. But it is hard to believe that, say, more than 1 in 10 mergers will generate an expensive suit. This portfolio approach reflects, of course, the possibility that investment bankers (or lawyers) diversify their risks in ways that board members or managers of a single firm cannot.

But if there is efficiency in that type of risk diversification, shouldn't competition bring down the cost of merger participation and consultation by other investment bankers eager to get into the game? Isn't this merger consultation arrangement analogous to the bidding for new issues that has driven down gross spreads?

The major difference here is the essentially confidential nature of merger advice and participation as opposed to the open competition for flotation of new issues (since shelf registration came on the scene) regarding gross spreads. Further, each merger or takeover conflict has elements that are not as readily converted to conventional bidding mechanics as are the rate (and nonrate) items of a new issue. Even innovative new issues carry wider gross spreads than those types of securities that have entered secondary trading.

Beyond all of the above are the elements of perceived quality differences among investment bankers. Such demand side elements (and negative agency attitudes) induce management to go with well-known, as opposed to newer, entrants even if the latter offer more competitive fees. In a crisis atmosphere when decisions must be made fast, who do you consult: the person with experience or the new guy on the block offering a cheaper service, especially if you're risking litigation as a board member and "spending" someone else's money?

Investment bankers represent what may be the nation's largest *unregulated* insurance business. The insurance process is an important aspect of the new-issues business as well, but there the competition tends to reduce fees (with the exceptions to be noted).

# Conclusion, Part I: Information Conflicts for Investment Bankers

As this book was going to press (June 1986) a number of insider trading cases surfaced. Inevitably, many professionals—lawyers, investment bankers, accountants—are involved in the planning of any major corporate change. Because such professionals take on the status of "insiders," they are subject to serious legal penalties if they use that information for personal gain.

In the process of attempting to land lucrative merger fees, investment bankers have cultivated arbitrageurs, and this use of information is what made Dennis B. Levine an important client getter at his firm.[1] What was not known at the time was that Levine used the inside information to buy and sell the companies' stock illegally. He pled guilty in June 1986. The same article suggested that others may have been involved in such illegal activities.

Inside information is difficult to handle even if all concerned attempt to stay within the law. In particular, the arbitrage department of an investment banker or the corporate finance department may be privy to inside information whose premature disclosure would breach the confidentiality of the

---

[1] See J. B. Stewart, D. Hertzberg, and Scott McMurray, "How Inside Knowledge Made, Ruined Career of Dennis B. Levine," *The Wall Street Journal*, May 15, 1986, p. 1.

banker-client relationship. If such disclosure is made to security traders of the investment banker, these traders have an unfair advantage over other market participants; under the Securities and Exchange Act, this is illegal as well. To avoid such disclosures, most firms have developed what is called a Chinese Wall between the inside information to which the investment banking group has access and the market information made available to market makers. This well-known procedure may not solve information conflicts as shown by a case brought in 1972, *Slade v. Shearson, Hammill & Co., Inc.* [CCH Fed. Sec. L. Rep. 94,329 (1974)].[2]

In 1972 a stockholder (Slade) in a firm called Tidal Marine charged that the firm's investment bankers, Shearson, Hammill & Co., had permitted its registered representatives to promote Tidal's stock even though Shearson's investment banking department knew that a large proportion of Tidal's fleet had been damaged. The registered reps were never told this news because Shearson, like many other Wall Street firms, had set up a Chinese Wall between the two departments.

This Shearson policy went so far as to preclude formal "buy" recommendations to be issued for securities of investment banking clients. But apparently, individual reps were permitted to research and free-lance recommendations, including the stocks of investment banking clients.

When Shearson's investment banking department first heard the adverse news regarding Tidal, they tried to persuade Tidal to disclose the information to the public. When Tidal stonewalled this request, Shearson threatened to go to the regulators with the story. After that, Tidal disclosed the information to the SEC, and Shearson terminated its investment banking relationship with Tidal.

The original court in the case held that Shearson (or its reps) were prohibited from soliciting customers without disclosing *all* adverse information. Since disclosure might violate Shearson's confidential relationship to its investment banking client, its only alternative was to actively *prohibit* stock trading of client stocks. Such a doctrine (though far from profitable) might be proposed in a period of stable banker-

---

[2]This section draws on N. Wolfson, *Conflicts of Interest: Investment Banking* (New York: Twentieth Century Fund, 1976), pp. 62–70.

client relationships, but in the trading environment of the 1980s, it was an almost impossible standard to sustain. In some particularly sensitive information environments (for example, a forthcoming merger), such a stop-trade order could be interpreted by itself as providing an inappropriate market signal.

Further information-exposure dilemmas have been raised in the superheated climate of the current merger wave. In the early stages of what was hoped to be a friendly takeover of a U.S. firm by a Swiss corporation, another form of information conflict occurred.

In the summer of 1984, a small group of Carnation Milk's owners and managers (the U.S. firm) were in discussion with the managing director of Nestlé (the Swiss firm) regarding a friendly takeover. In these discussions, Nestlé insisted that if absolute secrecy were not maintained, the discussion might be broken off. (There are no rules against insider trading in Swiss security markets.) In early August, the treasurer of Carnation, who had *not* been informed of these discussions, was quoted by the press as saying that a recent sharp run-up in Carnation's stock could not be attributed to "... news from the company and to corporate developments." What occurred was a clash of corporate cultures between the Swiss desire for absolutely secret discussion (as well as for least pressure from market forces to run up their acquisition price), and the U.S. requirement for full disclosure. But as the negotiations proceeded, the treasurer of Carnation, the target firm, was not fully informed by negotiators but was told to reply "no comment" if asked for information again. Such a statement, while more truthful, would, just because it represented a change from prior statements, also add to the market-price pressure on the target firm, thereby improving its purchase price.

The impact of *when* to go public with information may have a less-than-neutral effect in pricing takeovers. But the SEC's standard for releasing information is that "... to the extent that the standard for accuracy and completeness embodied in the antifraud statutes *is not met* [emphasis supplied], the company and any person responsible for the statement may be liable under the federal securities laws."[3]

---

[3] SEC, Securities Exchange Act Release No. 20560 (January 13, 1984).

# PART II

# The New-Issues Process

This part of the book covers the rationale, mechanics, and techniques involved in placing new issues in the capital markets. It begins with a transition from the market-making process discussed in Part I to suggest that the new-issue flotation process is another part of market making, albeit a rather special one. In the pricing of those securities, the issuer (that is, the corporation or the government) is brought directly into the market that determines its cost of capital for some time. The new-issue process can be made easier by market power as well as by market savvy. Accordingly, for the placement of large new issues, only the major investment banking firms in the industry play a significant role. This part begins with a general overview (Chapter 9) and then goes on to describe how a corporation decides that a new issue should be sold (Chapter 10) and how the work is done (Chapters 11–12).

# 9

## The New-Issue Underwriter: How to Price That Market-Making Service

The participation by investment bankers in any market-making activity, even as traders, is a necessary prerequisite for the primary service offered to the issuer, namely, the ability to put an appropriate price on a new issue. This is not a simple matter. Beyond satisfying a number of regulatory constraints, the price must be high enough to be acceptable to the issuer and simultaneously low enough to be attractive to the marketplace.

To develop and maintain pricing skills, underwriters for new stock and bond issues are involved in secondary-market trading (and market making). In those markets, such underwriters-dealers compete with all other broker-dealers who trade exclusively in the secondary market and only involve themselves in new-issue flotations (as small syndicate members) on occasion. From the point of view of managing a large investment banking firm, the secondary market is always an alternative to participation in the primary market. The underwriting firm thus has made a positive decision that, for a number of reasons, it will also participate in the primary market in that particular issue. At the same time, transactions in the primary market may include market making in a technical sense if, after the new issue is successfully launched, the investment banker continues to "make the market" in that issue.

For the initial public offering of, say, a common stock, only two basic decisions are open to the issuing firm: (1) a negotiated "fixed price" per share offering of which the underwriter buys the entire issue or (2) a "best-efforts" deal in which the underwriter provides technical or marketing assistance only, leaving to the issuing firm all of the risk with respect to price per share and total proceeds. Under the rules of fair practice of the NASD (a self-regulatory organization under the SEC), the dealer cannot sell the shares at a price higher than that set forth in the prospectus. If at that price the issue does not sell (the issue is said to be priced above the market), the underwriter is stuck with unsold inventory; that position, of course, is not the object of underwriting.

## NEW-ISSUE MARKET MAKING

A syndicate is a group of underwriters assembled to float a new issue. The firm in charge of the syndicate is called the managing underwriter or manager. To avoid accumulating unsold shares in the syndicate, the managing underwriter typically places a stabilizing bid in the market at the offer price to the public and, if the offering goes well, may sell short some supply of the stock during the offering. (See below for further discussion of syndicate tactics.) There are, to be sure, competitively set prices for new offerings such as, for example, electric public utilities. In an IPO for a new stock, however, it would be difficult to set up two (or more) competitive syndicates.

After the offering is completed and the syndicate is dissolved with little or no residual shares left, the managing underwriter may continue to act as a formal market maker, that is, as a dealer in secondary markets, especially if the new issue has not traded previously. This means hitting all bids and making offers at stated prices.

By contrast, in the typical best-efforts deal for issuing a new stock, the company is on its own unless it has arranged for price stabilization with an underwriter—of course, for a fee. The issuing firm might consider supporting its own stock price during the offering period, but this is unlikely. The new issue is sold to meet the need for added financing—and if financing is needed to support the issue price, the very purpose of the new issue is defeated dollar for dollar. The issuing firm is not likely to have market contacts and trading connections as good as professional underwriters—it is not a market maker. All else the same, the lesser market-making efficiency of a corporate issuer requires more financial capacity to support the same price than would be needed by an underwriter. (These points will be discussed further below.)

## THE INFORMATION SET FOR A NEW ISSUE

When a corporation decides to issue stock for initial sale to the public, it should provide potential buyers with information that makes the stock attractive or interesting for purchase. The new issue has to compete for the attention of investors with every better-known stock already trading. The buyer of an IPO doesn't buy the new stock to fill a conventional portfolio niche but, instead, has to be induced.

The need to attract information traders to IPO's is, of course, supported by the information requirements of the Securities Act of 1933, as amended. Legal sanctions force the investment banker to pursue energetically all material information from the issuer. This is called due diligence.

Further reasons induce the underwriter to pursue the information set with energy and effectiveness. If potential traders (individual or institutional) had better information than the underwriter in a fixed-price offering, they could short the new stock as it is issued or sell to the market maker after the offering is completed. This is another way of saying that the offering is mispriced. Copeland and Galai as well as Glosten and Milgrom have analyzed bid/ask spreads to offset adverse effects of information trading.[1] One defense of the underwriter against the ultimate negative information trader—the issuer himself—is the hold-down of the share of the company that is

---

[1]T. C. Copeland and D. Galai, "Information Effects on the Bid-Ask Spread," *Journal of Finance*, December 1983, pp. 1457–69; L. R. Glosten and P. Milgrom, "Bid/Ask and Transaction Prices in a Specialist Market with Heterogeneously Informed Traders" (Working paper, October 1982).

sold by the owner-entrepreneur in the new offering. This could be put into a risk/issue-price analysis. An underwriter who is really concerned about excess risk from the new issue might walk away from the deal or insist on such a low issue price that it amounts to the same thing. Finally, the underwriter could shift the entire price risk to the seller by proposing a *best-efforts* underwriting.

Figure 9–1 illustrates these alternatives. The vertical axis indicates price per share (PPS), while the horizontal axis indicates the number of shares to be sold; the PPS multiplied by the number of shares to be sold equals the size of the offering. The function that relates PPS to the number of shares to be sold represents a forecast of market receptivity to the IPO. That function is concave to the origin because, as more shares are expected to be sold, the stock market's information traders are expected to become less interested in the issue. This is the case because potential buyers of untested issues have to be concerned that a bailout by the owner-entrepreneur might be taking place. The figure also shows two functions: the outer one represents the owner's expectations, which are more optimistic than the investment banker's.[2]

The first agreement that must be reached between owner and investment banker involves market receptivity. If they cannot agree, the owner moves to another banker, or the banker might make a counteroffer of a best-efforts deal, in which the owner himself takes on the flotation risks. Suppose that the owner accepts the investment banker's view. Then it becomes a case of financial engineering to decide on the price per share of the new issue and on the number of shares to be sold. In Figure 9–1 PPS is set at $a$, the number of shares is then set at $L$, and the owner's proceeds will be $a \times L$, less flotation costs.

By contrast, if the owner insists on a best-efforts deal, based on the outer function, PPS will be set at $b$, the number of shares sold at $M$. The owner takes the risk of not selling many new shares for the chance to realize a much larger sum if the

---

[2] For a discussion of these issues and an empirical test of the attractiveness of (larger) owner retention in an IPO, see D. H. Downes and R. Heinkel, "Signaling and the Valuation of Unseasoned New Issues," *Journal of Finance*, March, 1982, pp. 1–10.

**FIGURE 9-1**
Optimal Size of IPO

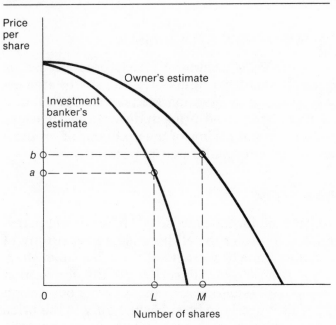

Number of shares

offering is successful. For the owner, accepting the lesser risks of a fixed-price underwriting, even though it may yield a lesser sum, may be a more attractive solution because few companies are sold in their entirety by a single IPO.[3] If, therefore, more growth is expected by firm, and more new offerings of stock are expected to be made in near future, the less necessary risks of an unsuccessful large IPO may also be taken into account by the owner because he might contemplate a second flotation and its potential reception even as he anticipates the initial public offering.[4] (Chapter 11 discusses the

_____

[3] In Chapter 11, the discussion of the *Informatics* case suggests that many IPOs may actually be done in more than one bite. To be sure, only the first issue is the initial public offering. Nevertheless, a second flotation will often follow the IPO within a year. This happens if the firm does well and the stock markets continue to be receptive. The last point is obviously the necessary condition for such an event.

[4] Recall that the *Morgan Stanley* IPO consisted of about 20 percent of the firm, and that Bear Stearns floated a new issue about six months after the first.

actual IPO of *Informatics*, its size, its pricing, and the follow-up flotation that took place.)

## PRICE ACTION FOR A NEW STOCK ISSUE

For the sake of simplicity, assume XYZ Corporation issues new stock without preemptive rights—that is, shares are currently trading in some organized market (say NASDAQ) and the offering is a negotiated fixed-price underwriting.[5] Because the stock is trading currently, some of the problems of setting a value per share are avoided, although not entirely.

### Preoffering Price Action

As negotiations proceed for the new issue, some current investors in XYZ stock will prefer to sell because a new supply of shares is expected to come to market. At the same time, stock market prices in general are subject to all the forces that continuously affect stock markets. Thus, XYZ's stock action cannot be said unequivocally to be subjected only to the price pressure of those stockholders who are apprehensive about the new stock sale. Nor is it possible to isolate empirically the price impact of those who will wait to buy the new issue from the secondary market rather than acquiring XYZ stock now. Nevertheless, assume that on balance the announcement effect of the new stock sale will drop the price. From the point of view of the issuer, that price drop especially depends on the market's action at one particular time: The signing of the underwriting agreement that sets the offering price generally occurs following market closing on the day prior to the public offering of the underwriting. If that day happens to be a "down" day (even in a bull market, the price averages go down on some days), the presumptive "preoffering price pressure" could have been interpreted as having been greater than if it had been an "up" day.

---

[5]This discussion is based, in part, on J. F. Childs, *Encyclopedia of Long-Term Financing and Capital Management* (Englewood Cliffs, N.J.: Prentice-Hall, 1976), chap. 9.

At the final price meeting, a number of pricing parameters are set but they boil down to just two:

1. The per-share offering price to the public.
2. The per-share proceeds to the company.

The difference between the two is the *gross spread* that accrues to the underwriter(s)—that is, the gross compensation. In that sense, the gross spread is analogous to the bid/ask spread that prevails in secondary dealer markets and represents the compensation to market makers. It is a fee for service. But the gross spread cannot be exactly the same as the bid/ask spread in concept since, for the period of the underwriting, the offer price to the public and the proceeds to the firm are obliged to remain the same regardless of general market price changes.

## Pricing Debates

The issuer (the XYZ Corporation) prefers as high a price as possible to maximize total proceeds for the firm. The underwriter, who is taking the risk of buying and then reselling the issue, would prefer a lower price to minimize selling risk. In most cases, during the preliminary discussions that precede the final price meeting and the signing of the underwriting agreement between issuer and underwriter, some limiting parameters are set.

Suppose the offering is "underpriced"—that is, the offering price to the public is set slightly below the closing market price that occurred just prior to the price meeting. To get the complete picture, let's review the data in Figure 9–2.

XYZ was trading at $100 a share prior to announcement of the new flotation, and at the market's close prior to price meeting, the preoffering pressure dropped that price to $99 per share. The underpriced offer price to the public is set, by negotiation, at 98½, or one half point below the closing price on the day prior to the offering.

In addition to the cost to XYZ company of these pricing reductions, the net proceeds are further reduced by the gross spread of 4½ points per share which, when subtracted from

**FIGURE 9–2**

Underpricing for a Direct Offering of Common Stock

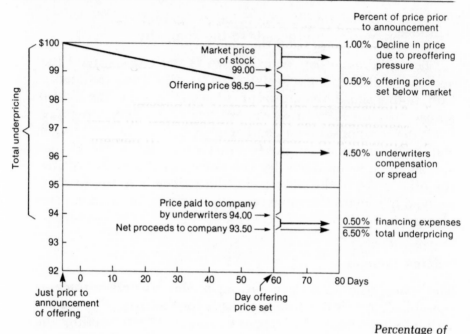

|  | | Percentage of Price Prior to Announcement |
|---|---|---|
| Market price of stock just before announcement | $100.00 | |
| Decline in price due to preoffering pressure | 1.00 | 1.00% |
| Market price on day offering price set | 99.00 | |
| Amount by which offering price is set under market | 0.50 | 0.50 |
| Offering price | 98.50 | |
| Underwriters' compensation or spread | 4.50 | 4.50 |
| Price paid to company by underwriters | 94.00 | |
| Corporate expenses | 0.50 | 0.50 |
| Net proceeds to company | $ 93.50 | 6.50% |

SOURCE: J. F. Childs, *Encyclopedia of Long-Term Financing and Capital Management* (Englewood Cliffs, N.J.: Prentice-Hall, 1976).

the offer price (to the public) of 98½, give the corporation gross proceeds of $94 per share. From these proceeds XYZ must also subtract another one half point in the underwriting expenses charged to the company.[6] In effect the firm realized about 93½ per share from the new issue.[7]

The gross spread includes the following major items (stated in percent of the $4.50 gross spread):

1. Allowance for selling costs:* 60 percent.
2. Management fee for lead underwriter: 20 percent.
3. Allowance to cover underwriting:† 20 percent.

*Also includes "dealer concession."
†Of this, 5 percent is for underwriting expenses.

By far the largest share of the spread, the allowance for the selling cost (sometimes called selling allowance) permits syndicate members to sell the stock to the public at $98.50 per share but to buy it at the following purchase prices.

If the dealer is a member of the "preferred" group agreed on by the syndicate of underwriters, he may buy the stock with a per-share discount equal to the selling concession: at $98.50 − .6($4.50) = $95.80. That seller's spread will be equal to $2.70 per share. If the dealer is not a member of the preferred group, he will earn only one half of that spread (or $1.35 per share). The major sales effort will be done by the first group; the second group is provided with some return not necessarily because they do a selling job but because, in accommodating their own clients, they are given a piece of the action called the dealer concession. In some sense, that distribution of the selling costs represents a substitute for selling commissions (or bid/ask spreads) on organized markets to the dealers (or brokers) who do the work.

The 20 percent of the gross spread called allowance for underwriting goes to the syndicate participants in proportion to their participation; the other 20 percent of the entire spread

---

[6] These expenses include SEC fees, listing fees, federal revenue stamps, state taxes and fees, transfer agent's fees, and printing, legal, accounting, engineering, and other miscellaneous expenses.

[7] Further expenses charged to the issuer over and above the direct costs incurred during the registration period include charges for counsel, for accounting services, for other technical and printing costs, and so forth.

goes to the lead (or managing) underwriter right off the top of the gross spread to cover his costs and risks for carrying the deal's major expenses—and risks.

Finally, from the issuer's point of view, any reduction of the per-share proceeds—whether by underpricing, by larger gross spread, or by expenses—clearly represents a flotation cost for the new issue. There appears to be a trade-off (neglecting tax effects) between (a) underpricing to the public and (b) a wider gross spread.

In that context, the issuer sees a wider underpricing as risk reducing for the underwriter, thereby suggesting a narrower gross spread (less return). In turn, the lead underwriter perceives a narrower gross spread as providing less sales encouragement to the syndicate members and to the other dealers who qualify for the selling allowance—and hence as riskier to the deal after it becomes effective. There is conflict in pricing any issue—even one that has a trading record on an exchange—and it must be resolved before a deal can go forward. For IPOs, that conflict can be more problematic since the basic parameter—the value per share—may itself be a subject of controversy. The fact that issues *do* go public indicates that even difficult conflict situations can be negotiated.

# 10

## The Nuts and Bolts of an
## Initial Public Offering

### PREPARATION

This chapter examines an initial public offering by a firm, beginning with a view from within the firm.[1] The decision to go public must be made by the owner-manager-entrepreneur. That decision, in turn, is rife with conflicting interests and emotions. For openers, the only reason successful businesspeople consider sharing their businesses with others is that they have financing needs they are unable to meet with present resources. Often those needs are the result of a firm's success. First, rapid growth in sales requires more working capital; second, a move to a higher level of sales may require a larger production base in the form of plant and equipment. Even the resources of a wealthy individual owner and an understanding commercial banker (given regulatory constraints on loans to a single borrower) may be insufficient. But because these financing needs result from a firm's success, outsiders *will* be interested in providing financing.

An owner is thus faced with the dilemma of holding back

---

[1]This chapter deals with a privately owned firm that is *not* financed by venture capitalists. For a discussion of venture capital, see Chapter 6.

the firm's growth or accepting outside financing. By bringing in more financing from the outside, the owner must share:

1. Potential growth in wealth.
2. Sole decision-making control.

Somewhere along the line, the owner perceives he is being constrained for lack of financing resources. He then has to consider the advantages of owning a smaller portion of a growing pie. If the owner-entrepreneur can be persuaded that the pie will grow enough, he will usually opt for added financing with outside funds.

## FIRST STEPS IN FINANCE FROM, AND INFORMATION FOR, OUTSIDERS

The emerging firm can go in a number of directions for financing and professional advice when it changes scale from a single proprietorship. It can acquire partners who provide funding as well as some expertise (accountants, lawyers, professors of philosophy). These partners, who incur unlimited liability for the enterprise (as well as rights to all of its earnings) will demand up-to-date and complete accounting of the firm's affairs if only to protect their investments and limit their risks.

If, on the other hand, the firm began its life as a corporation, the bank officer in charge of making short-term loans will require all the usual statements of financial information as well. Finally, if the owner-entrepreneur receives financing from a venture capital firm, that firm, and especially the officer in charge of the account, will likewise require financial statements that reflect the corporation's present position.

All providers of outside funds before the IPO will want "full disclosure" of the corporation's affairs—even before it goes public—as a means of safeguarding their interests, limiting risks, and evaluating the value of their assets. Moreover, the partnership phase as well as the venture capital process may involve group company policy decisions rather than individual ones.

These sources of outside participatory funding, while meeting the needs of one stage of company growth, will ultimately limit the size of the firm and its expansion, albeit on a larger scale than a single proprietorship. Conceptually, that limit is determined by the risk/return attitudes and portfolio decisions of a fairly small set of mainly professional investors. Moving to a still larger scale would require entry into the organized financial markets and the entire population of investors, broker-dealers, and regulators.

## PURPOSE OF PUBLIC FINANCING

The successful sale of new equity to the public generates cash for two main purposes.

1. To buy a share of the firm from the original owner(s)—called a secondary offering.
2. For general corporate expansion purposes, called a primary financing.

In every case that is not an exclusively secondary offering, both purposes are achieved by going public. In every primary offering, purpose 2 has to be satisfied to some extent. In fact, only purpose 2 generates cash from the public to deal with the firm's financing needs by adding to working capital or by the acquisition of additional corporate assets. In short, it permits the successful corporation to grow. Beyond this, enlarging the equity base permits improved qualification for long-term borrowing in the form of a term loan, a private placement, or a bond issue. For all these reasons, the initial public offering of stocks may be a financial prerequisite for the economic take-off of the firm beyond local resources even if subsequent financings are restricted to equity (more on this below).

Moving now to the financial market *after* the IPO has been sold, the mere fact that the stock is being traded makes it possible for all owners of the stock to gain liquidity by selling (or margining) the shares, including the sale sometime in the future of ownership position of the firm that remains. The expanded financial posture of the firm will not only help it become better known among local investors and lenders, but the financial information will also spread among a wider array of potential clients for the output of the firm. This serendipity may work particularly for firms that sell consumer goods or deal with a public that is in contact with financial markets.

But the very same advantage that spreads information through financial markets and generates publicity for the firm's output may be seen by some firm owners as a negative factor. The financial disclosure required under the Securities Act of 1933 may expose management salaries, transactions of key personnel (including the owner's relatives) within and without the firm, and other items that owner-managers may deem sensitive. Such disclosures are not often discussed in new-issue financing just because those problems get cleaned up early. The owner-entrepreneur may also be concerned about other items whose publication could be damaging. Among these are the firm's rates of return, its methods of operations, and its significant contracts. Owner-entrepreneurs often consider publication of such information as a gratuitous offering to competitors rather than as essential information required by law and by the necessity to attract potential new investors. Further, some entrepreneurs see constraints on managerial decision making, (e.g., limitations on salary and fringe benefits to key personnel) as a problem when going public. Sole proprietors fear a slowdown in implementing decisions when they have to seek approval from a board of (partly outside) directors or from shareholders.

And finally, from the owner's perspective, a financial marketplace that efficiently monitors management performance through the processing of newly public information likewise interferes with effective management. Every decision now has implications for the firm's stock price. For example, a willingness to hold out in a strike or to persist with a price policy that may imply short-term losses to maximize long-term gains may be inhibited by stock price reactions and pressures from stockholders. It takes a rare amount of character on the part of a chief executive to withstand such pressures, including those from company officials holding stock options.

In spite of these arguments, few large firms are *not* publicly held—that is, nearly all firms that expect to reach a certain size *do* go public at some time. Further, the oft-mentioned disadvantages of providing public information may reflect an executive's nostalgia for running a smaller firm.

## DECISIONS, DECISIONS. . .

In seeking added financing, an owner-entrepreneur may meet a new business representative of an investment banking firm just because both are searching for what each has to offer the other. And at that point, a process of mutual education begins.

The new-business representative of an investment banking firm is trained to spot small corporations that can use the services of an investment banker. This means that the new-business people have to analyze the growing firm's financial potential and its financing needs. Ultimately, these estimates have to be translated into the number of shares to be sold at a determined price to set the dollar proceeds to the owner (to the extent that the offering is a secondary) and to the firm itself. If the firm's change of scale has some minimum requirement, the price/proceeds relationship must satisfy the needs of the firm for the IPO to proceed beyond the discussion stage. And on an even more fundamental level, some size parameters are likely to be required before an underwriter will consider a review of the firm's prospects.

An analysis of recent IPOs suggests that the first offerings of stock by corporations cluster about the following levels:

Sales of $15–$20 million per year.
Net income of $1 million in most recent reporting year.
Annual growth rates of 30–50 percent, compounded, with reasonable expectations of meeting these projections for the next several years. To maximize interest by institutional investors, there should be realistic expectations of meeting sales projections of $50–$100 million in the near future.[2]

On the other hand, many smaller firms have successfully issued IPOs. Such firms have certain characteristics that encourage underwriters (and, ultimately, investors) to accept the risk of floating a new issue for an unknown firm. Among these characteristics are:

---

[2] If current sales are at $20 million and a 50 percent annual growth rate is maintained, that minimum level could be approached in another two years.

1. A strong management team with an earlier track record of accomplishment.
2. Strong or leadership position in the industry or a technology supported by patent ownership.
3. Strong outlook for the market and the firm's market share based on 2.
4. Good product with strong possibility for growth between 33 percent and 50 percent per year.

These characteristics are necessary for new hi-tech issues. But some closely held, well-managed firms in less exciting or even routine activities that can promise good, stable, future rates of return also have used the IPO market to expand their financing base.

One final point must be made regarding the *timing* of an IPO. The per-share price of the stock is, among other variables, crucially dependent on expected future cash flows, on the desired size of the stock offering, and last—and never least— the current state of the stock market (the level of average stock prices as indicated by the level of say, the S&P 500 stock average). The higher the average (or the higher the market's P/E multiple), the higher the potential per-share price of the IPO. In short, even an IPO that is exceptionally interesting to investors and could get a good reception any time would still produce a better price per share in a strong stock market than in a weak one. Thus factors beyond the control of issuers or underwriters, to some extent, influence the size of proceeds from any issue. This fact is often difficult for owner-entrepreneurs to accept, especially if the stock market is moving downward just prior to the issue's pricing.

## PREPARATIONS

If it is important to the success of any small business to establish good management techniques, including complete and up-to-date record keeping, it becomes doubly so when preparing to go public. In specific terms, the firm and its financial management can prepare for an IPO by producing reliable and analytically appropriate monthly financial statements from which quarterly data is easy to generate. This procedure leads executives of any firm—even one closely held—to make decisions that are based on analysis and control of current operations. When publication of these documents subsequently becomes a legal requirement, producing the documentation will be routine.

Financial statements that project a picture of growth and hold few surprises can be used by underwriters and syndicate members in selling stock. If those statements, when published, appear to reveal confidential data or, worse, some previously unknown problems, they will be harmful rather than helpful and may even result in cancellation of the offering.

## THE LEGAL SIDE

Counsel to the firm about to go public should be familiar with the process, the required procedures, and the problems related to working with the SEC and the underwriters in an IPO registration. This work is complex and time-consuming, and there are severe penalties for presenting false or misleading statements. Moreover, there is a fine line between (1) full disclosure and (2) presenting data in a less-than-appropriate form that may not help the firm give a fair picture of itself in its prospectus. An error on the side of excess caution, while not actionable in court, may cost the firm by dropping its new-issue price. Experience in this work is essential.

In fact, counsel's first useful job is to determine whether the firm, as currently constituted, can go public. Among the organizational housekeeping chores that must be undertaken is the simplification of ownership and control structure. If, for example, the closely held firm is really (1) a number of corporations under common ownership, (2) a partnership, or (3) some other combination of entities, simplifying the structure will produce an easier IPO (or, alternatively, a higher price per share). Counsel may then advise a merger, some liquidations, or simplification of company structure financed by ownership capital contributions. Similarly, an unnecessarily complex capital structure (including, say, preferred stock or special voting rights or preemptive rights provisions) or an unacceptably small (or excessively large) number of shares authorized may have to be dealt with. Finally, obsolete provisions in the corporate charter or bylaws may have to be changed. In short, many provisions in a closely held firm's organizational structure will be an unnecessary drag on the progress of a publicly held firm (or, once again, a potentially lower price per share in the IPO).

To move from the closet to the goldfish bowl, the firm must implement the information requirements of the Securities Act of 1933. Public disclosure, moreover, helps to generate interest in (or publicity for) the firm whose stock will be sold in the market. This means that *all* the information on the firm, if it is to help sell its stock at the best price, should provide answers rather than raise questions. Full disclosure includes:

1. Names of highly compensated employees and others, including relationships to owners, salary and other benefits, and so on.
2. Shareholder rights beyond those of ordinary stockholders, including rights of first refusal. [These should be eliminated.]
3. Insider loans to company; company loans to insiders. [The latter should be repaid.]
4. Fairness of contracts (for example, leases) between company and insiders. [These should be appropriately documented, altered, or canceled.]
5. All employment contracts including stock options, pensions, and stock purchase plans. [These should be reviewed, arranged, or canceled.]

On the asset side, documentation and the marshaling of ownership should be clear, as should documentation on loans and leases as well as assessment of all default clauses to prevent the inadvertent occurrence of the latter during the offering. In fact, all the foregoing clarify and simplify the firm's valuation.

As part of the preliminaries that precede publication of its registration statement, the firm should prepare to have its accountants produce up to five years' worth of audited earnings (Form S-1 statements require audits for the last three years; Form S-18, two years) if the underwriters require this. If unpleasant, unexpected surprises show up during this stage, the entire deal could be scrapped—after the firm has spent a good deal of nonrecoverable cash for professional services. Once again, if a firm routinely performs such analytical services as part of its prepublic activities, none of this need happen. And the underwriters' requirement for a five-year audited review of the firm's earnings performance is clearly a part of their risk-reducing, fiduciary responsibility.

Finally, the accountants' "comfort letters" to the underwriters that will attest to the dependability and accuracy of the financial information provided represent part of the underwriters' "reasonable investigation" of financial and accounting data. This subject will come up again in a discussion of the underwriters' "due-diligence" investigation.

## EXECUTION

### The Underwriting Problem Summarized

In one sense, the IPO procedure removes market imperfection and informational insufficiency. Contrast this with the textbook world of Modigliani and Miller (M&M), in which methods of financing are irrelevant because all information is available and free and market adjustments are frictionless and immediate. In the M&M world, the net present values (NPV) of projects and firms are produced by simple exercises in capital budgeting:

1. Forecast a project's after-tax cash flows.
2. Assess a project's risk.
3. Project the cost of capital.[3]
4. Calculate NPV by using DCF methods and data from 1, 2, 3.

Further, the aggregate value of the firm will be equal to the sum of all NPV's of currently owned assets, and that value is not affected by the equity/debt ratio of the firm's capital structure, at least in one version of the M&M theory. And in that simple version of the theory, the NPV of a new project, however financed, could be calculated the same way.

The sale of an IPO cannot be assessed quite so simply because of lack of informational openness on which the M&M formulation depends. In fact, the closely held firm could be

---

[3] More specifically, the expected rate of return available to investors by assets of the same risk classification traded in financial markets.

viewed as the theoretical opposite of the M&M world. Little, if any, information on firm value is published; no securities are valued in the market because none is traded; and in the end, the process of going public represents the presentation of the firm's information set to the market for the purpose of valuation *both by the firm and investors.*

### The Adjusted Present Value Rule[4]

Suppose an entrepreneur wants to expand his firm through a primary issue by engaging in a $10 million project that is expected to provide a cash flow (after-tax) of $1.8 million per year for 10 years. Assume that the project's opportunity cost of capital (adjusted for the project's risk classification) is 12 percent. This is another way of arguing that investors are indifferent between an existing (risky) market investment yielding 12 percent, or the IPO. For the new project, financed by IPO, the entrepreneur's calculation looks as follows (in millions of dollars).

$$\text{NPV} = -\$10 + \sum_{t=1}^{10} \frac{\$1.8}{(1.12)^t} = \$0.17$$

This means that NPV = $170,000. This also means, from the entrepreneur's point of view, that if the new-issue flotation cost of the IPO exceeds $170,000, he would *not* undertake the project. And since flotation costs usually range from 5 to 10 percent of the issue when all outlays are accounted for, that project would *not* be undertaken—if flotation costs of $500,000 to $1 million exceed the new NPV anticipated. In other words, after new-issue costs are met, NPV is negative.

It is not only in that sense that the special flotation costs make a naive analysis based on assumptions of efficient secondary-market trading inappropriate. Uncertainty associated with pricing the issue depends, not on some average rate of return, but on the one-time and unpredictable price level of stock averages at the moment of price meeting for the flotation. Further, issue proceeds depend on the bargain that will

---

[4]This discussion is based in part on Brealey & Myers, *Principles of Corporate Finance,* 2nd ed. (New York: McGraw-Hill, 1984), chap. 19.

be struck by the firm's owners and the underwriter(s). That price decision—which will be discussed at length in this and other chapters—involves two parties *only* in a fixed-price offering, and the same two parties are involved in pricing flotation service even in a best-efforts underwriting.

## DEALING WITH THE UNDERWRITERS

What issuers sometimes have difficulty accepting is that their own stock price is significant for the firm not only at new issue. Only at new issue, to be sure, do the dollar proceeds accrue directly to the stock sellers. Yet the stock price, even after it trades on a local exchange, over the counter, or nationally, influences the fortunes of the firm because it influences the firm's cost of capital and, by extension, its investment policies with respect to real capital and other projects. Especially important are the market-making services provided by the investment banking firm after the IPO has been marketed. Until the investor base for the new stock has enough breadth and depth, the investment banker may be the major counterpart to all sell and/or buy orders so that some aspects of an underwriting process may, for all intents and purposes, be extended after the offering has been technically completed.

From the company's point of view, the need for a specific package of services to float the issue and provide post-issue trading capacity narrows the choice among potential underwriters. If the firm previously employed a venture capital firm, that connection may lead to a particular underwriter being used. As with other professional relationships offered on a competitive basis, a certain amount of exploratory discussions are necessary. Factors considered are:

A. For choice of new-issue underwriter:
  1. Reputation (especially with IPO underwriting).
  2. Distribution capability:
     Institutional.
     Individual.
     International.
     Regional.
  3. Experience: Review experience of IPO's in similar industries and for firms of corporate size.

B. After issue is sold:
1. Market-making capacity: For how long and in what size will underwriter(s) continue to make a market? How good a dealer is the underwriter?
2. Research capacity: How many analysts does the underwriter carry for the industry in which the IPO firm is active? How much of a following do these analysts have?
3. Availability of financing advice by underwriter to firm: How helpful has the underwriter been to similar firms in developing new sources of financing; how well have the firms' stocks done subsequently?

Discussions with prior clients are essential in selecting an underwriter, even if these discussions involve competitors in the same industry. And discussions with competing underwriters are part of the game.

## THE UNDERWRITER'S SIDE

The managing underwriter of an IPO syndicate incurs quasi-fiduciary responsibilities with respect to the members of the syndicate he has put together. He also incurs risk from underwriting the lion's share of the offering, and he may face further risks as a market maker by serving as the major *contra* trader for all buy-and-sell orders in the aftermarket. Finally, by incurring due-diligence liabilities under the Securities Act of 1933, the lead underwriter has a powerful incentive to thoroughly investigate the affairs of the firm about to issue its IPO.

## SECURITY ANALYSIS VERSUS VALUATION OF A FIRM

It is tempting to view the underwriter's investigative function as an analog to security analysis. There are similarities. Both types of analyses attempt to forecast the future prospects of a firm and the impact of these flows on the stock price.

The differences are the same as those between an efficient and an inefficient market. The former reflects the efforts of many stockholders and analysts who review and assess the information that each publicly held firm must issue to the SEC and the public. Whenever that information induces owners (or potential owners) to change their portfolios, the price effect of such changes provides a continuous assessment of market valuation. By contrast, the investment banker looking at the affairs of a firm on its way to a first public offering is placed into the same situation as an appraiser. For assets that are not traded continuously, a price valuation estimate is subject to opinion. Market inefficiency, in fact, reflects that range, which, under a different market structure, would be described by a relatively wide bid/ask spread.

Further, that spread may also be related to the data's quality. A firm with a lengthy history of stock-market exposure is unlikely to have many substantive errors left in its financial statements. A relatively new firm, on the other hand, has not undergone the scrutiny of different accounting firms, security analysts, and other experts. Instead, the lead underwriter must satisfy himself that his own investigative team, as well as the multiple-year audited statements requested from the IPO firm, properly and fairly represent the firm's valuation. And in that evaluation, he must maintain a balance between the optimism of one group eager to win the account and the skepticism of analysts who can more readily see the negatives. That unknown balance (as contrasted with a market price) is another aspect of market inefficiency.

In the critical evaluation, the underwriter's investigation will consider:

Management:
  Experience.
  Depth.
  Leadership potential.
  Planning skills.
Product and industry:
  Quality of product.
  Competitors.
  Market segment.
  Growth potential.
  Expected life of product.
  Technology: Leader, follower?
  Research and Development: How close to the leader?
  How permanent is the industry?
Financial structure:
  How well are assets managed?
  How risky is credit rating; capital structure?

Earning capacity:
  History and growth of earnings.
  Upward trend?
  Compare to competitors.
Reputation:
  Are public, customer perception different from company's?
  Customer complaints, if any.
  Suppliers' complaints.
Use of proceeds:
  What proportion of offering is for corporate purposes?
  What proportion goes to selling stockholders?

That last element of the investigative process is a key variable to the underwriter and to eventual buyers of the firm's stock. If there is even a small possibility that the prime purpose of the stock issue is to transfer main ownership from selling stockholders-owners to the public, the notion could emerge that a "bailout" by present owners may be underway. Some underwriters are deterred from such an IPO. Others do not consider any but a best-efforts underwriting under such circumstances.

In appraising the company, each underwriter sets certain criteria to determine whether to offer the stock. For the underwriter, short-term benefits from the offering must be weighed against the risk of a tarnished reputation from underwriting a flop. In any case, underwriters spend several weeks or months investigating a firm. This includes some probing questioning of senior executives, key technical personnel, vendors, competitors, and clients of the company. In addition, underwriters may hold private meetings with the firm's accountants.

## THE TIME LINE OF AN IPO

Once the two parties (issuer and underwriter) agree to go ahead with the deal, the schematic below describes the general schedule that will follow after the IPO firm (called Company below) has decided on its counsel and its printer (for documents). Once that sequence starts, the company's officers and the managing underwriter will make no statements about the proposed new issue without clearance from company counsel and underwriters' counsel.

## APPENDIX

### Tentative Time Schedule for Public Offering of Common Stock

| | |
|---|---|
| Required actions prior to public offering | Company selects counsel and printer.

Company officers, directors, and managing underwriter make no statements about the proposed public offering without prior clearance from Company counsel and underwriters' counsel. |
| Nine weeks prior to offering date | Company, its accountants, and counsel begin assembling required data, including financial statements and exhibits, to be included in the registration statement.

Company makes available to underwriters' counsel the Board of Directors' meeting minutes for prior years and abstracts all important contracts for review by such counsel.

Company officer and Company counsel prepare and make available the first draft of the business, property, management's discussion of earnings, competition, and employee sections of Part I of the registration statement.

First draft of underwriting agreement to be available from underwriters' counsel.

Conference with managing underwriter, underwriters' counsel, and Company officers, counsel, and accountants to discuss the time schedule and initial document drafts. |
| Eight weeks prior to offering date | Board of Directors authorizes preparation of the registration statement and related documents.

Accountants prepare the audited financial statements for inclusion in the registration statement.

Company counsel begins preparation of Part |

II of the registration statement including exhibits.

Managing underwriter and underwriters' counsel begin preparing the first draft of the remaining sections of Part I of the registration statement, agreement among underwriters, underwriting agreement, underwriters' questionnaire, and underwriters' power of attorney.

Company counsel prepares questionnaires to be sent to officers and directors as to interest in material transactions.

| | |
|---|---|
| Seven weeks prior to offering date | Second draft of the registration statement and underwriting agreement to be available. |

Tour of principal Company facilities by managing underwriter and discussions with principal management personnel of the Company to assist managing underwriter in gaining a complete understanding of the Company.

Conference with managing underwriter, underwriters' counsel, and Company officers, accountants, and counsel to discuss second draft of the registration statement and related documents.

Reworked second draft of the registration statement and related documents sent to financial printer for page proof.

| | |
|---|---|
| Six weeks prior to offering date | Managing underwriter, underwriters' counsel, and Company officials, accountants, and counsel continue to work jointly on the preparation of the registration statement and related documents. |
| Five weeks prior to offering date | Company counsel and underwriters' counsel jointly prepare appropriate resolutions for the Board of Directors' meeting to be held at the time of the initial filing of the registration statement. |

Managing underwriter submits a list of the prospective underwriters for review by the Company.

Four weeks prior to offering date

Board of Directors (1) approves preparation, execution, and filing of the registration statement and all amendments thereto (except the price amendment) and related matters, (2) authorizes qualification under state "Blue Sky" laws, (3) authorizes Company officers to negotiate with the managing underwriter as to the terms of the offering, and (4) takes any other action necessary.

Registration statement filed with SEC and a copy of the tentative time schedule delivered to the branch chief of the SEC who will review the registration statement and related documents forming a part of the registration statement.

Preliminary prospectuses printed in quantity.

Managing underwriter issues press and "broad tape" releases relating to the filing of the registration statement.

"Blue Sky" action is initiated by underwriters' counsel on behalf of the Company to register the proposed offering with various state security commissions.

Managing underwriter forms underwriting group and mails copies of the registration statement and related documents to members of such group.

Preliminary prospectuses broadly distributed to prospective underwriters, dealers, institutional investors, and individuals.

Company orders initial quantities of stock certificates.

| | |
|---|---|
| Three weeks prior to offering date | Company counsel and underwriters' counsel prepare appropriate resolutions for the Board of Directors' meeting to be held at the time of the determination of offering terms and the filing of the price amendment to the registration statement. |
| | Underwriters' due-diligence meeting held in New York City to discuss the registration statement with Company officers, accountants, and counsel. |
| | Information meetings held in certain cities such as Chicago, Los Angeles, and San Francisco to acquaint underwriters and dealers with the Company and its management. |
| Two weeks prior to offering date | Executed underwriters' questionnaire forwarded to Company counsel. |
| | Company counsel contacts SEC branch chief to confirm anticipated date of receipt of SEC comments on the registration statement. |
| | Quarterly or "stub" financial statements made available, if applicable. |
| One week prior to offering date | Receive comments from SEC on the registration statement. |
| | Managing underwriter, underwriters' counsel, and Company officers, accountants, and counsel correct deficiencies in the registration statement and, if necessary, file amendment no. 1 to the registration statement with SEC. |
| | Preliminary prospectus distribution letter from managing underwriter sent to SEC along with letter requesting acceleration of the registration statement from managing underwriter and Company. |
| | "Tombstone" advertising proofs prepared by managing underwriter for release on |

the day following the effective date of the registration statement.

Company and managing underwriter prepare press release and "broad tape" release relating to the effectiveness of the registration statement and the public offering terms.

Week of offering

Managing underwriter meets with Company officers to negotiate terms of the offering.

Board of Directors (1) approves offering terms; (2) approves registration statement, including amendment no. 1 thereto, if any; ratifies actions of Company officers in executing and filing same; and authorizes Company officers to execute and file all further amendments and supplements thereto; (3) approves the form of underwriting agreement and authorizes Company officers to execute and deliver an underwriting agreement in substantially such form; (4) approves the indemnity agreement; (5) authorizes the issuance of the stock to be sold by the Company upon proper documentation; and (6) authorizes all further actions as may be necessary to give effect to and facilitate the public offering.

Managing underwriter and Company officers, accountants, and counsel prepare pricing amendment to the registration statement including the underwriting agreement and agreement among underwriters.

Offering date (New York City)

Managing underwriter and Company execute the underwriting agreement.

Price amendment filed with SEC (after underwriters execute agreement among underwriters).

Company receives SEC order declaring the registration statement effective and so advises the managing underwriter.

Registration statement and the final prospectus forming a part thereof printed in quantity.

Underwriting agreement delivered to respective signators.

Underwriters' counsel transmits relevant information to "Blue Sky" authorities.

Managing underwriter commences public offering of the stock and so advises the Company.

Managing underwriter releases "tombstone" advertisement for appearance on the day following the offering date and issues press release and "broad tape" release relating to the effectiveness of the registration statement and the public offering terms.

Day after offering date

"Tombstone" advertisement appears in selected newspapers throughout the United States.

Matters to be completed prior to closing

Managing underwriter provides registrar with the names in which the certificates are to be registered.

Managing underwriter packages certificates for delivery.

Day before closing

Preliminary closing with underwriters and Company counsel.

Closing (one week after the offering date)

Payment for and delivery of shares sold.

Documentation required from and by managing underwriter and Company delivered to appropriate parties in New York City.

Note: Special circumstances may require departures from the above outline, particularly as to the scheduling of Board of Directors' meetings, the period of time required to prepare audited financial statements and draft the description of business sections of the Registration Statement, and the period of time required by the SEC to review the Registration Statement subsequent to the initial filing. With regard to the SEC review of the Registration Statement, the above time schedule provides for a period of approximately four weeks from the date of initial filing to the effective date of the Registration Statement. This time period may vary depending upon the number of Registration Statements and Proxy Statements currently being processed by the SEC and certain other factors.

# 11

## New-Issue Underwriting as Insurance to the Issuer

It is no accident that the word *underwriting* has similar meanings and connotations in insurance and investment banking. The insurance function provided by investment bankers has become more important as rates in the capital markets have become more volatile.[1]

Put differently, the management of a firm placing an issue of new common stock in the market is aware that the price per share when sold might be lower than it should be willing to accept because it implies negative net present value for funds raised ("flotation risk"). As one approach to minimizing flotation risk, the firm will purchase two types of services from investment bankers:

1. Pricing services.
2. Marketing (or market-making) services.

---

[1]This insurance function has been pointed to in a general way by Mandelker and Raviv in "Investment Banking: An Economic Analysis of Optimal Underwriting Contracts," *Journal of Finance*, June 1977, pp. 683–94. Their emphasis on corporate risk avoidance generally is disputed by Mayers and Smith (see below). Further discussion in this chapter also suggests that risk avoidance by the issuing firms takes on quite a different form from that proposed by Mandelker and Raviv.

Based on expertise gained in continuous market participation, investment bankers set a realistic valuation on any new issue so that it can be sold. The second service, market making, refers to the capacity of underwriters to know who potential buyers are and to place the new issue at a price acceptable to both issuers and investors. This set of services and the conflicts that develop between issuer and investment banker can best be understood in the context of risk transfer from issuer to underwriter.

During the period when the issuer is waiting to go into the market or even waiting for SEC approval for the issue to "go effective," changes in security market prices will either raise the expected price of the new issue or lower it. Such waiting risk is borne exclusively by the issuer.[2] Adding in other risks against which the issuer attempts to insure himself with an underwriter results in the following flotation risk:

(1) Waiting risk + (2) Pricing risk + (3) Marketing risk
= Flotation risk

Of these components, the first is the least obvious.

## WAITING RISK

The investment banker and corporate client may have a long-standing advisory relationship, especially prior to the initial public offering. Even after the decision is made to go public, it usually takes three to five months for the corporation and its investment banker, counsel, accountants, and other experts to prepare the registration statement and all the other documents that are necessary before the initial public offering (IPO) is declared effective. To calculate the risk to the firm (XYZ) during that waiting period, assume that at the beginning of the period price levels in the stock market imply a price/earnings multiple of 20 for the stocks of corporations with characteristics similar to XYZ's. If market prices decline and reduce that multiple to 15 times several months later, XYZ may postpone the offering. In that case, the waiting risk has turned out to be too great.

---

[2]Shelf registration (SEC Rule 415) will be discussed in the next part.

A second type of waiting risk that affects the cash offers of new issues of large corporations was virtually eliminated by SEC Rule 415 (the shelf-registration rule) and its predecessor in the development of "instant bond issues," the S-16 form. Prior to Rule 415, for any new corporate issue—stock or bond—to be declared effective by the SEC, there was a three- to four-week wait between the time the registration statement was submitted and the SEC's release of securities for trading. That waiting risk was eliminated by the SEC's change in policy, and at this writing, the issues that qualify may be declared effective in *two days* or less, sharply reducing the waiting risk for large, seasoned issuers.

This policy change has had a policy by-product (probably not foreseen at the time) that influenced pricing risk as well.

When a new issue is decided on, the corporate client may require competitive bidding (a public utility holding company is obligated to do so by law), or it may be negotiated. Since shelf registration, corporations can choose the *timing* of their new issues. And firms that qualify for shelf registration can ask for pricing services (bids) from more than one investment banker. In effect, this gives these corporations the equivalent of a competitively set pricing service even though the formal rituals of competitive bidding mechanisms are not performed.[3]

With the continuing experience of shelf registration, the most sophisticated and most active issuers in 1985 have gone as far as completing all of the prospectus mechanics up to and including having a note or bond issue *declared effective* by the SEC. The document declared effective will contain all but the pricing terms. At that point, waiting risk is totally eliminated since the issue can go at a moment's notice. This does not mean, however, that all issuing risks are eliminated. In effect, issuers trade off waiting risk for market-timing risk. The issuer's management must decide when to go and they have to

---

[3] The Dutch-auction scheme used by some corporations represents still another mechanism for developing a competitive pricing process. For further discussion of new-issue flotations under Rule 415, see S. Bhagat, "The Evidence on Shelf Registration," *Midland Corporate Finance Journal* 2, no. 1 (Spring 1984), pp. 6–12. For discussion of competitive bidding mechanics, see Chapter 12.

take the heat if, in a period of volatile rates and markets, they picked the wrong phase of the cycle.

In volatile markets, all issues are subject to such timing risks. Under the present (1986) mechanics of shelf-registration issues, the manager who decides to go can be identified. In earlier days, random events during the waiting period could be blamed. The new rules may make the issuer more conscious of pricing problems and more prone to lay them off on the underwriters.

## PRICING RISK

The purchase of the pricing service is designed to minimize pricing risks:

1. Improper pricing in a stable market.
2. Proper pricing overwhelmed by an unstable market.

Improper pricing refers to the problem of setting an IPO price on a firm whose securities have not traded (if privately held) or are not traded as widely (if registered, say, on a local exchange) as they are expected to be after the new issue is sold. The major pricing service purchased, therefore, is a transactions price that comes closer to an equilibrium price than the bid/ask spread prior to the time the issue is traded. Put bluntly, the pricing service the company wants is a price as high as possible that will still appeal to the market. If the price is too high, the issue won't sell after it is underwritten, and a significant portion of securities will have to be sold at a sharp discount to the offering price. By that time, the firm has received its cash proceeds—the slow or discounted security sales will be a loss only for the underwriters. It is often said that a firm will not be as happy with a slow flotation than if its issue had done well.[4] That notion, however, may be one of the many Wall Street adages whose truth is appreciated mostly in lower Manhattan. The alternative, and a better known one, is

---

[4] A conflict in attitudes may develop between: (1) old (or selling) stockholders, who would clearly benefit from getting as high a price as possible from the market and (2) the new stockholders who, like everyone else, prefer capital gains to capital losses.

the notion that new issues tend to be underpriced; a number of studies suggest that underpricing improves market reception and reduces underwriting risks to investment bankers, all for the obvious reasons.

The second pricing risk generally refers to those exogenously determined price changes that depress stock market prices occasionally (for example, a rise in the Federal Reserve discount rate). Because a newly priced issue then carries a price fixed to the public on its prospectus (as long as syndicate restraints prevail) that is above its prior relationship to the market, it will be difficult to sell. By that time, as noted, the flotation risk of an underwritten issue would be carried by the underwriters and not by the issuing company.

## THE DEMAND FOR RISK SHIFTING

The demand for risk shifting by large corporations can no longer be discussed in terms of general risk avoidance. Instead, the theory emphasizes the impact of insurance on maximization of stockholder wealth.[5] Stockholders—that is, holders of stock portfolios—can generally eliminate corporation-specific risks by portfolio diversification. As Mayers and Smith put it, a corporation's purchase of insurance is no guarantee of stock price improvement since "...the purchase of insurance by firms at actuarially unfair rates would represent a negative net present value project, reducing stockholder wealth."[6] They go on to argue that closely held corporations, on the other hand, like individuals, have an incentive for risk avoidance in general. They prefer (1) a less risky average outcome to (2) a range of less predictable outcomes that may be higher or lower than the average. Likewise, for the one large stockholder in a firm, the diversification type of wealth self-insurance is not directly feasible. In order to diversify his wealth, he must first sell a share of his company. Consequently, like any other insurance buyer (individual or corporate), he acquires flotation insur-

---

[5] The following derives insights from the current literature on insurance, especially, D. Mayers and C. W. Smith, Jr., "On the Corporate Demand for Insurance," *Journal of Business* 55 no. 2 (1982), pp. 281–96.

[6] Ibid., p. 282.

ance—that is, insurance against an "accident" for his IPO by having his new issue underwritten.

That isn't the end of the insurance story, however. Consider the asymmetry in the capacity to bear risks between even large firms that may face an occasional (or rare) accident in their own new-issue flotation and those firms (called insurance companies or, in our special example, investment bankers) that specialize in dealing with potential accidents. Insurance specialists deal with (1) a large number of policies and (2) a more predictable set of accident-related claims per unit of time. As a result they get the benefit of:

  a. Better actuarial predictability of *aggregate* accident costs.
  b. Improved claims management and settlement.
  c. More-effective spreading of the costs and burdens of accidents among the insured population.

Finally, a number of factors tend to hold down the "loading fee"—that is, the difference between the premiums paid by policyholders and the insurance companies' aggregate payoff after an accident. First, as the loading fee rises, fewer corporations will be interested in buying insurance services. Second, this potential decline in demand will be met by a supply that becomes increasingly competitive among the insurance firms offering risk protection.

Investment bankers have a comparative advantage in risk bearing. Most of the Fortune 500 firms, which enter the financial markets fairly regularly to float bond issues and, less frequently, stock issues, have found that the flotation of new issues carries an insurable risk which investment bankers have a comparative advantage in covering for a number of reasons.

## SUPPLY OF RISK SHIFTING BY UNDERWRITERS THROUGH DIVERSIFICATION, MARKETING, HEDGING, AND INSTITUTIONAL SALES

### Diversification

**1.** Most large new issues are sold by syndicates. This spreads the total risk in any one flotation among the participating underwriters according to the size of each firm's participation or as spelled out in the underwriting agreement.

**2.** On the same day that the managing underwriter is carrying the largest single share of risk in any given flotation, he is also participating in other flotations already open for trading or about to. To that extent, any single flotation risk exposure may be diversified throughout the new-issues market (a sort of portfolio effect).

**3.** In the days following, all these underwriters will be participating in other new offerings, thereby diversifying flotation risks through time.

### Marketing

Marketing reduces flotation risk as follows: the syndicate manager will "build a book" prior to the time the issue becomes effective. Further, after the offering is made effective, the overallotment of securities to syndicate members and others and the price stabilization actions undertaken by the syndicate manager during the flotation period are all designed to improve reception of the new issue (or reduce underwriting risks). Under the present legal constraints of the Securities Act of 1933, only the underwriter can so support the offering. The underwriter has an *absolute* advantage in providing this service.[7] The issuing firm is prohibited from market stabilization of its own securities at new issue or thereafter for many valid reasons.

The chart below illustrates how these risks may be perceived by the issuer (XYZ Corporation) and its investment bankers. To simplify the example, assume XYZ stock sold in an OTC market at $100 per share prior to the announcement of a new issue. In the three weeks after the announcement of the new issue that is accompanied by the distribution of the red-herring prospectus, the firm expects the stock price to rise $5 per share, to remain the same, or to drop by $5.[8]

---

[7] He also has a liability regarding due-diligence efforts with respect to material information misstated or omitted in the prospectus and so forth.

[8] The red-herring prospectus contains all the information of the new-issue prospectus except for the price and size of the new issue.

| Stock Price Change | A | B |
|---|---|---|
| Rise by $5 | 50% | 35% |
| Stable | 15 | 15 |
| Down $5 | 35 | 50 |

In case A, waiting risk is favorable; there is a bull market. In case B, waiting risk is not favorable; there is most likely a bear market. XYZ Corporation projects that, with net proceeds of $95 per share, there is a small net positive risk-adjusted present value for the project to be financed. With a gross spread of $6 per share, even in a bull market, if the stock price drops to $95 in the market during the waiting period, the issue will be postponed at best, or canceled. If the price remains at $100 during the waiting period then drops during the pricing day to $99, XYZ will fight hard for a higher price to the public (that is, no underpricing) or for a narrower spread (for example, price to public, $99; gross spread, $4; net proceeds, $95), or it will insist on a postponement.

From the underwriter's point of view, if the expected worst-case price drop during the marketing (or syndicate) period is $3 per share, a narrower ($4) spread at a $99 price that could decline to $96 when the syndicate breaks does not necessarily imply an immediate out-of-pocket loss since proceeds to XYZ are $95. If, however, out-of-pocket costs exceed $1 per share, the underwriter will incur a loss. It is to avoid the equivalent of these losses that the issuing firm engages an underwriter in the first place.

## Hedging

After a syndicate dissolution, any unsold securities in excess of the supply desired by the underwriter represent the outcome of an unforeseen (and risky) market event. For the syndicate operation involved, it would constitute a "loss event," but the securities can be placed in the portfolio of the investment banking firm or sold subsequently in the normal course of business. In any case, because these "leftovers" represent only a part of the underwriter's unsold share of any offering (other syndicate members also absorb their share), they are easier to hedge or diversify than the equivalent total leftover, following its own flotation, by the issuing firm.

## Institutional Sales

While the concept of institutional sales may not appear to be directly related to the new-issue process, the capacity of investment bankers to deal on a large scale in secondary markets generates economies of scale for primary-market trading or the placement of securities generally. Knowledge of the market and its major institutional buyers helps investment bankers place large pieces of large new issues whatever the aggregate current volume of new issues. In fact, many new issues are largely presold to institutions prior to the formal offering. The usefulness of these contacts in placing new issues represents a type of scale economy that is not easy to achieve except by continuous market participation; moreover, it is difficult to measure. For that reason, the underwriter's market contacts tend to be ignored in discussions of flotation risk. After all, the continuous exercise of placing large blocks and of pricing skills (in large-scale buying and selling) provides relative stability (or narrow bid/ask spreads) in market pricing as well as generating transferable expertise to new-issues pricing.

For all of these reasons, investment bankers have "sold" their risk services to new issuers, and for all underwritten securities, corporations have effectively shifted new-issue risks to the underwriters.

After any issue is proposed for sale, the flotation may be executed in an open market or by negotiation. In more-familiar jargon, the competitive process is called a public offering, while the negotiated flotation scheme is called a private placement. For a private placement, the negotiations for pricing and for flotation schemes are collapsed into one process.[9]

---

[9]The final bargain struck for a private placement probably includes some opportunity-cost factor for avoiding flotation risk. To some extent, this may be encompassed in the rights of holders of privately placed issues to trade these securities prior to maturity either among each other or back to the issuer. There is no neat way of estimating the cost of such options in private placements.

## PRICING SERVICES

For investment banking firms and particularly for special-bracket firms (or lead underwriters generally), the sale of pricing services extends into many areas. For example, the sale of pricing expertise may occur by itself in consultations with firms that acquire other companies through mergers (see Chapters 7 and 8). As noted above, the pricing expertise of investment bankers is continuously exercised (or tested) in the performance of their dealer activities. Further, those tests are intimately related to marketing skills (for example, institutional sales) and risk-taking capacity (capital available to finance the inventory of securities). Most special-bracket firms perform these functions in a number of secondary markets as well as in the primary (new-issues) market where they lead syndicates.

### New-Issues Pricing

Setting a price on a new issue is similar to setting a futures price: the flotation process is not completed until some time hence—that is, when securities trade on their own without syndicate support. That time can be shortly after the issue date if market prices rise for any reason or if the new issue has been underpriced (see below for further discussion of underpricing).

Many new-issue transactions, however, don't close out in a short period, and syndicates may be maintained for more than a week (although rarely) if markets move down or if, for any other reason, the issue won't sell. All the securities in the underwriting must be sold at the same price (to issuer, to the public) as long as the syndicate is maintained. This means that in terms of the new-issue price relative to prices on other securities, the new issue will appear more expensive to buy the longer it takes to close out the syndicate.

If the security were clearly underpriced relative to the market, syndicates would not have to be maintained for longer than minutes or hours regardless of whether the issue adds to the securities already in the market ("seasoned issuer") or whether it is an initial public offering. To price an initial offering, a substitute must be found for a trading history of

existing stock, or earlier bond issues, by examining comparable companies to develop a general valuation model for the
new securities. Once that valuation is done, the final price
adjustments are then made for futurity—that is, the price risks
associated with a lengthy flotation period. The next section
examines the valuation process and futurity adjustments. Recall the types of new stock flotations offered. A *general cash*
offer is a flotation to the market at large as contrasted with a
*preemptive rights* offer, which is made to current stockholders. General cash offers, in turn, may be sold to underwriters at a firm price; many rights offers are supported by a
process that is clearly an insurance-type of underwriting
called a standby.

## Valuation of an Initial Public Offering

The initial public offering (IPO) of a firm involves either (1)
raising funds for executives (owners) selling off a share of the
firm for cash to diversify their *own* wealth and/or (2) raising
funds to expand the scale of the firm's operations. Depending
on when in the firm's history the IPO occurs, reason (1) or (2)
predominates, and at its earliest stage, reason (1) may involve
financing the industrial implementation of a technological
advance or scientific breakthrough. The valuation process
thus may start with something as intangible as the financial
marketing of an idea. Or in a conventional financial analysis,
an investor may decide to participate in the further development of a well-established concern.

In a technical sense, then, a valuation (price per share) that
is the equivalent of the present value of the future stream of
dividends must be place on a security some time before any
initial dividend may be paid or even expected. In many cases,
there may be no history of market evaluation to go by. Nevertheless, a price must be set.

At the next stage of corporate development, when a company is well established, setting a price on a new issue still
remains an exercise in futures pricing. With the proceeds of
the new issue, the firm will not only be larger but may be
different (in assets, outputs, financial characteristics) than

before. Finally, the price must be set some time before trading can begin. These time lags are:

1. The SEC lag until the issue is declared effective for trading.
2. The flotation lag—that is, until the issue is all sold.

The SEC lag is presently about two days or less assuming the prospectus contains no significant technical errors and the backlog at the SEC is no greater than average.

The second time lag—the flotation lag—reflects the problem of scale: not only is the stock traded for the first time, but a large quantity must be sold at one offering. The mechanism for setting a price in that large-scale context implies the involvement of a dealer rather than a broker. And the aftermath of the large-scale trade carries marketing and inventory implications for the dealer. Leaving these aside for the moment, let's first consider the typical spreadsheets used by corporate finance departments to set reasonable parameters for new-issue pricing.

## VALUING INFORMATICS: A CASE STUDY

The exercise below is an attempt to place a valuation on a cash offer, using data from comparable firms to set the new-issue price. As the cover of the Informatics prospectus indicates (Figure 11–1), the initial offering made on October 4, 1979, carried a price to the public of $12.50 per share (and proceeds to the selling shareholders of $11.56 per share). The $12.50 price to public represents a multiple of about 11 times the reported income per share for 1978; a comparison of these data with the spreadsheet data used by the underwriters in pricing the issue (shown in Figure 11–2) indicate that the issue price is right in line with market experience (compare price-earnings ratios for mean and median of comparable firms on pages 166–69). Some other comparisons (e.g., sales growth rate), to be sure, show somewhat better results for Informatics but that suggests that, at new-issue, those better results may have helped to move up the P-E multiple to the mean industry level.

**FIGURE 11–1**
Informatics Prospectus

---

600,000 Shares

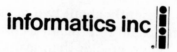

Common Stock

---

All of the shares of Common Stock offered hereby are being sold by the Selling Shareholder, The Equitable Life Holding Corporation, a wholly-owned subsidiary of The Equitable Life Assurance Society of the United States. See "Principal and Selling Shareholder". None of the proceeds from the sale of the shares will be received by the Company.

Of the shares offered hereby, 18,700 shares are being reserved for sale by the Underwriters to certain officers and employees of the Company as described under "Offering to Employees". Such offering will terminate on the date of this Prospectus. Any shares not purchased by officers or employees will be reoffered to the public.

Prior to this offering, there has been no public market for the Company's stock. For the method of determining the initial public offering price, see "Underwriting".

---

**THESE SECURITIES HAVE NOT BEEN APPROVED OR DISAPPROVED BY THE SECURITIES AND EXCHANGE COMMISSION NOR HAS THE COMMISSION PASSED UPON THE ACCURACY OR ADEQUACY OF THIS PROSPECTUS. ANY REPRESENTATION TO THE CONTRARY IS A CRIMINAL OFFENSE.**

---

| | Initial Public Offering Price | Underwriting Discount(1) | Proceeds to Selling Shareholder(2) |
|---|---|---|---|
| Per Share .................... | $12.50 | $.94 | $11.56 |
| Total ..................... | $7,500,000 | $564,000 | $6,936,000 |

(1) For information concerning indemnification of the Underwriters, see "Underwriting".

(2) Before deducting expenses of the offering payable by the Selling Shareholder estimated at $278,000. In addition, the Company has agreed to pay certain expenses of the offering estimated at $112,000. See "Management — Certain Transactions".

---

These shares are offered severally by Underwriters as specified herein, subject to receipt and acceptance by them and subject to the right to reject any order in whole or in part. It is expected that certificates for the shares will be ready for delivery at the offices of Goldman, Sachs & Co., New York, New York on or about October 11, 1979.

---

## Goldman, Sachs & Co.

The date of this Prospectus is October 4, 1979

**FIGURE 11-1** *(concluded)* _____

## PROSPECTUS SUMMARY

*The following summary is qualified in its entirety by more detailed information and consolidated financial statements appearing elsewhere in this Prospectus. Unless the text indicates otherwise, all share and per share information in this Prospectus gives effect to the recapitalization of the Company which became effective on October 1, 1979 as described under "Management — Certain Transactions" and in Note 6 of Notes to Consolidated Financial Statements.*

### THE COMPANY

Informatics, Inc. provides a variety of computer-related products and services to both private industry and government. The business of the Company includes the design, development, marketing and maintenance of proprietary computer programs, the furnishing of professional services, consisting principally of programming, system development and facilities management, and the furnishing of information processing services, including timesharing and data management and analysis.

The Common Stock offered hereby may involve special risks. See "Certain Factors".

### THE OFFERING

600,000 shares of Common Stock are being sold by the Selling Shareholder (The Equitable Life Holding Corporation). After the offering, the Selling Shareholder will own approximately 63% of the Company's Common Stock and 97% of the Company's Preferred Stock, and will possess approximately 83% of the voting power of the Company's capital stock with respect to the election of directors.

### SELECTED FINANCIAL INFORMATION

| | 1974 | 1975 | 1976 | 1977 | 1978* | Six Months Ended June 30, | |
| --- | --- | --- | --- | --- | --- | --- | --- |
| | | | | | | 1978* | 1979* |
| | | (In thousands, except share and per share amounts) | | | | (Unaudited) | |
| **INCOME STATEMENT DATA:** | | | | | | | |
| Revenues | $ 29,527 | $ 38,982 | $ 58,743 | $ 74,768 | $ 92,507 | $ 41,908 | $ 52,970 |
| Income (loss) from continuing operations before extraordinary item | (1,300) | (4,365) | (1,865) | 620 | 1,497 | 85 | 935 |
| Net income (loss) | (1,398) | (4,468) | (1,905) | 940 | 2,703 | 153 | 1,492 |
| Income (loss) from continuing operations before extraordinary item per common share | (.68) | (2.28) | (.98) | .16 | .58 | .02 | .38 |
| Net income (loss) per common share | (.73) | (2.33) | (1.00) | .31 | 1.15 | .04 | .65 |
| Weighted average number of common shares outstanding | 1,910,622 | 1,914,045 | 1,912,708 | 2,140,348 | 2,118,396 | 2,131,427 | 2,080,873 |

*As explained under "Management's Discussion and Analysis of the Consolidated Statements of Operations", reported results have been affected by certain costs incurred in connection with an acquisition and reorganization in 1974. Such costs have made the comparison of results for the first half and second quarter of 1979 with the corresponding periods of 1978 more favorable than a comparison giving effect to the elimination of these costs. The effect of these costs was to reduce per share income from continuing operations by $.48 to the reported $.58 per share for 1978, by $.17 to the reported $.02 per share for the first six months of 1978 and by $.03 to the reported $.38 per share for the first six months of 1979. After giving effect to the elimination of these costs, income from continuing operations before income taxes declined $84,000, or approximately 8%, in the second quarter of 1979 compared with the second quarter of 1978.

| | December 31, 1978 | June 30, 1979 |
| --- | --- | --- |
| | | (Unaudited) |
| **BALANCE SHEET DATA:** | | |
| Working capital | $ 7,945,000 | $ 8,537,000 |
| Total assets | 40,025,000 | 39,566,000 |
| Total debt | 10,341,000 | 10,860,000 |
| Total liabilities | 28,299,000 | 26,672,000 |
| Deficit | 6,906,000 | 5,414,000 |
| Shareholders' equity | 11,726,000 | 12,894,000 |

3

# FIGURE 11-2

| | INFORMATICS, INC. ESTIMATED 12/31/78 | APPLIED DATA RESEARCH 12/31/77 | AUTOMATIC DATA PROC 6/30/77 | BRADFORD NATIONAL CORP 6/30/78 | COMPUTER SCIENCES CORP 6/30/78 |
|---|---|---|---|---|---|
| | | | (DOLLARS IN MILLIONS) | | |
| **CAPITALIZATION** | | | | | |
| SHORT TERM DEBT | $ 4,789 | $0.1 | $2.0 | $135.8 | $57.2 |
| LONG TERM DEBT | $6,934  36.1 | $0.9  14.1% | $9.2  6.9% | $10.8  17.6% | $57.2  57.0% |
| PREFERRED STOCK (LIQ VAL) | 69  0.3 | 0.0  0.0 | 0.0  0.0 | 0.0  0.0 | 0.0  0.0 |
| COMMON EQUITY | 12,197  63.6 | 5.5  85.9 | 124.8  93.1 | 50.7  82.4 | 43.1  43.0 |
| TOTAL CAPITALIZATION | $19,200  100.0% | $6.4  100.0% | $134.0  100.0% | $61.5  100.0% | $100.3  100.0% |
| **COMMON SHARES OUTSTANDING** | 608,000 | 1,306,000 | 14,867,000 | 4,044,000 | 12,913,000 |
| **NET SALES/NET INC/NET MARGIN** | 12/31/78 = 1978 | 12/31/77 = 1977 | 6/30/77 = 1977 | 12/31/77 = 1977 | 3/31/78 = 1977 |
| | $ N/A | | | | |
| 1973 | 29,560 (1,344) N/A | $7 $0.5 6.6% | $102 $9.2 9.0% | $41 $2.3 5.6% | $147 $1.1 0.7% |
| 1974 | 38,982 (4,392) N/A | 8 0.5 6.1 | 130 12.0 9.3 | 50 2.0 4.1 | 177 3.6 2.1 |
| 1975 | 58,743 (1,882) N/A | 10 0.3 3.5 | 163 14.3 8.8 | 57 4.0 7.0 | 220 7.2 3.3 |
| 1976 | 74,768 570 0.8% | 13 1.0 7.4 | 199 18.7 9.4 | 66 3.2 4.7 | 235 11.6 5.0 |
| 1977 | 90,400 1,834 2.0 | 17 1.8 10.5 | 245 23.3 9.5 | 94 3.5 | 277 13.9 5.0 |
| 1978 | N/A | | | | |
| COMPOUND GROWTH/AVG MAR (1973-77) | 32.2% N/A | 24.7% 40.2% 6.8% | 24.5% 26.2% 9.2% | 23.1% 11.5% | 17.2% 89.6% 3.7% |
| **EPS(PD)/DPS/PAYOUT RATIO** | $ N/A | | | | |
| 1973 | 1.04 .00 N/A | $0.32 $0.00 0% | $0.70 $0.00 0% | $0.56 $0.00 0% | $0.08 $0.00 0% |
| 1974 | (6.97) .00 0% | 0.16 0.00 0 | 0.82 0.05 5 | 0.50 0.00 0 | 0.26 0.00 0 |
| 1975 | .08 .00 0 | (0.29) 0.00 0 | 0.96 0.10 10 | 1.00 0.15 15 | 0.51 0.00 0 |
| 1976 | 1.99 .00 0 | (0.82) 0.00 0 | 1.22 0.21 16 | 0.74 0.20 25 | 0.81 0.00 0 |
| 1977 | 4.08 .00 0 | 1.30 0.08 6 | 1.58 0.28 17 | 0.88 0.20 23 | 0.97 0.00 0 |
| 1978 | 4.08 .00 0 | 1.26 0.16 1% | 1.84 0.43 23 | 1.03 0.20 19 | 1.04 0.00 0 |
| NEXT YR EST/IND ANN RATE | .00 0 | 0.16 | 2.20 0.52 24 | 0.20 | 1.25 0.00 0 |
| COMPOUND GROWTH/AVG PAY (1973-77) | 40.7% | 42.0% | -8 9% | 2.46 -8 13% | 68.6% -8 0% |
| **INTERIM EPS (THIS YR/LAST YR)** | N/A | $0.51 $0.56 6 MONTHS JUN | $1.84 $1.58 12 MONTHS JUN | $0.55 $0.40 6 MONTHS JUN | $0.28 $0.21 3 MONTHS JUN |
| **MARKET RANGE (CALENDAR YR)** | | | | | |
| 1977 | N/A | 9.625 - 5.125 | 30.50 - 21.50 | 10.625 - 7.50 | 9.875 - 6.75 |
| 1978 | N/A | 17.50 - 7.875 | 36.375 - 23.00 | 13.75 - 6.75 | 17.00 - 8.00 |
| 10/6/78 | N/A | 14.125 AMEX | 32.875 NYSE | 10.75 AMEX | 14.375 NYSE |
| **P/E RATIO** | | | | | |
| 1977 | N/A | 7.7 4.1 | 16.6 11.7 | 10.3 7.3 | 9.5 6.5 |
| 1978 | N/A | 14.0 6.3 | 19.8 12.5 | 13.3 6.6 | 16.3 7.7 |
| LATEST 12 MONTHS EPS | N/A | 11.3 | 17.9 | 10.4 | 13.8 |
| NEXT YR EST EPS | N/A | - | 14.9 | - | 11.5 |
| **TANG BOOK VAL/MKT AS A % BOOK** | N/A | $4.20 336.6% | $6.69 491.4% | $7.95 135.2% | $2.73 526.6% |
| **DIVIDEND YIELD** | 0.0% | 1.1% | 1.6% | 1.9% | 0.0% |
| **CERTAIN RATIOS (LAST FISC YR)** | | | | | |
| PRE TAX MARGIN | 3.9% | 17.9% | 18.7% | 5.9% | 9.4% |
| TAX RATE | 48.0% | 41.1% | 49.3% | 36.3% | 46.8% |
| NET MARGIN | 2.0% | 10.5% | 9.5% | 3.8% | 5.0% |
| ASSET TURNOVER (AVG) | N/A | 2.1X | 1.6X | 0.2X | 2.0X |
| RETURN ON ASSETS (AVG) | N/A | 21.7% | 15.4% | 0.7% | 9.8% |
| TOTAL LEVERAGE (AVG) | N/A | 1.8X | 1.4X | 10.8X | 3.7X |
| RETURN ON EQUITY (AVG) | N/A | 39.2% | 20.9% | 7.5% | 36.4% |

# FIGURE 11-2 (continued)

(DOLLARS IN MILLIONS)

| | INFORMATICS, INC. ESTIMATED 12/31/78 | ELECTRONIC DATA SYSTEMS 6/30/78 | LOGICON INC 3/31/78 | NATIONAL CSS INC 5/31/78 | TYMSHARE INC 3/31/78 |
|---|---|---|---|---|---|
| **CAPITALIZATION** | | | | | |
| SHORT TERM DEBT | $4,789 | $0.9 | $0.0 | $0.7 | $3.5 |
| LONG TERM DEBT | $6,934 / 36.1 | $2.6 / 2.6% | $0.0 / 0.0% | $6.9 / 29.4% | $15.6 / 26.4% |
| PREFERRED STOCK (LIQ VAL) | 69 / 0.3 | 0.0 / 0.0 | 0.0 / 0.0 | 0.0 / 0.0 | 0.0 / 0.0 |
| COMMON EQUITY | 12,197 / 63.6 | 97.6 / 97.4 | 8.1 / 100.0 | 16.6 / 70.6 | 43.5 / 73.6 |
| TOTAL CAPITALIZATION | $19,200 / 100.0% | $100.2 / 100.0% | $8.1 / 100.0% | $23.5 / 100.0% | $59.1 / 100.0% |
| **COMMON SHARES OUTSTANDING** | 608,000 | 12,828,000 | 888,000 | 2,174,000 | 4,348,000 |
| **NET SALES/NET INC/NET MARGIN** | 12/31/78 = 1978 | 6/30/78 = 1977 | 3/31/78 = 1977 | 2/28/78 = 1977 | 12/31/77 = 1977 |
| 1973 | $N/A / $N/A / N/A | $114 / $15.3 / 13.4% | $23 / $0.7 / 2.9% | $24 / $1.6 / 6.7% | $40 / $2.3 / 5.8% |
| 1974 | 29,560 / (1,344) / N/A | 119 / 14.6 / 12.3 | 33 / 0.9 / 2.7 | 33 / 1.8 / 5.6 | 53 / 3.4 / 6.5 |
| 1975 | 38,982 / (4,392) / N/A | 129 / 13.6 / 10.5 | 32 / 0.8 / 2.7 | 36 / 2.2 / 6.1 | 64 / 5.0 / 7.7 |
| 1976 | 58,743 / (1,882) / N/A | 157 / 16.4 / 10.5 | 28 / 1.3 / 4.6 | 42 / 3.2 / 7.7 | 82 / 6.7 / 8.2 |
| 1977 | 74,768 / 570 / 0.8% | 211 / 19.7 / 9.3 | 33 / 0.8 / 2.5 | 49 / 3.9 / 7.9 | 101 / 8.0 / 7.9 |
| 1978 | 90,400 / 1,834 / 2.0 | – / – / – | – / – / – | – / – / – | – / – / – |
| COMPOUND GROWTH/AVG MAR (1973-77) | 32.2% / N/A | 16.5% / 6.4% / 11.2% | 10.2% / 6.3% / 3.1% | 19.8% / 25.0% / 6.8% | 26.3% / 36.7% / 7.2% |
| **EPS(PD)/DPS/PAYOUT RATIO** | | | | | |
| 1973 | $N/A / $N/A / N/A | $1.28 / $0.25 / 0% | $0.50 / $0.00 / 0% | $0.72 / $0.00 / 0% | $0.58 / $0.00 / 0% |
| 1974 | 1.04 / .00 / 0% | 1.21 / 0.50 / 22 | 0.78 / 0.00 / 0 | 0.84 / 0.00 / 0 | 0.85 / 0.00 / 0 |
| 1975 | (6.97) / .00 / 0 | 1.10 / 0.50 / 48 | 0.98 / 0.00 / 0 | 0.95 / 0.08 / 5 | 1.19 / 0.00 / 0 |
| 1976 | 1.30 / .00 / 0 | 1.54 / 0.60 / 48 | 1.50 / 0.00 / 0 | 1.41 / 0.20 / 11 | 1.55 / 0.00 / 0 |
| 1977 | 1.99 / .00 / 0 | 1.46 / 0.72 / 49 | 0.92 / 0.00 / 0 | 1.68 / 0.23 / 13 | 1.82 / 0.00 / 0 |
| 1978 | 4.08 / .00 / 0 | 1.90 / 0.84 / 47 | 0.99 / 0.00 / – | 1.82 / 0.25 / 14 | 2.04 / 0.00 / 0 |
| NEXT YR EST/IND ANN RATE | 4.08 / .00 / 0 | – / 0.84 / 44% | – / – / – | 2.25 / 0.32 / – | 2.40 / 0.00 / 0 |
| COMPOUND GROWTH/AVG PAY (1973-77) | 40.7% / N/A | 4.7% / 30.3% | 16.5% / – % | 23.8% / – | 36.1% / 0% |
| INTERIM EPS (THIS YR/LAST YR) | N/A / N/A | | $0.37 / $0.30 3 MONTHS JUN | $0.53 / $0.39 3 MONTHS MAY | $1.33 / $1.11 6 MONTHS JUN |
| **MARKET RANGE (CALENDAR YR)** | N/A | NYSE | AMEX | AMEX | NYSE |
| 1977 | N/A / N/A | – / – | 17.625 – 7.25 | 18.00 – 9.50 | 23.625 – 14.00 |
| 1978 | N/A / N/A | 24.875 – 14.625 | 19.50 – 11.00 | 36.00 – 15.375 | 34.375 – 17.00 |
| 10/6/78 | N/A | 21.375 | 15.75 | 29.375 | 28.00 |
| **P/E RATIO** | | | | | |
| 1977 | N/A / N/A | – / – | 17.8 / 7.3 | 9.9 / 5.2 | 11.6 / 6.9 |
| 1978 | N/A / N/A | 16.3 / 9.6 | 19.7 / 11.1 | 19.8 / 8.4 | 16.9 / 8.3 |
| LATEST 12 MONTHS EPS | N/A | 14.0 | 15.9 | 16.1 | 13.7 |
| NEXT YR EST EPS | N/A | 11.3 | 11.1 | 13.1 | 11.7 |
| TANG BOOK VAL/MKT AS A % BOOK | N/A | $7.61 / 280.9% | $9.14 / 172.3% | $6.70 / 438.7% | $8.38 / 334.0% |
| DIVIDEND YIELD | 0.0% | 3.9% | 0.0% | 1.1% | 0.0% |
| **CERTAIN RATIOS (LAST FISC YR)** | | | | | |
| PRE TAX MARGIN | 3.9% | 15.4% | 4.6% | 15.3% | 15.6% |
| TAX RATE | 48.0% | 39.4% | 46.0% | 48.5% | 49.3% |
| NET MARGIN | 2.0% | 9.3% | 2.5% | 7.9% | 7.9% |
| ASSET TURNOVER (AVG) | N/A | 1.7X | 2.5X | 1.2X | 1.6X |
| RETURN ON ASSET (AVG) | N/A | 16.2% | 6.2% | 12.2% | 12.2% |
| TOTAL LEVERAGE (AVG) | N/A | 1.3X | 1.8X | 2.2X | 1.8X |
| RETURN ON EQUITY (AVG) | N/A | 21.3% | 11.3% | 26.9% | 22.7% |

## FIGURE 11-2 *(continued)*

FOOTNOTES:

APPLIED DATA RESEARCH :

EARNINGS ARE STATED BEFORE EXTRAORDINARY ITEM OF $  -0.1 MILLION OR $ -0.11 PER SHARE IN 1974
EARNINGS ARE STATED BEFORE EXTRAORDINARY ITEM OF $   0.2 MILLION OR $  0.16 PER SHARE IN 1975
EARNINGS ARE STATED BEFORE EXTRAORDINARY ITEM OF $   0.4 MILLION OR $  0.29 PER SHARE IN 1976
EARNINGS ARE STATED BEFORE DISCONTINUED OPERATIONS OF $  -0.1 MILLION OR $ -0.10 PER SHARE IN 1975
EARNINGS ARE STATED BEFORE DISCONTINUED OPERATIONS OF $  -0.1 MILLION OR $ -0.11 PER SHARE IN 1977
AVG INVENTORY METHOD USED SINCE 1974

AUTOMATIC DATA PROC :

FIFO INVENTORY METHOD USED SINCE 1973

BRADFORD NATIONAL CORP :

EARNINGS ARE STATED BEFORE EXTRAORDINARY ITEM OF $   0.0 MILLION OR $  0.01 PER SHARE IN 1973
EARNINGS ARE STATED BEFORE EXTRAORDINARY ITEM OF $   0.1 MILLION OR $  0.03 PER SHARE IN 1974
EARNINGS ARE STATED BEFORE EXTRAORDINARY ITEM OF $   0.1 MILLION OR $  0.02 PER SHARE IN 1975
EARNINGS ARE STATED BEFORE EXTRAORDINARY ITEM OF $   0.3 MILLION OR $  0.06 PER SHARE IN 1977

COMPUTER SCIENCES CORP :

EARNINGS ARE STATED BEFORE EXTRAORDINARY ITEM OF $   3.0 MILLION OR $  0.23 PER SHARE IN 1976

ELECTRONIC DATA SYSTEMS :

NO APPLICABLE FOOTNOTES

LOGICON INC :

FIFO INVENTORY METHOD USED SINCE 1973

NATIONAL CSS INC :

EARNINGS ARE STATED BEFORE EXTRAORDINARY ITEM OF $   0.2 MILLION OR $  0.10 PER SHARE IN 1973

TYMSHARE INC :

EARNINGS ARE STATED BEFORE EXTRAORDINARY ITEM OF $   0.3 MILLION OR $  0.08 PER SHARE IN 1973
EARNINGS ARE STATED BEFORE EXTRAORDINARY ITEM OF $   0.2 MILLION OR $  0.03 PER SHARE IN 1974
EARNINGS ARE STATED BEFORE EXTRAORDINARY ITEM OF $   0.1 MILLION OR $  0.03 PER SHARE IN 1975
FIFO INVENTORY METHOD USED SINCE 1973

| Per Share | Year-End | | Six Months Ended June 30 | |
|---|---|---|---|---|
| | 1978 | 1979 | 1979 | 1980 |
| Net income | $1.15 | $2.03 | $0.65 | $0.81 |
| Change in net income | $0.88 | | $0.16 | |
| Percent change | 80% | | 25% | |

The sale of the new issue went so well that in less than one year, the selling shareholder (a subsidiary of Equitable Life Assurance Society) saw the stock trade on NASDAQ at a price above $20 per share. Consequently, on September 18, 1980,

**FIGURE 11-2** *(concluded)* _____

| CAPITALIZATION | RANGE FOR COMPANIES IN THIS REPORT | MEDIAN FOR COMPANIES IN THIS REPORT | MEAN FOR COMPANIES IN THIS REPORT |
|---|---|---|---|
| STOCKHOLDERS' EQUITY | | | |
| AS A % OF CAPITALIZATION | 100.0% - 50.1% | 83.9% | 81.1 |
| PAYOUT RATIO | | | |
| LATEST YEAR | 28.1 - 0.0 | 9.5 | 11.1 |
| AVG OVER 5 YEARS | 25.8 - 0.0 | 3.1 | 6.4 |
| PROFITABILITY | | | |
| NET MARGIN (LATEST YEAR) | 14.9 - 2.1 | 8.4 | 7.9 |
| NET MARGIN (5 YEAR AVERAGE) | 11.8 - 2.0 | 6.8 | 6.9 |
| RETURN ON AVG ASSETS (LATEST YEAR) | 21.8 - 4.0 | 10.6 | 11.6 |
| RETURN ON AVG EQUITY (LATEST YEAR) | 29.9 - 13.9 | 18.8 | 19.3 |
| COMPOUND ANNUAL GROWTH RATES | | | |
| NET SALES | 48.0 - 8.1 | 17.2 | 21.1 |
| NET INCOME | 72.7 - 5.0 | 27.0 | 30.7 |
| EARNINGS PER SHARE | 61.3 - 5.7 | 29.8 | 28.6 |
| DIVIDENDS PER SHARE | 31.3 - 31.3 | 31.3 | 31.3 |
| MARKET DATA | | | |
| P/E RATIO ON LATEST 12 MO. EPS | 12.2X - 11.9X | 12.0X | 12.0 |
| P/E RATIO ON NEXT YR EST EPS | 19.7 - 11.6 | 11.9 | 14.4 |
| MARKET AS A % OF BOOK | 645.4% - 194.2% | 252.3% | 322.3 |
| DIVIDEND YIELD | 2.4 - 0.0 | 1.3 | 1.2 |

Equitable Life Holdings sold another 1,267,250 shares at a price between the bid/ask quotation (20½ and 20¾) on the close of the preceding day. At that time, market data and spreadsheets tended to confirm the pricing of the issue. This suggests that the pricing process for this firm appears to be less traumatic than it might be in other cases. Because the selling stockholder is a major institutional client, that issuer may be more knowledgeable about capital markets than many other IPO clients (see Figure 11-3).

## Avoidance of Flotation Risks: Management's Point of View

Corporations that are expanding rapidly have opportunities to make real investments (with positive net present values) in excess of their internal funds currently available for investment. They will raise outside funds as long as internal rates of return on the new projects exceed the firm's cost of capital. At the margin, however, some projects are necessarily more sensitive to unforeseen rises in cost of capital (that is, flotation risk); and, for all new projects, an unforeseen rise in the cost of capital has the same impact as an unforeseen rise in business risk on expected net present value. Alternatively, an unforeseen rise in the firm's cost of capital could be interpreted as a

**FIGURE 11–3** _____

1,267,250 Shares

# informatics inc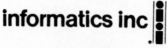

Common Stock

_____

All of the shares of Common Stock offered hereby are being sold by the Selling Shareholder, The Equitable Life Holding Corporation, a wholly-owned subsidiary of The Equitable Life Assurance Society of the United States. See "Principal and Selling Shareholder". None of the proceeds from the sale of the shares will be received by the Company.

The Company's Common Stock is traded in the over-the-counter market and quoted on the National Association of Securities Dealers Automated Quotation System ("NASDAQ"). On September 17, 1980, the closing bid and asked prices as reported by NASDAQ were $20½ and $20¾, respectively. See "Market Prices of Common Stock".

_____

**THESE SECURITIES HAVE NOT BEEN APPROVED OR DISAPPROVED BY THE SECURITIES AND EXCHANGE COMMISSION NOR HAS THE COMMISSION PASSED UPON THE ACCURACY OR ADEQUACY OF THIS PROSPECTUS. ANY REPRESENTATION TO THE CONTRARY IS A CRIMINAL OFFENSE.**

_____

|  | Initial Public Offering Price | Underwriting Discount(1) | Proceeds to Selling Shareholder(2) |
|---|---|---|---|
| Per Share ..................... | $20.625 | $1.100 | $19.525 |
| Total ........................ | $26,137,031.25 | $1,393,975.00 | $24,743,056.25 |

(1) For information concerning indemnification of the Underwriters, see "Underwriting".

(2) Before deducting expenses of the offering payable by the Selling Shareholder estimated at $214,000. In addition, the Company has agreed to pay certain expenses of the offering estimated at $6,000. See "Management — Certain Transactions".

_____

These shares are offered severally by Underwriters as specified herein, subject to receipt and acceptance by them and subject to the right to reject any order in whole or in part. It is expected that certificates for the shares will be ready for delivery at the offices of Goldman, Sachs & Co., New York, New York on or about September 25, 1980.

_____

# Goldman, Sachs & Co.

The date of this Prospectus is September 18, 1980

new tax on new investment. If that "tax" threatens to make the new investment unattractive—that is, carry negative net present value—the new issue may be postponed or canceled.

In view of the foregoing arguments, consider the following propositions:

**1.** Most corporations that sell a new issue come to market only occasionally; their experience with flotation risks will be limited.

**2.** Economies of scale with respect to fixed costs abound in new flotations; as a result, ventures into the capital markets are necessarily concentrated into fewer, rather than more frequent, new issues.

**3.** The chief financial officer (CFO) may be induced to be satisficing rather than maximizing corporate net worth (in connection with flotations). He may feel (probably correctly) that the sale of an issue at a better-than-anticipated price will not generate as much *credit* for him as a failed issue will raise *doubts* about his abilities and promotability. This induces managerial risk avoidance in flotations. In other words, it raises corporate management's demand to shift incidence of flotation risk.

**4.** Suppose that the decision to sell a new issue is made by a mostly outside board of directors. Aside from their prior responsibilities with due diligence, they have now added a fiduciary responsibility regarding new-issue *timing*. Their demand for insurance protection will not be reduced.

Summing up, economies of scale limit the number of trips to market, and the fewer the trips to market, the thinner management's experience. Risk avoidance in new-issue pricing and in flotation risks generally leads, in turn, to calls for "the experts." Beyond finding another handy group to blame if things go wrong, the CFO may also conceive of the new-issue underwriting process as a useful insurance scheme that limits the variance of net present value—or risk—as much as possible from the cost-of-capital side.

Perhaps the most direct way to confront these issues and the demand for insurance is by a simple matrix (see Figure 11–4) that takes into account both market environment and pricing characteristics. Assume in the *ex ante* context where pricing must take place before *trading*, both issuer and under-

**FIGURE 11–4** _____

Market Environment during Syndicate

| Pricing | Stable | Uncertain |
|---|---|---|
| Correct | 0 | 1 |
| Incorrect | ½ | 1 |

writer have no asymmetry of information (i.e., both parties, after agreeing on a price, are about equally uncertain that it is the right price). Of course, uncertainty is likely to be small in a stable market. When convinced that the issue is correctly priced, the issuer may not request insurance; as a result, the northeast cell has a zero. But even in a stable market, uncertainty regarding appropriate pricing may induce some issuers to request underwriting—hence the value given to the southeast cell is ½.

Clearest of all are the cases that take place in an uncertain market where the risks related to greater environmental variance are most likely to be underwritten (here the symbol 1 is used), whether or not the issuer feels that the security has been properly priced. (In an uncertain market, none of the participants may have confidence in the pricing decision). Note the explicitly assumed symmetrical expectations on the part of issuers and investment bankers; that the demand for, and supply of, underwriting services is no more than a reflection of greater capacity to diversify risks on the part of underwriters; and that differential demands for insurance are based on environmental uncertainties. Thus in an overall market cycle, even assuming equal proportions of certainty/uncertainty periods, the demand for insurance will dominate since it adds up to 2½ out of 4. This also assumes more managerial confidence than may be found in practice by potential issuers (and the desire to exercise it) in the pricing of new issues and the willingness to forgo the insurance factor in stable market periods.

This desire of management (or the board of directors) to accept responsibility for pricing decisions is obvious in the one kind of flotation that comes closest to a do-it-yourself effort.

### "Privileged Subscription" for Rights Issues and Standby "Insurance"

Most articles of incorporation give shareholders preemptive rights to new-issue stock subscriptions. This provision reflects the common-law practice of reserving to current owners—that is, stockholders—rights associated with their property (common stock), including a potentially valuable opportunity to acquire new stock.

Most preemptive rights are presented to current stockholders as the "right" (hence the name) to acquire new shares in some proportion to their present holdings at a preferential price. Since only present owners benefit from such "underpricing," the nominal price set on rights offers—however low the price might be—does *not* affect stockholder value or any other aspect of ownership status. These offerings must be registered with the SEC (like any other new-money issue), and the prospectus, like any other, states the volume of funds to be raised, the price per share, the purpose of the flotation, and so on. The rights issued to each stockholder may be in the form of warrants (for example, the holder can use five warrants to buy one share of additional stock at $50 within 20 days of the offering date). Rights may be exercised, sold, or thrown away; they have value only if the market price at the end of the subscription period is above the exercise price. Assume that the market price on the exercise date is $52 per share. Most often, a subscription agent is named to receive the rights for the purchase of new stock or for resale by those not exercising their rights. Finally, most of these options (for these are, indeed, call options) are exercised by holders at the end of the subscription period because only by then will it be clear and certain (that is, risk will approach zero) that holders can buy $52 market-price stock at the bargain price of $50.

From the point of view of the issuing corporation and, more specifically, the CFO, this is a desirable and useful result. But to avoid flotation risk (or waiting risk as defined earlier), many corporations even have rights issues underwritten by an investment banking firm on a *standby* arrangement. This means that the underwriter *will not* buy the issue on subscription day if the issue is a success. Instead, the issuing firm pays a standby fee (1 percent of the value of the issue is customary). For that premium (or, in effect, the equivalent to the firm of a *standby put option*), the underwriter stands ready to buy any unsubscribed shares at the subscription price less an additional *take-down discount* (or fee) of 2.5 percent.[10]

If everything works out as planned, the fees paid to the underwriter are the equivalent of an insurance premium. What is insured against is the vagaries of a market where the price might drop below $50 per share and where the standby put option in effect covers flotation risk as defined. That risk is the possibility that the stock market will decline so far—say, below $50 per share—during the subscription period as to make the put option (rights) worthless (out of the money). In fact, the cost of the standby insurance can be calculated as a pay-as-you-go proposition by a set of steps that move the security issuer into a fully hedged ("certainty equivalent") position.

Assume that most current owners—that is, rights holders—will wait until the exercise date to proffer their rights. By the exercise date the stock price has fallen through $50 per share to, say, $48 per share. At that point, the standby put option is invoked, and the corporation sells the shares to the underwriter at $50 per share less the following fees: 1/2-point standby fee (1 percent) + 1 1/4-point take-down discount (2.5 percent), leaving the issuer proceeds of 48 1/4 per share—1/4 point better than the current market price. And the risks of an even lower market price as well as all other transaction costs of selling new shares are progressively shifted to the underwriter.

---

[10] That last option will also be exercised by the underwriter to the extent that subscribers ignore their valuable rights and do not exercise them. Typically, the underwriter's profits in such transactions are split 50/50 with the issuer.

To consider that problem from the issuer's point of view, start with the assumption that the stock issue to be sold had a par value of $20 million (at a $50 exercise price on 400,000 shares). The worst-case scenario then gives the corporation fully hedged minimum proceeds of $20 million less $700,000 [400,000 shares (.01 + .025)($50) = $700,000]—all from owners of the firm. The net proceeds then come to $19.3 million.[11]

If the price on exercise day is above $48\frac{1}{4}$, the proceeds to the firm will be higher, reaching a maximum of $19.8 million (all from owners of firm) at the exercise price of $50. If the projects for which the new funds are needed require a minimum of $19.3 million cash, then the fully hedged position, having shifted the flotation risk to the underwriter, becomes a rational policy. If on the other hand, the cost of the hedge is too high or if the issuer can afford to be less risk averse, a rational decision might be made not to underwrite the stock issue. Nevertheless, some 70 percent of rights offers are underwritten.

## SOME CONCLUSIONS

There is a demand for risk shifting to the underwriter even among the do-it-yourself issuers that use preemptive rights offerings. From a stockholder's point of view, that flotation cost can be avoided if the rights offering is priced very substantially—say, 25 percent—below the current market price. In a narrow stockholder's viewpoint, there should be no concern whatever no matter how low the new stock price is set because each stockholder will maintain the same proportionate ownership share. Even if the stockholders *sell* their rights, an efficient market will price that value appropriately. Why, then, are some 70 percent of new-rights offerings underwrit-

---

[11] Note that the spread between the stock price at the announcement date ($52 per share) and the ultimate floor price ($48) came to $4, or nearly 8 percent of the exercise price. Adding to that spread the 1 percent standby fee and the 2.5 percent take-down discount, a total spread of about 10 percent (typically assumed) is obtained. But the standby arrangements reach their maximum spread only if market decline raises costs to the maximum.

ten at significant expense, while using only a modest price discount below market?

The question really being asked here is: Why is the trade-off between a substantial price discount as an insurance premium (that is, presumably costless to the stockholder) foregone in favor of a costly underwriting (standby) premium associated with a lesser price discount? One possible (and plausible) explanation could be management's fear that the market might misperceive the large discount as an information signal rather than as a flotation-insurance mechanism. This is a generally unexplored area of agency theory where management may prefer easier (even if more expensive) stockholder relations and a consequently higher cost of capital.

This proposition, finally, should be kept conceptually separate from the more general aspect of the payment of a flotation-related insurance fee if that payment appears to have been a "useless" expense. Such a payment can appear useless if the offering goes well and if the underwriting support is unnecessary because of a rise in market prices. But that is the nature of all insurance fees. If the accident insured against does not occur, the payments seem unnecessary. A rational corporate decision to use insurance *before* the coverage period is like any other capital budgeting decision. If it appears to carry positive net present value when made, the decision should be judged accordingly.

# 12

## New-Issue Underwriting of Stocks and Bonds: Another Application of Options Theory

This chapter explores the concept of securities underwriting further, taking as a model the notion of the flotation process as a put option. Using that concept, the Black/Scholes model is evaluated as a representation of a new-issue flotation "premium." The model is then used to value changes in flotation cost—or changes in put-option *premium* cost—as Rule 415 has changed the process by reducing flotation risk.

### THE BLACK/SCHOLES MODEL AS AN UNDERWRITING PROCESS

The Black/Scholes model of option pricing develops an equilibrium solution for option premiums by substituting the value of underlying securities for option value.[1] By adjusting the components of the Black/Scholes substitution model, the new-issues process for stocks and bonds may also be modeled. The following are the necessary adjustments:

1. For option "premium," read "gross spread."
2. For "exercise price," read "proceeds to company."

---

[1]This presentation is based in part on Sharpe's *Investments*, 2nd ed., Prentice-Hall, Inc., Englewood Cliffs, N.J., 1981, chap. 6.

3. For "exercise price, plus premium," read "price to public."
4. For "value of dividends," read "accrued interest" (for bonds only).

With respect to the Black/Scholes assumptions, there appears to be a good fit (with one exception to be noted) in the actual conditions for a new issue underwriting. These assumptions and conditions are listed in Table 12-1.

The last item appears well within the boundaries established for the B/S model. Even though the prices on the prospectus (to public, to firm) are fixed, these prices must be seen relative to the market environment and in only one way: If market-environment prices move down, and move down substantially, the issue becomes unattractive, and the syndicate will break up eventually. From the underwriters' point of view, the flotation is a loser.

If, on the other hand, market prices rise, the issue will sell out quickly at the price to public stated on the prospectus ("go out the window"), and the securities will then trade in secondary markets; the subsequent capital gains accrue to buyers rather than to syndicate members. Accordingly, from the point of view of syndicate members, the flotation process implies a limited possibility of gain and some downside risk. They do it because the flotation gains (and other benefits) outweigh the potential for loss.

The B/S security replication model can now be restated as a flotation proxy. Consider that the underwriting syndicate buys the stock (which it is obligated to do as the offering becomes effective); the financing assumption of the B/S model is not necessary since no cash to pay for the stock (or bonds) needs to change hands prior to the closing of the underwriting deal (this typically occurs five working days later). As soon as the underwriting is declared effective by the SEC, it is open for trading, and syndicate members will sell to the public at the new-issue price. In fact, the syndicate has written a costless call (to the public) at that price. The "premium equivalent" for the call has been paid by the issuer (the gross spread). This produces the combination of the syndicate (a) stock purchase and (b) call that constitute the equivalent of a "synthetic put" option.

**TABLE 12-1**

| Assumptions, Black/Scholes | Terms and Conditions, Underwriting |
| --- | --- |
| 1. No transaction cost, no differential taxes. | 1. No commissions, no immediate tax affect. |
| 2. Borrowing and lending, at same rate, are unrestricted. | 2. New stock issue will not produce dividends; underwriters receive no funds and will not pay funds until deal closes five days after trading begins.* (No funds change hands during syndicate period.) |
| 3. Short-term risk-free rate of interest is known and constant through time. | 3. If issue sells quickly, assumption is not relevant. If issue sells slowly, underwriters will need financing only for unsold portion of their own shares *after* syndicate deal closes. |
| 4. Short sales with full use of proceeds are not restricted. | 4. Price support operations, including short sales, are permitted during syndicate period. |
| 5. Trading takes place continuously through time. | 5. Trading takes place continuously through time. |
| 6. The movement of the stock price can be described by a diffusion process. | 6. The price to the public (as well as the price to the issuer) is fixed by prospectus for the syndicate period (or until the sale is completed if the issue goes out the window). |

*For a new bond issue, accrued interest is charged (to the buyer) and paid at same rate; the borrowing-lending condition is satisfied.

The foregoing uses the option valuation model only as an analog. The model helps by focusing analysis on the valuation of the underwriting service cost. No option is written or purchased in any syndicate deal; the foregoing suggests how the pricing of the gross spread and some other factors in such deals can be interpreted *as if* an option had been written.

As Figure 12–1 indicates, the two top charts describe the situation of the syndicate as evaluated by the B/S model:

a. The syndicate is committed to buy the new stock; *its* cost (at closing) is the proceeds per share to the company. We assume that all out-of-pocket costs are reimbursed by the company.

b. The published prospectus shows two prices per share:
   1. The proceeds to the company.
   2. The (higher) price to the public.

The difference between (1) and (2) is the gross spread—that is, the gross revenue to the syndicate. In effect, the syndicate sells a call to the public at the price to public, and the (implicit) option premium is paid by issuer as the gross spread.

In the third chart, called composite position, we show the two parts of the model that are *not relevant* to the syndicate flotation, namely, the situation when the stock price rises above the price to the public. At that time, the issue sells out immediately at the price to public. Line f (stock valuation) and line g (call valuation) exactly offset. As a result, they are shown as broken lines.

In the fourth chart, the situation as seen by a syndicate participant is called a synthetic put precisely because that is the situation in which the syndicate operates.

Thus are illustrated (1) the substitution process of the B/S model and (2) the resultant option value.

Consider now that the new-issue spread in a flotation is a straightforward put premium, as indicated earlier, and is set equal to the gross spread. The syndicate will earn the premium only if the public buys at the price stated on the prospectus. If the offering will not sell out at that price, the syndicate will earn less than the premium as average sale price (after close of deal) declines below the price to the public. At "break-even" (on an option value when the premium is equal to zero), the syndicate will be out of pocket an amount equal to expenses plus foregone opportunity earnings on resources employed. At prices below that point, losses will rise dollar for dollar per share (or bond) as the price falls below stated proceeds to company.

**FIGURE 12-1**
Syndicate's Position in a Black/Scholes Setting

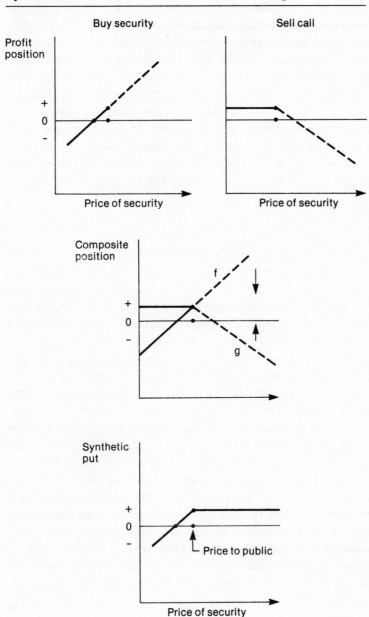

## UNDERWRITING AS A PUT OPTION

The purchase of a standby (put) option for a rights issue of new stock has the purpose of hedging flotation risks. The rights issue is a special case where the firm is dealing mainly with its own owners but where it may still feel it remains potentially exposed to severe downward pricing risks that might affect all markets. *All* underwritings (rights or cash, stocks or bonds) incorporate a put option for the issuer. And as noted, the volatility of market prices, when perceived as a dimension of risk, may induce issuers to have their new issues underwritten. By the same token, the valuation of the underwriting spread (as a put option) is also sensitive to price volatility.

### Volatility

Figure 12-2 examines the price environment of a market for a security for which a current option price—as distinct from current spot price—is established with a contract date set for the near future (say, an issue date one month hence). Point X is the execution price. It could represent the consensus of market expectations of the spot prices anticipated in the market for maturity of the contract one month away. If market prices are expected to be relatively stable, the range of strike prices on put and call options on the two sides of the futures price would be described between points A and B, which are relatively close to X. Conversely, if the market is expected to be volatile, the range of strike prices widens to the points between C and D. With greater volatility, the premiums for puts and calls will rise substantially, especially as more extreme strike prices are covered. This occurs partly because insurance against greater declines in value is more costly than insurance against smaller declines and partly because greater rate volatility usually is accompanied by higher interest rates (that is, carrying costs). Recall, finally, that a new offering has a fixed sales price so that rises in price will not benefit the issuer.

### Insurance Components of New-Issue Flotation

From the issuer's point of view, insurance coverage against a large drop in the bond (or stock) price on the new issue *before*

**FIGURE 12–2**
Volatility Examined

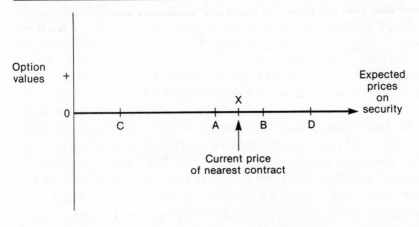

pricing is essential because, if the issue is sold below a certain price, it implies a rise in the firm's cost of capital. In turn, that possibility may raise the risk that the real investment financed by the proceeds from the new issue may carry a negative net present value and should therefore *not* be undertaken. Because the firm that can sell bonds nearly always has the option of financing at short term, it might look on, say, bank loans as a temporary expedient, anticipating consolidation of those bank loans subsequently through a bond issue (when long-term rates have receded). That willingness to pay current short rates that are higher than long rates[2] could be seen as an opportunity cost for insurance (or option) payments to hold current long rates at present levels. In another sense, current short rates may also represent a boundary condition, setting a limit to the price charged for providing a flotation hedge against flotation risk. (Such insurance fees in the form of options or in higher short rates are, however, more likely to be paid the higher the level and the greater the anticipated volatility of future rates.) From the point of view of the bond issuer, how can such insurance be purchased? The shift to the shelf-registration process does just that and is, in effect, equivalent to reducing premiums on a put option.

---

[2]Higher rate volatility frequently occurs when yield curves have a negative slope; that is, when short rates are higher than long.

## Put Option Valuation

The syndicate is in a position where it sells a put (only *one* strike price) as long as the syndicate is maintained. That strike price is the price to the public. If it is set at a discount to market price, as shown in Figure 12–3, that implies only a reduction of risk to the syndicate, not a rise in return. Indeed, if the market price does not recede to the level of the price to public, so that the syndicate's offering is sold out right away since it represents (now) a special bargain, the issuer's management will raise some incisive questions regarding pricing with the lead manager. In turn, the lead manager will be besieged with all kinds of requests for more securities in the "hot" new issue. In all of the post mortems of an excessively successful offering, the syndicate manager will point out that he got no more than the (bargain) price to the public for each security sold, and the issuer knows only too well that all *he* got was the (still lower) price to the company.

Conversely, suppose that the market declines sharply during the syndicate period to, say, price X. At that point, the put option value is clearly out of the money since, ultimately, the syndicate will break up at a price *below* that paid to the issuer. To be sure, not all securities may have been sold at price X; on the other hand, to the extent that syndicate expenses chew up a share of the gross spread, the syndicate loss (per security) may be greater than what has to be a minimum syndicate-loss measure.

As can be seen from the preceding, such market-loss accidents can occur even if, *ex ante* syndicate trading, the issue was underpriced. In fact, what the preceding may illustrate equally well is that if the issue was priced "at the market," a rise in market prices during the syndicate period will produce the same out-the-window flotation result as an underpriced issue. To be sure, if asked about that resemblance to underpricing results, the syndicate manager can point to the rise in prices *during* the flotation period and to the equality of the market price and the offer price at close of day preceding the flotation. This type of analysis works only for large cash stock offers. For IPOs, secondary trading information prior to flotation is at best partial and unrepresentative, and for the major share of new flotations, namely bond issues, secondary trad-

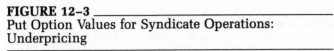

**FIGURE 12–3**
Put Option Values for Syndicate Operations:
Underpricing

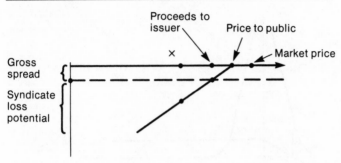

ing data are too fragmentary to be helpful. And getting back to
the cash stock offers, to the extent that these (for public utilities or under 415) are priced by competitive underwritings,
the underpricing issue will not be a relevant one.

## CALCULATION OF PUT PREMIUM

Let's now consider the issuer's position in two interest-rate (or
capital-market) environments:

1. Low price variance.
2. Volatile price variance.

### Low Price Variance

Figure 12–4A examines case 1. The frequency distribution of
security prices in the time period around the new flotation has
a small variance; this is, when the flotation is announced and
if the mean value is set at the price paid by the public, it
appears there is but a small chance (perhaps 1:5) that the last
security will be sold out of the syndicate at a price below that
paid to the company. Under those circumstances, the issuing
firm does not have too much of a problem waiting out a period
of, say, 21 days during which the SEC examines the prospectus, indenture, and so forth before declaring the issue effective
for trading. If, in addition, low volatility prices are associated
with low interest rates, as they usually are, the two variables

**FIGURE 12–4**
Payoff to Syndicate as an Option Premium

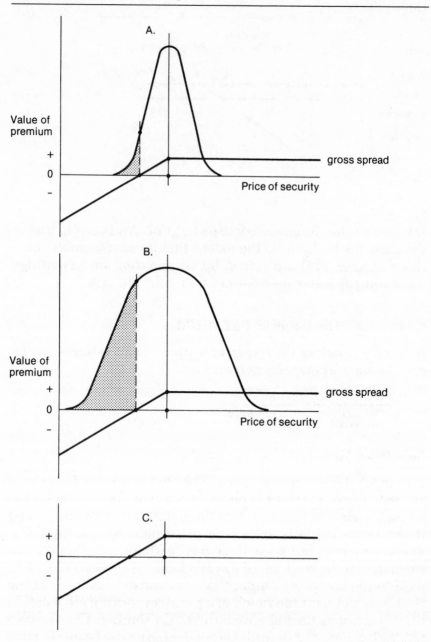

that typically raise the cost of an option premium will be at low levels. This implies that the cost-of-waiting risk is low when variance is low.

**High Price Variance**

Figure 12–4B illustrates a flotation in a high-variance price (rate) environment. It assumes that gross spreads are the same and that the new-issue price paid by the public is the same, but now the probability that the market price during syndicate operations may fall below the price paid to the company is nearly 1:1. Moreover, the cost of the option (or gross spread), which has been held constant, necessarily has to finance a higher rate (carrying) cost if any securities remain unsold after new-issue closing. Does this mean that the insurance feature has now fallen in cost? Not necessarily, for the higher price volatility is generally a feature of a high interest rate environment which, by itself, tends to discourage new long-term flotations. In other words, the cost side of the gross spread may be squeezed somewhat by greater competition among underwriters for the lesser volume of new merchandise. But beyond this market effect is the *policy* effect of SEC changes that led to a shortening of waiting period.[3] The first of these changes was the shift to S-16 "instant bond issue" flotations; the second, the shelf registration (Rule 415) mechanics. Under both changes, the effectiveness period between the corporation's decision to go and sale of new issue was cut back to about 2 days from the prior 21 days, and this cut in option duration *of time to maturity* was equivalent to a reduction in flotation risk. In more direct language, the probability in a volatile environment of prices falling substantially is far less for a two-day period than it is for a three-week period.

Figure 12–4C only traces through the put option cost, indicating that the greater the variance, everything else the same, the higher the cost of the option premium. Recall, finally, that the Black/Scholes option valuation formula shows a rise in value with (a) the product of time to maturity and the interest rate and (b) the product of variability of the security and time to maturity.

---

[3] For discussion of these policy changes, see Chapter 13.

Valuation calculations using the B/S model that evaluate the costs to the syndicate of a price drop under different levels of volatility and time lapse.[4] Consider the costs to the syndicate of a price drop under such differences of terms when the following assumptions hold:

Stock price = $50 per share.
Risk-free rate = 8 percent.
Price difference = $5 (equals gross spread).

When variance is only 20 percent, the value of a put premium (per share) is 0 for 1 day, 0 for 15 days, and only 3 cents for 30 days. (See Table 12–2.)

But suppose that volatility rises to 40 percent. At that time, the premium on a 1-day put is still worth 0, but now the 15-day put rises to 16 cents, and the 30-day put costs 47 cents. How much is the shortening of the waiting risk by SEC's Rule 415 worth? Since the average flotation gross spread is in the neighborhood of 10 percent per share, for a $50 stock that comes to about $5 per share. By contrast, in the *low volatility* phase, the cost of a put option (at current, relatively high interest-rate levels) came to 3 cents per share at 30 days; in the quiet days of low volatility, that put value should be close to zero.

Now consider the cost of a put premium for 30 days when volatility is high. It comes to 47 cents, or to about a one-tenth equivalent of the gross spread of $5. Of course, if the gross spread were less than 10 percent of the share price—say, 5 percent, or $2.50 for our $50 stock—the SEC-induced collapsing of the waiting period from 30 days to 1 day in a high-variance environment would have cut the cost to the issuer of the gross spread not by a tenth but by a fifth.

The preceding analysis indicates that the shift to shelf registration (Rule 415) has cut the waiting risk. Using the B/S model as a valuation tool in the context of setting the gross spread (for a stock) equal to a put option premium, we can

---

[4]The calculations in Table 12–2 are based on the model presented by G. Courtadon and J. Merrick in "The Option Pricing Model and the Valuation of Corporate Securities," *Midland Corporate Finance Journal*, Fall 1983, pp. 43–57.

**TABLE 12-2**

Calculation of Option Premiums for a New Flotation

| Standard Deviation | Price per Share | Premiums | | | |
|---|---|---|---|---|---|
| | | 1 day | 15 days | 30 days | |
| .20 | $45.00 | $5.01 | $5.15 | $5.32 | |
| .20 | 50.00 | .21 | .89 | 1.31 | |
| .20 | 55.00 | .00 | .01 | .08 | |
| .30 | 45.00 | 5.01 | 5.19 | 5.48 | |
| .30 | 50.00 | .32 | 1.29 | 1.88 | Calls |
| .30 | 55.00 | .00 | .09 | .35 | |
| .40 | 45.00 | 5.01 | 5.31 | 5.77 | |
| .40 | 50.00 | .42 | 1.70 | 2.45 | |
| .40 | 55.00 | .00 | .27 | .75 | |
| .20 | 45.00 | 0.00 | .00 | .03 | |
| .20 | 50.00 | .20 | .73 | .98 | |
| .20 | 55.00 | 4.99 | 4.83 | 4.72 | |
| .30 | 45.00 | .00 | .04 | .18 | |
| .30 | 50.00 | .31 | 1.13 | 1.55 | Puts |
| .30 | 55.00 | 4.99 | 4.91 | 4.99 | |
| .40 | 45.00 | .00 | .16 | .47 | |
| .40 | 50.00 | .41 | 1.53 | 2.12 | |
| .40 | 55.00 | 4.99 | 5.09 | 5.39 | |

Assumptions:  Stock price = $50
Interest rate = 8 percent

SOURCE: G. Courtadon & J. Merrick, "The Option Pricing Model and the Valuation of Corporate Securities," *Midland Corporate Finance Journal*, Fall 1983, pp. 43–57.

show that the SEC's shift to shelf registration has reduced the cost of the waiting risk (in a high-variance market) as follows:

1. If the gross spread is set at 10 percent of the new-issue price, the waiting risk in a high-volatility market falls by a tenth.
2. If the gross spread is smaller, the relative value of the waiting-risk reduction will be further improved.
3. If the price variance is small, the waiting risk is small, and shelf registration would not substantially reduce the waiting risk.

The foregoing analysis may, in fact, suggest a different rationale for the narrowing of new-issue spreads under Rule

415 than the one to which many analysts have alluded. The conventional wisdom has it that 415-type issuers can now get the equivalent of a competitive bid because issuers can request quick responses from one or more investment bankers when they take the issue off the shelf.

The option analog used here, which holds true for calls as well as puts, tends to place buyers of new issues (that is, institutional investors) in a risk-type bind similar to that of issuers when rate volatility is high because the cost of a call also rises sharply with the passage of time. Consequently, investment bankers will attempt to presell the largest possible share of an issue on short notice even while they are making a bid for a shelf issue, thereby reducing risks all around. And as risks are minimized, so is the cost of insurance. In that sense, then, Rule 415 is a rational public-policy response by the SEC to the rise in rate volatility. Finally, the behavior of market participants to speed up the new-issue process reduces the cost of the process because the cost of the risk offset is reduced. This argument is not inconsistent with the competitive bidding argument but may, instead, represent a larger share of reduction of flotation cost. In turn, this suggests that the conclusion that 415-type new issues constitute the "ultimate competitive bid" (see Bhagat reference in an earlier chapter) may be an overstatement because, behind the scenes, a 415 flotation is also the ultimate "instant offer" to investors.

**Moving from High Variance to Low Variance**

Suppose the environment for flotation of new issues is conditioned to competition in a period of high price variance. Suppose further that the markets perceive a reduction in risk—that the variance of price fluctuation (that is, price volatility) begins to recede. In this environment, the flotation risks are reduced, and competition among investment bankers will squeeze gross spreads closer to the now lower cost of the insurance premium. Further, an understanding of the lessened variance-related risks to underwriters would enable issuers to bargain more effectively for a narrower gross spread even if they continue to use shelf-registration mechanics for

**FIGURE 12–5**

**FIGURE 12–5**
Price Volatility in the Debt and Equity Markets (annualized percentage change, trend adjusted, based on closing prices of previous 60 days)

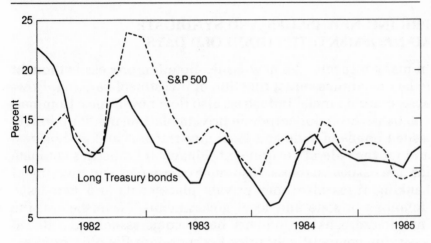

new stocks. The fact that underwriters are aware of the lessened variance of all markets (in mid-1985) is shown by Figure 12–5, prepared by Salomon Brothers.

Returning to Figure 12–4, the market change to lower volatility in 1985 has shifted the risk-analysis replication from the middle panel back to the upper panel. Chapter 14 discusses how that change in risk perception, along with shelf registration, has changed the syndicate game. Suffice it to say at this point that the sharp reduction in risk perception among underwriters can help explain the sharp reduction in the number of underwriters participating in each syndicate to the ultimate minimum, namely, the bought deal where the lead underwriter is the sole underwriter and the syndicate consists of one investment banking firm. If risk is less, syndicate diversification can be less, and in that fashion, even a thin spread of about one fourth of 1 percent for the issue can be made to work for the single underwriter.

This contraction of syndicate size is the counterpart to the collapse of the time delay from the leisurely two- to three-week time span needed to organize the large syndicates of the

1960s.[5] The following discussion of a typical large new syndicate flotation of the 1960s shows that the problems and concerns of flotation managers remain the same.

## PRICING NEW ISSUES AND SYNDICATE MANAGEMENT: THE GOOD OLD DAYS

In many respects, the new-issues flotation process is thought to be the quintessential function of investment banking. However, other financial industries also float new issues. Commercial banks do so for corporate private placements, for publicly issued bonds of state and local governments and authorities, and for the federal government. Financial industries compete for new-issues business. Insurance companies and investment banking firms also offer private placements and new-issue flotations of state and local governments. Nevertheless, the investment banking industry has become associated with, at least, the competitively priced corporation flotation process.

### Bidding Mechanics in the 1960s: A Case Study

The following section describes the competitive bidding process for a new AT&T bond issue.[6] Because that issue was very large for the time ($100 million), the pricing decision was made by members of a large underwriting group acting as a syndicate. Each member had been tentatively assigned a share of the new issue. The pricing decision, to be successful, had to better that of a strong rival syndicate.

### Preparation for a Large Issue

When a corporation planned a large financing in the 1960s, it announced its intention some time before scheduling the issue to warn other issuers to stay out of the way and to prepare the

---

[5] Among the other changes brought about by shelf registration is the virtual elimination of regional investment bankers in routine syndicate operations.

[6] The following is taken from E. Bloch, "Pricing a Corporate Bond Issue: A Look behind the Scenes," *Federal Reserve Bank of New York Monthly Review,* October 1961.

capital market. In line with this practice, AT&T announced its intention to borrow $100 million several months before the date of actual issue. The early announcement gave potential investors, such as insurance companies, pension funds, and bank trust accounts, the opportunity to adjust their financial commitments to make room, if they wished, for sizable chunks of the issue. At the same time, other potential corporate borrowers were made aware that the AT&T underwriting would bring special pressures on the market, making it unwise to schedule other sizable flotations around that period.

A light calendar of flotations, then, made possible a more eager participation in the underwriting by syndicate members because their overall market commitments during the flotation period would have been less. And the better the demand for bonds among syndicate members, the stronger their bid would be and the lower the borrowing cost to the borrowing firm. In the underwriting of the AT&T issue, two competing syndicates were formed. One of the groups, managed by X Investment Bank, consisted of more than 100 investment firms, and the competing syndicate, led by Y Investment Bank, was about as sizable.

Managing such large syndicates was the business of about a half-dozen large investment banking houses. Only the largest among them had the capital, the manpower, and the market contacts necessary to propose the proper price for a large offering. If a given house, acting as syndicate manager, wins what the market considers a fair share of the bidding competitions in which it participates, it gains in a number of ways. Not only is its prestige enhanced—which helps in managing future syndicates—but the house that continuously proves the high quality of its market judgment may be more successful in attracting negotiated financings. This concern for the future tends to intensify present competition among managing underwriters.

But while the half-dozen syndicate leaders were rivals, they were also potential allies because a grouping of underwriters exists only for a given flotation and the next offering on the market will involve a different group. During the preparation for the AT&T issue, two of the major firms in the rival syndicate led by Y Investment Bank knew they would be associated with X Investment Bank in a large secondary stock

offering within two weeks. Because of the shifting associations and combinations of firms from syndicate to syndicate,
current associates in an underwriting insist on conserving
their independence of action, and this has an important
bearing on the pricing process, as we shall see below.

The first informal price meeting on the forthcoming issue
took place at X Investment Bank two days before the actual
bidding date set for the issue. Fifteen senior officers of X
Investment Bank actively engaged in trading and underwriting met to discuss pricing recommendations that would win
the issue and at the same time find ready acceptance in the
market. The terms of the new issue were discussed in light of
current market factors, and each pricing suggestion was, in
effect, an answer to a double-barreled question. First, how
attractive was the issue in terms of quality, maturity, call
provisions, and other features, and, second, how receptive
was the market at this time? Among the factors discussed as
leading to a lower yield was the new bonds' Aaa rating, while
factors leading to a higher yield included the lack of call
protection and the large size of the issue.

The preliminary discussion of the offering price then
shifted to the "feel of the market." Even the proponents of a
relatively high yield recognized that the final bid should be
closer to current market yields on similar securities, owing to
the relatively light calendar of forthcoming new corporate
flotations. Another sign pointing to aggressive bidding was a
relatively light dealer inventory of corporate securities. The
discussion of competitive demands for funds was not confined
to the corporate-securities market, however, but extended to
the markets for municipal and Treasury issues. Here the picture was mixed. The light calendar of forthcoming municipal
issues was cited by proponents of a lower yield, while those in
favor of a higher yield pointed to expectations of a relatively
heavy volume of Treasury financing. Finally, the discussion
moved on to assess the possibility of changes in significant
market rates such as the prime loan rate and Federal Reserve
bank discount rates during the flotation period. It was agreed
that the likelihood of such changes during the financing period was small. Each of the officers of X Investment Bank then
independently set down his opinion of the proper pricing of
the issue (the combination of coupon rate and price offered the

borrower) and the reoffering "spread" (the difference between the bid price and the reoffering price to the public).

The majority of the 15 members of the group agreed that the new bonds should carry a rate of 4¼ percent to the borrower with the bonds priced at par and with a reoffering spread of about $7 per $1,000 bond.[7] One member of the group thought that a lower yield might be needed to win the bid, and two or three others indicated yields higher than 4¼ percent. The aggressiveness of X Investment Bank's price ideas can be judged from the fact that newspaper comment on the likely level for the winning bid on the day of this meeting indicated a yield in the neighborhood of 4.30 percent.

## Marketing Strategy

Simultaneously, assessments of the market for the purpose of establishing a proper bid for the issue were under way in the offices of the allied syndicate members. The comparison of various opinions of the "best" bid of the syndicate members took place a day later, the day before the actual opening of the bids by the borrower. This was the preliminary price meeting, to which each firm in the syndicate was invited. At the meeting, each participant firm named the price it was willing to pay for the number of bonds tentatively assigned in the underwriting.[8] The poll of the 100-odd allied syndicate members revealed far less agressiveness (that is, willingness to accept a low yield) by the smaller firms than was shown by the syndicate manager. Relatively few ideas were at 4¼ percent, while one of the "major underwriters" (that is, a firm tentatively assigned $3 million of bonds or more) put his offering yield at 4.35 percent, and a small firm went as high as 4.40 percent.

In this particular underwriting, X Investment Bank seemed quite eager to win the bid, partly because of its optimistic appraisals of the state of the bond market and partly because it is the syndicate manager's responsibility to push for a winning

---

[7]These rate numbers may look small, but the spread is not that different from more recent experience.

[8]In this meeting, as in the final price meeting, a number of security measures were taken to prevent a leak of information to the competing syndicate.

bid and to exercise the proper persuasion to carry his syndicate along. Syndicate managers are particularly concerned with prestige because, rightly or wrongly, the market apparently does not attach nearly so much significance to membership as to leadership in a losing syndicate.

This factor explains the paradox that the followers, rather than the manager, may be more responsible for the failure to win a bid for lack of aggressiveness, even though the market tends to place the blame on the manager. But smaller syndicate members may be reluctant participants at lower yields because their commitment of funds for even a relatively small portion of a large underwriting may represent a larger call (or contingent liability) against the small firm's capital than it does for a bigger firm. Even though the larger firm's capital may be as fully employed as that of the smaller firm in its total underwriting business, the commitment of a large portion of capital for a single underwriting may make the smaller firm more hesitant to take that particular marketing risk.

In preparing for the final price meeting, the syndicate manager held the first of a number of behind-the-scenes strategy sessions. At these meetings, some basic decisions were made about ways and means of holding the syndicate together. During the final price meeting, any firm believing that the market risk of the proposed group bid was too great (that the yield was too low to sell well) had the right to drop out of the syndicate. Conversely, syndicate members who liked the group bid could raise the extent of their participation. Of course, if many syndicate members drop out, particularly major underwriters, too much of a burden is placed on the remaining members, and the result is, in effect, to veto the proposed bid. The aggressive manager thus is placed squarely in the middle of a tug-of-war. If his bid is too aggressive and carries a relatively low yield, the syndicate may refuse to take down the bonds; if the bid is too cautious and carries too high a yield, the syndicate may lose the bidding competition to the rival group. This conflict was resolved at the final price meeting.

## Syndicate Tactics

On the morning of the day on which the final bids were made to the borrower, officers of the syndicate manager held their final conference to decide on their own share of the underwriting. In effect, a manager who believes in an aggressive bid puts up or shuts up by his willingness to absorb a greater or a lesser share of the total underwriting as firms drop out of the syndicate at lower yields. A manager's strong offer to take more bonds may induce a number of potential dropouts to stay at a lower yield, partly because their share of the flotation won't be raised by a given number of dropouts since the manager is picking up the pieces. But beyond the arithmetic effect, a strong offer may have a psychological impact, and some reluctant participants may decide that the manager knows more than they do and that his willingness to raise his share at a given yield is his way of backing the strength of his judgment.

This psychological downward push on yields may be small, but sometimes even a tiny difference can mean the difference between success and failure. For example, in late 1959, the winning syndicate for a $30 million competitive utility issue bid 1/100 of a cent more per $1,000 bond than the losing syndicate—$3 more for the whole $30 million issue![9]

Another important factor in holding the syndicate together is the strength of the "book" for the new issue. The book is a compilation of investor interest in the new bonds. This interest may have been solicited or unsolicited and may have gone directly to X Investment Bank or to other members of the syndicate from institutional investors. Thus the book is a sample of market strength. All the interest in the book is tentative since no lender would commit funds for an issue of unknown yield. Nevertheless, it is impossible to exaggerate the importance of a large book to an aggressive syndicate manager in holding his group together at the lowest possible yield. Because reluctant participants in an underwriting are particularly concerned about the selling risk, the larger the book, the more reassured they will feel at any given rate. Put another way, the better the book, the more bonds a firm will take at a given rate, thus absorbing more dropouts. Indeed, the size of the book was considered so important that the final price meeting on the AT&T underwriting was interrupted a

---

[9]At times, tie bids are received. On September 12, 1961, two underwriters bid identical amounts, down to the last 1/100 of a penny per $1,000 bond, for a $3 million issue of municipal bonds. Such tie bids are as rare as a golfer's hole in one, however.

number of times by the latest indications of interest in the
issue.

### The Final Price Meeting

As a means of preventing information leaks, representatives of
the firms attending the final price meeting were locked in a
room. The meeting was opened by a vice president of X
Investment Bank with a brief review of the good state of the
book—about half the issue had tentatively been spoken for. He
had derived further encouragement for an aggressive bid from
the healthy state of the bond market. Thus he proposed to
make his bid at the 4¼ percent rate agreed on at the X
Investment Bank preliminary meeting two days earlier.

The immediate reaction to this statement was a chorus of
moans. Apparently, the book was not sufficiently broad to
carry the doubters along with the first bid, nor did the manager indicate any other action that would have made his
proposal more acceptable. When the group was polled, large
and small dropouts cut the $100 million underwriting by
about a third. The failure to carry the syndicate at the first go-
round was later attributed by some X Investment Bank people
to the fact that three dropouts occurred among the first set of
major underwriters polled (the eight largest firms, each of
which had been tentatively assigned $3 million of bonds).
And in the second set ($2 million assigned to each firm),
another few had fallen by the wayside.

Thus a new bid proposal had to be presented to the group.
Following another behind-the-scenes consultation of the senior officers of the managing underwriter, a 4⅜ percent coupon
with a price above par was proposed with a bid yield of 4.27
percent. Amid continued grumbling of the majority of the
members of the meeting, this was readily accepted by nearly
every firm.

Judging that they might have leaned over too far in the
direction of their reluctant followers, the officers of the syndicate manager consulted once again and decided to present a
somewhat more aggressive bid to the syndicate. In the third
proposal, the bid price on the 4⅜ coupon was upped by 20
cents per $1,000 bond. The underwriters, still grumbling,

were polled again and, following a few minor dropouts, approved the new price. The final allocation of the bonds differed relatively little from the tentative original allocation except that the manager picked up the allotments of the dropouts by adding about $3 million to his own commitment. By this time only a few minutes were left until the formal opening of the competitive bids by AT&T. The final coupon and price decisions were telephoned to the syndicate's representative at the bidding, who formally submitted the bid to AT&T.

Promptly at 11:30 A.M. the doors of the price committee meeting were thrown open, and within 30 seconds of that time, the news was shouted from the trading room that the X Investment Bank bid had lost. The difference in the bid prices between the two syndicates came to a little more than $1 per $1,000 bond.

The bonds were released for trading by the Securities and Exchange Commission at around 4 P.M. and were quickly snapped up by market investors. At X Investment Bank the feeling of gloom hung heavy, particularly since the first bid offered to the price meeting would have won the issue.

Would a better X Investment Bank book have carried the defecting major underwriters along on the first bid? Should the manager have been willing to take more bonds to carry the group along in the first recommendation which would have won the issue? And would market acceptance of that bid have been as good as that accorded the actual winning bid of Y syndicate? These post mortems were bound to be inconclusive, and the unremitting pressures of the underwriting business soon cut them short. Within the next several days, a number of other securities were scheduled to come to market. Tomorrow was another day and another price meeting.

To syndicate participants in the 1980s, the foregoing will appear almost quaint in the leisurely pacing of the pricing process and its modest rate levels. Today, the availability of shelf-registration issues to corporations forces lead underwriters to come up with a bid for a new issue in as many hours as it used to take days a generation earlier. However, the earlier experience provides a slow-motion replay of the motivation of syndicate managers and the love-hate relationship between them and other syndicate participants.

# PART III

# Public-Policy Issues in New-Issue Flotation

This part of the book examines the policy issues that arise in the process of floating new securities. It reenters the deregulation debate from a different perspective because it examines the supervisory responsibilities with which investment bankers are charged, as well as the role played by the SEC, in new-issue placement. More specifically, it discusses the policy change called Rule 415 that was instituted on a temporary basis by the SEC in 1982 and was made permanent in 1984.

First, a few parameters regarding the sources of funds for corporate finance and the volume of new-money issues floated deserve some attention. Let's examine the total sources (which equal the uses) of funds of nonfinancial corporations as described by the Federal Reserve's flow-of-funds data. Table III–1 looks at a period covering seven recent years to get some notion of the relative importance of internal sources—namely cash flow—and external sources. The latter consists of new-money equity and corporate debt—both long-term and short-term. Table III–1 shows that new debt far exceeds the importance of new equity even when corporate repurchase of equity does not make the volume of new-equity issues a negative number. Recall that this sector only covers *nonfinancial* firms.

In the SEC's data for new-money issues for *all* corporations in Table III–2 (including some financial firms), new-debt is-

**TABLE III-1**

Sources of Funds of U.S. Nonfinancial Corporations, 1976-1982*
(dollars in billions)

|  | 1976 | 1977 | 1978 | 1979 | 1980 | 1981 | 1982 |
|---|---|---|---|---|---|---|---|
| Retained earnings | $ 44 | $ 49 | $ 52 | $ 28 | $ 25 | $ 39 | $ 31 |
| Depreciation | 91 | 103 | 117 | 134 | 153 | 177 | 203 |
| Cash flow | 135 | 152 | 169 | 172 | 178 | 216 | 234 |
| New stock issues | 4 | 4 | - 2 | - 4 | 17 | 6 | 13 |
| New debt† | 44 | 72 | 99 | 97 | 88 | 96 | 79 |
| Outside funds | 48 | 76 | 97 | 93 | 105 | 102 | 92 |
| Total sources | $183 | $228 | $266 | $265 | $283 | $318 | $326 |

*Totals may not add due to rounding.
†Short-term and long-term.
SOURCE: Federal Reserve Flow of Funds tables and Salomon Brothers.

sues still exceed new-equity issues but not by the same margin. These different results were produced by differences in industry coverage as well as the maturity of the debt issues: The Fed's data cover short-term as well as long-term debt.

Returning to overall corporate sources of funds (Table III-1), it is clear that: (a) internal finance by far exceeds outside financing by both bonds and equity and (b) bond finance by far exceeds equity financing even prior to the surge in new bond issues during the mid-1980s. This relationship gives relevance to criticism of the SEC's argument in favor of 415. In fact the SEC followed an appropriate policy but its reasoning was flawed.

As Figure III-1 shows corporate bond issues, both financial and nonfinancial, totaled $48.2 billion before deducting some $16.5 billion of retirements or calls. (The word *straight* used in the title of Figure III-1 only refers to the nonmerger or takeover purposes of the funds raised by the debt securities added up in the bars of the chart.) That $48 billion is an all-time record, exceeding the prior record of $34.6 billion set in 1980. Moreover, the new record is attributable to the surge in *financial*-sector issues because, as Figure III-1 shows, the issuance of nonfinancial-sector bonds has remained much more stable over the six years shown in the chart. Accordingly, some of the new-issue discussions below will also refer to financial-sector securities.

**TABLE III-2**

New Business Securities Offered for Cash, All Industries, 1976–1982
(dollars in billions)

|                | 1976 | 1977 | 1978 | 1979 | 1980 | 1981 | 1982 |
|----------------|------|------|------|------|------|------|------|
| Bonds and notes | $26 | $24 | $20 | $26 | $45 | $39 | $44 |
| Preferred      | 2    | 2    | 2    | 2    | 3    | 2    | 5    |
| Equity         | 8    | 8    | 8    | 9    | 19   | 25   | 23   |
| Totals         | $37  | $34  | $30  | $37  | $67  | $66  | $72  |

SOURCE: SEC *Monthly Statistical Review.*

**FIGURE III-1**

Gross Straight Corporate Bond Issuance—
Financial versus Nonfinancial Corporations
(dollars in billions)

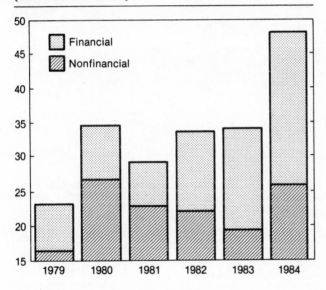

# 13

## Full Disclosure
## and Securities Regulation:
## The Change to Shelf Registration

One of the many ironies that turn up in studies of regulatory policy is that any regulatory shift is likely to have two effects: (1) the one intended by the change and (2) the one not foreseen by the regulators. Of the two, the second is frequently the most significant.

The Securities Act of 1933[1] and the Securities Exchange Act of 1934[2] provide separate, although related, regulatory disclosure systems. The first act (to be called Securities Act) requires the registration of new issues and disclosure of relevant information regarding the issuer corporation and prohibits misrepresentation and fraud related to the new security. The second act (to be called Exchange Act) extended the same disclosure principles to secondary-market trading and required the registration of national exchanges as well as of brokers and dealers for the purpose of self-regulation. Since 1934 both acts have been administered by the Securities and

---

[1] 15 U.S.C. 577a et. seq.
[2] 15 U.S.C. 578a et. seq.

Exchange Commission (SEC), a quasi-judicial agency of the U.S. government.[3]

Federal securities legislation of all types relies heavily on the principles of (1) *full disclosure* and (2) *self-regulation*. The first of these is reflected in the publication of data for the use of investors. Each firm whose securities are traded publicly is expected to publish its balance sheet and operating data within a specified time after completion of its fiscal period. Further, if a new-money issue is to be sold, these data (specific to the company) as well as other data specific to the new issue must be presented to potential buyers. As a result, virtually all firms with securities listed on exchanges publish audited annual reports and 10-K statements on a routine basis as well as new-issue prospectuses when a new issue is to be sold. In support of the self-regulatory principle, the SEC has delegated to the various exchanges its power to control trading practices for securities listed on those exchanges while retaining the final authority to supplement, alter, or reject an exchange's rules and regulations.

The SEC has delegated similar powers to the National Association of Securities Dealers (NASD), a private trade association of over-the-counter dealers and traders.[4] The SEC manages policy changes (like most other bureaucracies) by suasion and discussion rather than fiat; when these methods prove ineffective, the SEC acquires quasi-judicial powers to discipline violators. And in the end, not only is the SEC a creature of the Congress, but major changes can be made by legislation, such as the advent of negotiated commissions for trades on the NYSE.[5]

## FULL DISCLOSURE

The disclosure process refers to new issues as well as to trading in secondary markets. It is a fact of financial life that

---

[3] Initially, securities regulation was a state function that began in 1911 with the passage of the first "Blue Sky laws." Resulting variances were brought into some degree of order by the proposal (as late as 1956) of the Uniform Securities Acts.

[4] Similar statutes have been enacted by Congress to permit self-regulation of futures and option markets.

[5] That change was mandated by the Security Act Amendments of 1975.

the largest issuers of new-money securities are also those firms whose securities trade in large volume on secondary markets. Full disclosure under the Exchange Act, which provides investors in existing securities with up-to-date and audited information on these stocks and bonds, suggests that there is little need to repeat the same information when the same issuers place *new* securities on the market. Any review of prospectuses[6] up to 1981 shows that such documents largely duplicate accounting information already disclosed in annual reports and 10-Ks. The combination of the two disclosure systems or, in practical terms, the incorporation by reference—rather than reprinting—of annual reports and 10-K data into a prospectus was seen as an efficiency move as far back as 1966, when Milton Cohen suggested integrating the two reporting systems.[7]

Subsequent to Cohen's seminal article, the SEC established two sets of study groups whose recommendations produced a sequence of modest policy changes to simplify new-issue registration documents. In 1967, the SEC took its first small step toward integrating the two systems adopting Form S-7, a somewhat shorter registration form than the S-1 form it replaced. The S-7 form relied on the availability of some information contained in Exchange Act filings, but it did not permit any reporting by reference.[8] In 1970, the SEC adopted Form S-16 (following the issuance of the Wheat Report) that permitted issuers who qualified for Form S-7 to register certain *secondary* distributions by *incorporation by reference* of information contained in Exchange Act reports.[9]

This apparent breakthrough in combining the two reporting systems is not as profound a change as implied by the issuance of a special SEC ruling. For secondary trades, the

---

[6] Required by the Securities Act of 1933.

[7] Milton Cohen, "'Truth in Securities' Revisited," *Harvard Law Review* 79 (1966), p. 1340. The SEC commissioned two reports to examine the disclosure systems. (1) *Disclosure to Investors: A Reappraisal of Administrative Policies under the 1933 and 1934 Acts*, 1969 (called the Wheat Report); and (2) *Report of the Advisory Committee on Corporate Disclosure to the Securities and Exchange Commission*, 95th Congress, 1st session, 451 (Comm. Print 1977).

[8] SEC Release No. 4886, November 1967.

[9] SEC Release No. 5117, December 1970.

citation *by reference* is just repetition of information previously published under the Exchange Act. And as Table 13–1 indicates, the number and volume of formal secondary distributions had declined quite sharply by the end of the 1970s to about one fifth of that in the early 1970s. By contrast, block trades became the method of choice for distributing large (secondary) trades in the 1970s. For example, in 1981 block trades at about 3.8 billion shares constituted nearly one third of all of the trading volume done on the NYSE, while in 1981 secondaries (at a mere 14 million shares) barely exceeded 1/10 of 1 percent.

## SHORT-FORM REGISTRATIONS

Following the recommendations of the Advisory Committee on Corporate Disclosure,[10] the SEC in 1978 produced a more significant change by making Form S-16 available to the same qualified issuers for *primary* (or new-money) offerings in firm-commitment underwritings.[11] The mere availability of the short-form registration statement was only a beginning, however. What made that form most useful to issuers was, paradoxically enough, the sharp rise in interest rates as well as the even greater rise in rate volatility that occurred shortly thereafter. As the charts in Figure 13–1 indicate, the most sensitive short-term rates (Federal funds rates as published by the Federal Reserve Bank of Chicago)[12] not only reached all-time highs in the 1980s but also showed a substantial rise in variability per unit of time.

These increases in rate fluctuations were replicated in bond issues, thereby producing much greater bond-price changes per unit of time than previously experienced. In part, the rise in short-term rates in early 1980 reflected a shift in corporate borrowing (or demand for funds) toward short maturities to avoid locking in record interest rates on bonds. And

---

[10] *Report of the Advisory Committee on Corporate Disclosure to the Securities and Exchange Commission*, 95th Congress, 1st session, 451 (Comm. Print 1977).

[11] SEC Release No. 5923, April 1978.

[12] Federal Reserve Bank of Chicago, *Economic Perspectives*, January–February 1983, p. 11.

**TABLE 13-1**

Large-Scale Trades on the NYSE by Secondaries and Blocks, 1972, 1981, and 1982 (in number of transactions and by thousands of shares traded)

| | NYSE Secondaries and Other Special Methods | | | NYSE Block Trades | | | Percent of Block Trades in Total NYSE Trading Volume |
|---|---|---|---|---|---|---|---|
| Year | Number of Trades | Number of Shares Traded | Average Size of Trans-action | Number of Trades | Volume of Shares | Average Size of Trans-action | |
| 1972 | 154 | 64,067 | 423 | 31,207 | 766,406 | 25 | 18.5% |
| 1981 | 34 | 14,351 | 422 | 145,564 | 3,771,442 | 26 | 31.8 |
| 1982 | 71 | 39,047 | 550 | 254,707 | 6,742,481 | 26 | 41.0 |

SOURCE: New York Stock Exchange, *NYSE Fact Book 1983* (New York: 1983), pp. 11, 14.

when, in the aftermath of the 1980 recession, a large volume of that short debt was refinanced at lower long-term rates, the S-16 registration form—called instant bond issues—gave corporations the equivalent of a costless two-day put as compared to the earlier three- to four-week delay (in the put) for the SEC to permit a new bond issue to become effective.

## PERSPECTIVES ON THE PROSPECTUS UNDER RULE 415

In the context of the recent policy changes for broker-dealer firms, it is interesting to compare the regulation of depository-type institutions. Banking supervisors (the Controller of the Currency, FDIC, and the Federal Reserve) send examiners into each bank institution about once each year to perform *confidential* reviews of past performance and current lending practices. By contrast, the securities industry, its member firms, and its products (whether new-money issues or secondary offerings) are subject to public disclosure, including data specific to the issuers (corporations, states, public authorities, and so forth). New-money securities issued under Rule 415 may now satisfy the public-disclosure provisions of the Securities Act by including Exchange Act information by reference only.

However, some additional changes were associated with the shelf-registration process, such as a sharp reduction in the

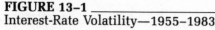

**FIGURE 13–1** _____
Interest-Rate Volatility—1955–1983

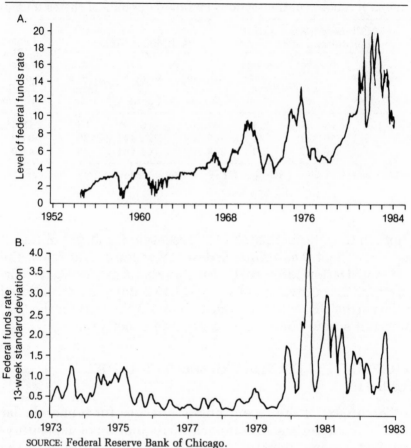

SOURCE: Federal Reserve Bank of Chicago.

time delay before a new issue might be sold. In a narrow sense, there is an analogy between the SEC's internal staff review of information presented in a new-issue prospectus before the issue becomes effective (or is permitted to be sold) and the bank examination process. One critic of that process observed that SEC staff efforts involved, in their reviews of full disclosure, " . . . filtering out everything but objective facts, as if the investor could not focus a suitable skepticism on estimates of value or projections of future earnings."[13] Kripke goes further

_____
[13] H. Kripke, _The SEC and Corporate Disclosure_ (New York: Harcourt, Brace Jovanovich, 1979), p. 14.

in suggesting that the prospectus, which was to have been the "primary document intended by the statute to inform the investor...has been a negativistic, pessimistic document, lacking in forward looking information which can affect securities prices and sales."[14] In short, Kripke believes that the potential investor does not refrain from reading a prospectus because of its boilerplate language and legalese (as is frequently argued by others) but because the thorough drycleaning efforts of the SEC staff have robbed the document of any information that cannot be absolutely sustained by 20/20 hindsight—or found in previously published documentation.

So why all the fuss over shelf registrations and the shortened time for an offering to become effective?

## UNDERWRITER LIABILITY AND DUE DILIGENCE

The best answer is that the full-disclosure provisions of the Securities Act attach parallel liability to the experts (e.g., lawyers, accountants, issuers, and investment bankers). Section 11 of the Securities Act imposes absolute liability on the issuer (for example, the corporation) for securities registered under the act for "material misstatements in and omissions from registration statements"[15] and, going beyond this, it imposes a liability on new-issue underwriters (as well as some others) based on a negligence standard with respect to disclosure of "material information."[16]

Thus both the corporate issuer and the investment banker are liable for selling securities on the basis of erroneous or omitted information. The rationale for this provision of the act is twofold:

**1.** To set up an adversarial relationship between the issuer and the investment banker to provide the investing public with the best possible information set.[17] "The act seeks not

---

[14]Ibid., p. 15. Kripke argues further, "...the [SEC] staff is fearful that the investor will misconceive the probabilities of expectations, and therefore most registration statements contain repeated warnings that 'there can be no assurance' that an expectation will be borne out."

[15]Section 11(a).

[16]*Ernst and Ernst* v. *Hochfelder*, 425 U.S. 185, 208 (1976).

[17]As cited in *Escott* v. *Leasco Data Processing Equipment Corp.*, 332 F. Supp. 544, 567 (1971). Citation is from Shulman, "Civil Liability and the Securities Act," *Yale Law Journal* 43 (1933), p. 227.

only to secure accuracy in the information that is volunteered to investors but also, and perhaps more especially, to compel the disclosure of significant matters which were heretofore rarely, if ever disclosed."

**2.** To enforce (1) by making lack of "due diligence" costly to the underwriter. From the investment banker's point of view, he would be relieved of liability under the statute if he could demonstrate that he had fought the good fight: that "he had, after reasonable investigation, reasonable ground to believe, and did believe, at the time such part of the registration statement became effective, that the statements therein were true and that there was no omission to state a material fact required to be stated or necessary to make the statements therein not misleading."[18]

If the investment banker can demonstrate that he followed due diligence in investigating the issuer-client's representations (rather than accepting them at face value), he has a *procedural* defense against negligence suits by investors.

However, neither the SEC nor the courts have ever offered specific guidelines for investment bankers in conducting such investigations, and the court has indicated that the investment banker's investigation (and verification of the issuer's statements) are matters of judgment that vary with the circumstances of the issuer.[19] Perhaps such uncertainty, along with the fear of potential negligence suits, was designed to encourage investment bankers to press their issuers to a high, rather than a low, disclosure standard.[20]

Suppose that the time lag between a corporation's decision to sell a new issue and its offer for resale by an underwriter has been collapsed from five weeks to two days and that the new-issue prospectus is reduced to boilerplate summary language. For companies with an Aaa or Aa rating, such a cursory review of available data, given substantial and continuous company

---

[18] Sect 11(b)(3) of Securities Act.

[19] In *Escott* v. *Bar Chris Construction Corp.*, (332 F. Supp. at 582).

[20] Full-disclosure standards are not universally accepted as the means of regulating securities markets. For a generally negative view, see G. Benston, "Required Disclosure and the Stock Market: An Evaluation of the Securities Exchange Act of 1934," *American Economic Review* 63 (1973), no. 1, pp. 132–55.

research by outsiders, may be sufficient. And yet, as the following section suggests, investors use historical accounting data (from annual reports, 10-Ks, prospectuses, and so forth) only as a base from which to form expectations.

## CAPITAL-MARKET EFFICIENCY: HOW RELEVANT?

Capital-market efficiency in the finance literature is almost exclusively discussed in terms of equilibrium stock prices. Research papers suggest that the secondary stock market is quite efficient with respect to:

1. Information contained in stock prices prior to date examined by analyst.
2. Publicly available information regarding company.
3. All information.[21]

From this most writers have concluded that returns in excess of the risk-free rate can be earned only by an investor's acceptance of systematic (that is, market), or undiversifiable, risk.

Capital-market efficiency is thus comparable to a response to "stale news."[22] For a market to be considered efficient, the current price of, say, IBM stock takes account of last year's earnings and necessarily reflects that figure. Last year's IBM earnings per share is a number readily and cheaply available from IBM's annual report, 10-K, and other sources.

With respect to this year's earnings, the situation is quite different. Many securities analysts and institutional and private investors spend substantial time and effort researching and forecasting this year's (and further-out years') IBM earnings, knowing that the further away, the more erroneous their estimates are likely to be. The more at variance each an-

---

[21] This information hierarchy is contained in E. Fama, "Efficient Capital Markets: A Review of Theory and Empirical Work," *Journal of Finance*, May 1970, p. 383.

[22] For further discussion, see K. Garbade, *Securities Markets*, (New York: McGraw-Hill, 1982), esp. pp. 236ff. The earlier discussion of SEC staff reviews of prospectus language basically refers to improving accuracy in presenting the most recent of stale news, while "due diligence" by the investment banker could be said to refer, by the same standards, to accuracy of stale news immediately prior to a new-issue flotation (or in legalese, "material new information").

nouncement of actual earnings is from the (consensus) antici-
pations, the greater the market's response to the (then newly
stale) news.

In effect, the substantial amount of work done on stock-
market efficiency reflects both the ready availability of price
and trading volume data collected for long periods of time for
many NYSE-listed firms and the related research designs that
developed a number of statistically testable hypotheses. (Sum-
maries of the literature are available in a number of sources.[23])
The statistical inference techniques employed by scholars in
this field boil down to a rejection of the hypothesis that the
markets are *not* efficient. Because many papers examine different facets of market efficiency, it is convenient to discuss
the issue under three headings:

1. Weak form.
2. Semistrong form.
3. Strong form.

Briefly put, the weak form rejects the hypothesis that stock
selection can be enhanced by analyzing past stock-price behavior (technical analysis); the semistrong form rejects the
hypothesis that present prices do not reflect all publicly available information (that is, stale news) regarding each company.
The strong form considers the hypothesis that those with
insider information can, consistently and often, use it to produce superior investment results. Here the studies suggest
that insiders make gains prior to release of publicly available
information; at least, that insider trades are particularly well
timed in relation to market behavior. Thus the strong form of
the efficient-market hypothesis is generally rejected. To sum
up, the efficient-market hypothesis represents a series of tests
by which to reject the proposition that NYSE stock prices *do
not* efficiently reflect publicly available information.

It is important to recall this research literature in spite of its
more-cumbersome language (based on statistical inference)
because these probabilistic judgments should not be collapsed
into possibly misleading, albeit simpler, positive statements
(such as the markets *are* efficient). One cannot assert the truth

---

[23] See, for example, Garbade, *Securities Markets*, chap. 13; and Lorie
and Hamilton, *The Stock Market* (Homewood, Ill.: Richard D. Irwin,
1973), chap. 4.

(or error) of the weak or semistrong or strong form of the efficient-market hypothesis. One can only argue that the evidence supporting their validity is persuasive and that the investment community is in general, but not necessarily unanimous, agreement on this.

## BOND SHELF ANNOUNCEMENTS AND MARKET-EFFICIENCY HYPOTHESIS

The major volume of shelf-registration issues are bond issues not stock issues (see introduction to Part III). In part this follows from the nature of U.S. corporate finance where much more new equity value is created by retained earnings than by net new stock flotations. Even if there were no decline in the equity/debt ratio,[24] that particular by-product of U.S. dividend payout policy ensures a continuing preponderance of new-money debt financing over new stock flotations. Under these conditions, the efficient-markets hypothesis will apply not to the lion's share of new flotations, namely new debt financings, but to the much lesser (albeit important) volume of new-equity issues. M. Weinstein studied the price behavior of newly issued corporate bonds, following some problems with earlier studies that referred mainly to differences in coupon yield between new and seasoned issues or between new issues and bond-price indexes. Weinstein's study contrasts new-issue yields (which he found underpriced) and the adjustment of new-issue yields to market and yields to be completed within one month. He does not give his sources of data for market yields; they are probably NYSE bond prices, which are subject to all the problems suggested above. Moreover, the period covered (1962–74) is one of relatively greater rate stability than more recent experience.[25]

In addition, the question may be raised whether the efficient-markets hypothesis applies with the same force to new-issue stock pricing as it does to secondary-market trading. One major difference has to be relative supply. In the new-issue

---

[24] Since the ratio has been declining secularly, that change will further raise the ratio of new debt to new-equity flotations.

[25] See M. Weinstein, "The Seasoning Process of New Corporate Bond Issues," *Journal of Finance*, December 1978, p. 1334.

case, each new flotation raises the volume by some proportion to outstanding shares. That rate of increase may be decided by each firm's management on the basis of parameters that may or may not be the same as that of other firms or from one time in history to another. In secondary trading, on the other hand, market participants are involved in the same playing field at the same time (each sale is also a purchase). The perceived need to use an investment banker for virtually every new issue, while market mechanics including most large block trades are routine, suggests a distinction with a difference.

Taking this argument still another step, consider Commissioner Thomas's arguments in her dissent to the temporary 415 rule extension.[26] She specifically objected to the use of the shelf-registration process for new primary equity offerings.[27] Her objections were twofold: (1) The foreshortened offer period would reduce opportunities to build nationwide syndicates, thereby cutting out regional dealers and making the industry less effective. (2) Individual investors would not receive timely enough information to make decisions " . . . because in non-Rule 415 offerings, the underwriters are selected before a filing [and] the underwriters' due diligence can begin early in the process, and the resulting give-and-take among the parties and their counsel should produce a higher-quality disclosure document than one prepared unilaterally by the issuer."[28]

The second objection suggests that Commissioner Thomas does not expect the efficient-markets hypothesis, cited by those commissioners voting in support of Rule 415, to work within the markets for which most supporting evidence is available, namely, the stock market.[29] None of the commis-

---

[26] SEC Release No. 6423, September 2, 1982.

[27] Commissioner Thomas does not object to existing rules that permit shelf registration for *secondary* equity issues.

[28] SEC Release No. 6423.

[29] In Commissioner Thomas's discussion of debt offerings, on the other hand, she refers to commission discussion and industry testimony that debt issues without notice "periods" are acceptable because the issuing companies " . . . are widely followed by financial analysts, and therefore, under the efficient-market theory, it is reasonable to assume that information about these companies is generally available." ("Debt Offerings by S-3 Issuers," SEC Release No. 6423, September 2, 1982, under #6.)

sioners distinguished between the evidence developed (1) for empirical research on the efficient-markets hypothesis (this covered mainly secondary-market equity trading) and (2) its policy application, pro or con, to primary equity markets. Worse still, all the commissioners broadly assumed that the general and bland presumption of "efficiency" applies to the largest part of the primary markets, namely, new *bond* issues. The small amount of evidence in the literature on bond-market efficiency at best leaves open the question whether efficiency in those markets is even comparable to stock markets.

There are understandable reasons for the absence of market-efficiency studies for secondary bond trading. Almost the entire bond market consists of institutional trading, mainly among principals and over the counter. Therefore, there is little empirical evidence on, say, corporate bond transactions (or on municipals or foreign issues, and so forth) in secondary markets even though trading volume is heavy. Nearly all bond traders consider the volume of daily trading in corporate bonds alone (1984) to be about $4 billion.[30] But because many trades involve swaps and because the merchandise traded is continuously changing (many AA and AAA firms *each* have some tens or dozens of bond series outstanding), even a cross-sectional study involves horrendous data-discovery and analytical problems.[31]

On the other hand, a good record of trading data and of some inventory figures for government securities and the dealers in that market is available, as are some price and volume data. As a result, most non-government bond traders use the market for governments as a *numeraire* data set. This permits pricing and trading in high-quality non-government securities to proceed as if there were a continuous information and trading system in each issue. The fact that pricing and trading can take place by using the equivalent of an indexing system attests to traders' ingenuity and flexibility. That substitution mechanism, likewise, suggests how difficult it would

---

[30] The data of bond trades recorded on the NYSE floor—about $7 billion for *a year* (par value in 1982)—thus represents no more than one or two *days'* worth of over-the-counter trading.

[31] For example, AT&T *alone* has nearly two dozen separate bond and note issues outstanding, not counting any of its operating subsidiaries.

be to develop efficiency studies based on actual bond trades (either on a cross-section or a time-series basis).[32] Or put another way, the fact that traders use index (or government securities) data as substitute data indicates that the corporate-bond market does not have direct data available in usable form.

## COULD RATING AGENCIES PROVIDE A SUBSTITUTE FOR EFFICIENCY HYPOTHESIS?

Some might argue that new bond flotations are carefully examined by bond-quality rating agencies, such as Moody's and Standard & Poor's, and that professionals in these agencies provide risk evaluations for new and existing issues, while the data produced by government securities markets can continue to serve as a proxy for current returns and expected returns. Does this mean that the legal concept of public disclosure and the adversarial relationship between issuer and investment banker and the agency conflicts between corporate management and stockholders are to be surrendered to rating agencies? Will these agencies then be subject to investor damage suits (under Section 11 of the Securities Act) if material information was not properly evaluated? Will quality assessments even be possible as a practical procedure (or at reasonable cost) in such a case?

New bond flotations are carefully watched by the bond-quality rating agencies, and some may argue that professionals in those rating agencies provide another evaluation set regarding new or material information. It probably should not be argued with equal force that the rating agencies may provide something like the due diligence of investment bankers since they do not carry the same liability as does the issuer, the directors of the issuer, or even the investment banker.[33] If

---

[32] Moreover, any such empirical analysis should encompass not only publicly issued (and occasionally traded) corporates but the large volume of private placements as well.

[33] Section 11(a) of the Securities Act (15 U.S.C. 577 K (a)). Section 11 of the act attempts to protect the investor by setting up a purposely adversarial relationship between issues and the investment banker.

rating agencies had a greater legal responsibility at new issue, their more intense and continuous involvement with the issuer (to protect themselves against damage suits) might be a conflict of interest with regard to rating independence and neutrality.

# 14

## Shelf Registration of Bond Issues: The Current Situation

With the experience of shelf financing still new (in fall 1982), the majority of SEC commissioners argued that the "experiment" (i.e., "temporary" Rule 415) should be continued. For most of the summer and fall of 1982 and 1983, the financial markets were rising in price and receding somewhat in volatility compared to the preceding period since October 1979. How would the markets (and issuers) respond should a more hostile environment return? To examine this issue, let's look at the problem of waiting out a 21-day (as opposed to a 1- or 2-day) effectiveness period in a volatile market.

### THE SHIFT IN RISK

To assess the shift in the incidence of risk, consider, first, the problem of a single corporation placing one issue of new bonds in the market prior to Rule 415. Proceeds will be used for expanding plant and equipment and related corporate purposes. The company's CFO feels the bond issue will be acceptable only if the interest rate is low enough so that, in view of the risk adjusted cash flows of the new project, the project will yield a positive net present value.

The CFO is well through the new-issue preliminaries, due-diligence meetings, and so on, and is currently sweating out the waiting period before the new issue becomes effective. He has always been aware of market volatility, but now, when he reads the papers, he lives and dies as interest rates fall and rise. Until the new issue becomes effective, he still has one option—he can cancel the deal altogether if he feels that some intermediate rise in rates has significantly shifted the odds and pushed the project into negative net present value territory. If his peers in his industry are turning to shorter-term financing, he faces all the more pressure to cancel the issue. Arguing *against* cancellation is the fact that all the new-issue costs already incurred must be paid. And, as indicated elsewhere, these costs are substantial.[1] Finally, even if the new issue is canceled and short-term financing substituted, the fact that the new loan comes at a time when rates are higher does not help present value estimates either.

All else the same, the more volatile the bond market, the less predictable the cost and, hence, the more costly the funds that are raised in it. Bond issues can be sold at rates so high that their proceeds will be invested in projects with low or even negative net present value. Even the cancellation (formal or informal) of a number of issues because of these uncertainties necessarily adds to effective flotation costs.

At best, the as yet unpriced, but announced bond issue was in the past subject to the vagaries of the bond market while the SEC and the lead underwriters reviewed the prospectus. But a single issue could have produced a more generic "waiting risk." Suppose that, in a volatile market, a company perceives a temporary "window of opportunity"—that is, a temporary market decline in yields. A bond issue is then announced, a syndicate formed, and a preliminary prospectus sent to the SEC. However, in the three- to four-week waiting period, other firms in a similar situation also bring out their issues with the result that the "window" slams shut, and bond prices begin to fall. Thus the very perception of an opportunity can cancel it out before the bond sale becomes effective.

Conversely, when bond sales are pressed on the market as

---

[1] The problem is further complicated by concerns about relationships with the syndicate's lead investment banking firm, although in a crunch, the syndicate will have bigger things to worry about.

bond prices are declining, the competition for new-issue placements is less, whatever the wait. The risk asymmetry in a volatile market is clear: If the market is perceived as relatively receptive, issuer competition makes it less so; if the market is unreceptive, lack of competition will not improve receptivity. Thus market volatility imposes unpredictable waiting risks on new issues equal to the unpredictable yields of bonds waiting to be made effective by the SEC staff. And with a longer waiting period, these risks are borne mainly by the issuer.

Now consider the shortened S-16 registration process which could be completed in two days. In spring 1980, a bond market rally developed, and bond financings hit record highs in June and July. Then the market rally began to reverse, partly because of a flood of new offerings. As yield volatility up began to replace yield volatility *down*, bond issuers began to perceive the risk reduction implicit in speeding up every element of the new-issue process, including the underwriting arrangements. Issuers expected lead underwriters (under Form S-16) to come up with firm price bids for a new issue within hours of a request.

Issuers under the S-16 registration form enjoy over time a reduction in risk-adjusted waiting costs even if *ex-post* underwriting spreads *have not changed!* On the other hand, lead investment bankers asked to make bids on new issues, especially as temporary windows get crowded, are now exposed to price-change risks for a *longer* period than previously. Consider the underwriter's waiting period under the old three- to four-week waiting period. Once the issue's nonprice terms were decided and the issue's effectiveness period neared its close, a price meeting was held, and if the issuer was willing to go, the issue could be placed on the market immediately, or overnight at the latest. Under the 415 rules, the issuer requests a bid, and the lead underwriter makes an offer that is accepted within, say, three hours. The price risks of a firm offer are shifted to the underwriter and the syndicate for the next 45 hours. The issuer is now exposed for, at most, the three-hour period of waiting out his bid request that he can reject in any case.

Given this downstream shift in price risk in the issuing process (not to mention increased due-diligence risks), why do lead underwriters step up to bid? To retain the prestige associated with being a leader (or special-bracket) firm in the syndicate game, underwriters must maintain a high profile by managing a large volume of new offerings. For such firms the risk-adjusted proceeds of new underwritings would now be less even if the underwriting spreads did not change! To that extent, the foreshortened new-issue process has helped the issuers not only to reduce risks but also to shift at least a share of the waiting risks forward from the borrowing firm to the investment banker.

The pressure to compete in the underwriting area and the reduction in risk-adjusted returns also spread competitive forces to other financial services. The result is a shift to "transactional finance"—that is, the breakdown of long-term professional relationships between a given corporation and a specific investment banker. The shift to "instant new issues" with the S-16 form helped sharpen competitive pressures in the industry and served as a transitional instrument to the shelf-registration process.

## SHELF REGISTRATION: CURRENT SUPPLY PROBLEMS

Major-bracket underwriters could protect themselves against market vagaries over the two-day effectiveness period by using financial satellite markets (financial futures, among others). The special-bracket firm that engages in continuous bidding for new issues could secure an automatic dollar averaging of volatility costs (unanticipated rises in rate after a successful bid) and gains (unanticipated rate drops). Unfortunately, however, the asymmetries of flotation agreement prohibit this. Because of the crowding effects of windows, a flood of new issues would tend to reduce the benefits of unanticipated gains.

## HEDGING

From the point of view of investment bankers, the greatest difficulties are encountered when the inventory of unsold bonds grows (because prices are dropping as rates rise). To make life more difficult, inventory carrying costs move up with the general rise in rates. Thus the investment banker faces the same hedging problem as other commodity dealers, namely, that inventories tend to surge as prices fall. Of course, sales at prices below cost—that is, at a capital loss—may be made to cut losses and/or the certainty of rising carrying costs.[2] Accordingly, syndicate managers may use the classic short hedge of commodity traders (or farmers). For example, in the expectation of declining prices, the investment banker could decide to sell 10-year Treasury bond futures (take a short position) on some proportion of his anticipated average unsold inventory. Some do so. Others emphasize dealing with each bond underwriting syndicate on its own terms. For lead underwriters, this practice at least appears to carry the advantage of relating risks and returns to each flotation and simultaneously integrating those results with the accounting of expenses to the syndicate membership.

Consider the unusual combination of items that are priced jointly on the face of a prospectus: first, the price to the company and, second, the price to the public. The difference between the two is, of course, the underwriting discount. This means that, as long as the syndicate agreement is in force, no sales to the public may be made at a price different from that set on the prospectus—the equivalent of placing a put-option price on each new stock or bond.

There are, however, two uncertainties. (1) The maturity period of the in-the-money options cannot be known because expiration is coterminous with the conclusion of a successful syndicate. Such deals may sell very quickly—within a day or less—especially if market prices are expected to move up more. (2) If market prices move down far enough, the put-option equivalent becomes an out-of-the-money option to the underwriters as soon as the bond price falls more than the

---

[2]The question of carrying cost relates only in part to financing an undesired rise in inventory. Because all bonds are sold with accrued interest, the direct carrying cost may be largely offset by such interest accruals. However, the following factors make the offset less than perfect: (1) As rates rise, so do all carrying costs. (2) In bond bear markets (with negative yield curves), short-term carrying costs may be higher than the accrued interest rate per unit of time (although that differential is helped by the tax deductibility of carrying costs).

algebraic total of: (a) share of gross spread less (b) expenses charged. The maturity period of that option (or syndicate) will be determined when the syndicate breaks its price-maintenance agreement, and this may take weeks. Finally, the actual loss may be greater than an option premium or its theoretical equivalent because there is no limit to the size of the price drop at the point of the syndicate's breakup.

The hedging process thus may be divided into in-the-money and out-of-the-money strategies. In-the-money strategies are simple because they involve a community of interest between the issuing company and its underwriters. The company places its issue at an agreed price; the latter collects its spread (the premium) very quickly and at no further risk. Indeed, for many new stock issues, a "Green Shoe" option on the face of the prospectus is customary (the corporation grants the underwriters the option of acquiring up to 15 percent more shares than indicated in the prospectus at the same terms as the new-issue prices).[3] Many prospectuses carry the notation that the Green Shoe option is exercisable for 30 days from issue date "solely for the purpose of covering overallotments." The community of interest between syndicate and issuer involves the company issuing 15 percent more shares than indicated in the original offering *and at the same price.* For the underwriters, the advantage lies in the fact that if, in its market stabilization transactions, the syndicate manager had taken a short position in a rising market, that position could be covered by the Green Shoe option at the offering price as opposed to a more expensive market price.

On the other hand, in a falling market, the attempt to place the new offering may involve overallotments to syndicate participants as a way to encourage sales efforts. Of course, if a market drop is correctly foreseen, the only way an acceptable bid can be made to the issuer is for the lead manager to accept an unusually large proportion of the offering himself. Such a situation implies that overallotments to other syndicate members represent smaller shares of the total offering. The ques-

---

[3] This option was first used in an offering by the Green Shoe Co., and the name stuck.

tion of aggressive bidding and related risks was discussed in Chapter 12.

## DOING A DEAL

Assume a corporation registers a 415-type offering with the SEC. The issuer has completed virtually all decision-making on nonrate issues. For a bond issue, this involves security factors (for example, debenture issue or mortgage bond, sinking fund, maturity and/or call protection). In fact, the issue is ready to go except for some fine-tuning on nonrate aspects (if required) and the interest rate/issue price decision. Since the major practical purpose of the 415 exercise is to give issuers the chance to catch interest-rate dips,[4] a go decision by an issuer may involve a request for bids from two or more special-bracket firms. In effect, what occurs is a speeded-up version of the competitive bidding process described earlier.

On the other hand, some corporations who maintain long-term relationships with a specific investment banking firm then negotiate the terms (including contract rate and price) of the new issue with that firm.

However the price is decided, once it is agreed to by the issuing corporation and the purchasing syndicate, the investment bankers in effect agree to buy the new issue and will own it until they sell it to the public. Syndicates sell issues for an amount higher than the proceeds to the company; the difference is the underwriting discount and commission or underwriting spread.

Once the terms, conditions, and all the other features of a new bond issue are set up, a *registration statement* is filed with the SEC, as well as a *preliminary prospectus* that discloses material relevant to any prospective buyer, with the exception of final price and contract rate.[5] The registration statement, filed with the SEC, becomes effective, and a *final prospectus* is issued as soon as, in the opinion of the SEC, there has been adequate disclosure to the public. Because nonrate terms of previously registered shelf issues are well

---

[4]Or at least avoid unanticipated rate surges.

[5]Because some of the printing on the preliminary prospectus is colored in red, it is often called the red-herring prospectus.

known in the markets and large issuers' activities are closely followed by security analysts, the waiting period for shelf-registered issues may be as short as two days. As the prospectus copy shows, however, (see Figure 14-1) the SEC does not take a position with regard to investment merits of the issue or the reasonableness of the offering price or yield. As noted above, while the issue is in the process of being sold by the syndicate, the risk that the price of the issue may fall—conceivably even below the price paid to the borrowing firm—is borne entirely by the investment banking members of the syndicate.

While the red-herring prospectus is outstanding and during the actual selling period of the new issue, the lead manager runs the book. This means that prior to the final price setting the lead manager keeps a record of indications of interest of potential buyers and, after the price is set, maintains a record of actual sales to new buyers by members of the syndicate and by members of the selling group. If a portion of the new issue remains unsold because market interest rates are rising, the syndicate manager can stabilize the new issue's price and market by standing ready to make purchases at or above the offering price. The syndicate manager may take a short position in the issue, and the price pegging may be continued for a time or stopped.[6] In most cases, the underwriters' agreement that establishes the syndicate limits the amount of stabilizing purchases that can be made. Syndicate members want to have some control over the share of the offering and the costs allotted to them (see below for further discussion).

## Underwriting Spreads and Discounts

The difference between the price paid by the public and the proceeds to the company is the underwriting discount or spread; frequently that number is referred to as the gross spread. In recent years and for most significant bond issues, the gross spread has been less than 1 percent of the issue ($10

---

[6] The following appears in every prospectus: "In connection with this offering, the underwriters may overallot or effect transactions which stabilize or maintain the market price of the securities offered hereby at a level above that which might otherwise prevail in the open market. Such stabilizing, if commenced, may be discontinued at any time."

**FIGURE 14–1** _____

---

### $100,000,000

# Dayton-Hudson Corporation

#### 10¾% Sinking Fund Debentures due 2013

---

The 10¾% Sinking Fund Debentures due 2013 (the "Securities") will be redeemable at any time at the option of the Company, in whole or in part, at declining premiums as described herein. However, they will not be redeemable before May 1, 1993 as part of any refunding operation involving the incurring of indebtedness having an interest cost of less than 10¾% per year. The Securities will be entitled to a sinking fund beginning May 1, 1994 in annual instalments of $5,000,000 (with a non-cumulative option of the Company to increase each such annual payment to a maximum of $12,500,000), calculated to retire at least 95% of the Securities prior to maturity. Interest is payable semi-annually on May 1 and November 1, commencing November 1, 1983. See "Description of Securities".

---

The Company intends to make application for the listing of the Securities on the New York Stock Exchange.

---

**THESE SECURITIES HAVE NOT BEEN APPROVED OR DISAPPROVED BY THE SECURITIES AND EXCHANGE COMMISSION NOR HAS THE COMMISSION PASSED UPON THE ACCURACY OR ADEQUACY OF THIS PROSPECTUS SUPPLEMENT OR THE PROSPECTUS. ANY REPRESENTATION TO THE CONTRARY IS A CRIMINAL OFFENSE.**

---

| | Initial Public Offering Price (1) | Underwriting Discount (2) | Proceeds to Company (1) |
|---|---|---|---|
| Per Security ............................. | 100.00% | .875% | 99.125% |
| Total ................................. | $100,000,000 | $875,000 | $99,125,000 |

(1) Plus accrued interest from May 1, 1983. The proceeds are before deducting expenses payable by the Company, estimated to be $215,000.

(2) The Company has agreed to indemnify the Underwriters against certain civil liabilities, including liabilities under the Securities Act of 1933.

---

The Securities are offered severally by Underwriters as specified herein, subject to receipt and acceptance by them and subject to the right to reject any order in whole or in part. It is expected that the Securities will be ready for delivery at the office of Goldman, Sachs & Co., New York, New York, on or about May 12, 1983. The Securities will be issued only in fully registered form.

## Goldman, Sachs & Co.

---

The date of this Prospectus Supplement is May 5, 1983.

on a $1,000 bond). To that sum the underwriter adds some out-of-pocket expenses (for legal fees, due-diligence meetings, and so on) which appear on the front page of the prospectus as "expenses payable by the Company."[7]

Out of the gross spread, the lead underwriter customarily collects a management fee of 20 percent. If the bond issue comes to $100 million, the management fee to the lead underwriter is $200,000. Syndicate members selling directly to the public then get, in the aggregate, about $8 per bond so sold. Dealers who are *not* syndicate members but are part of the selling group get a share of the spread called the selling concession. Table 14-1 illustrates a preliminary distribution of the gross spread. Note that only $785,000 of the $1 million spread is accounted for. The manager earns an (implicit) management fee for selling 30,000 bonds directly to public. In fact, he collects an additional $140,000 (or the equivalent of an additional 70,000 bonds' worth). The manager and syndicate members split the $2.50 underwriters' discount for the 30,000 bonds distributed by the selling group members in proportion to their original subscription stated in the prospectus (say, in a 30 percent manager/70 percent member proportion). The selling group is only committed to sell the securities without committing its capital to risk taking. Put differently, if the bond market were to drop the price of the new bond to, say, $985, the cost of the $5 net loss per bond *plus* the added expenses incurred by the manager in stabilizing the issue would also be shared on 30/70 ratio between the manager and the syndicate membership.

## Reallowance

Reallowance is a share of the selling concession (usually less than 50 percent of the sum—say $2 per bond in this case) paid to members of the syndicate or of the selling group for the sale of bonds to the public over and above those acquired from the manager. A reallowance is paid to the firm that actually makes

---

[7] These nonmarket costs such as printing, due-diligence meetings, and legal fees to outside counsel are not trivial and may come to between 1/4 to 1/2 of 1 percent of the proceeds of a new issue.

**TABLE 14–1**
Preliminary Distribution of Gross Spread

|  | Manage-ment Fee | Underwriter Discount | Sales Concession | Bonds Sold to Public | Direct Income |
|---|---|---|---|---|---|
| Manager | $2.00 | $2.50 | $5.50 | 30,000 | $300,000 |
| Syndicate member | — | 2.50 | 5.50 | 40,000 | 320,000 |
| Group member | — | — | 5.50 | 30,000 | 165,000 |
| Total |  |  |  |  | $785,000 |

the sale, but the balance of the spread is retained by the member who agreed to release the bonds.

The manager is the ultimate and final payer of all of these amounts—only he has all the data since he runs the book. Figure 14–2 indicates the distribution of the bonds as set by the Underwriting Agreement; the lead underwriter for the Dayton-Hudson Corporation, Goldman, Sachs & Co., took down $37.5 million of the $100 million issue. The next largest set of underwriters are the major special-bracket firms: First Boston, Merrill Lynch, Morgan Stanley, and Salomon Brothers, all of which took $3.5 million each. Goldman, Sachs will treat these firms as well as it wants to be treated by them when they run the book in another offering.

## BOUGHT DEALS, PRE-MARKETED DEALS, AND COMPETITIVE BIDS, CIRCA 1985

For some bond flotations in mid-1985, gross spreads substantially narrowed. The first sample below, Norwest Financial, Inc., (see Figure 14–3) shows a gross spread of 0.268, or slightly above ¼ of 1 percent. The description of the underwriting agreement in the prospectus (see Figure 14–4) names Merrill Lynch as the *sole* underwriter, and Merrill Lynch "proposes initially to offer part of the notes directly to the public at the public offering price. . . and part to dealers at a price that represents a concession not in excess of .2 of 1 percent of the principal amount." Under the latter circumstance, Merrill Lynch would keep no more than .068 percent

**FIGURE 14-2**

### UNDERWRITING

Subject to the terms and conditions set forth in the Underwriting Agreement, the Company has agreed to sell to each of the Underwriters named below, and each of the Underwriters, for whom Goldman, Sachs & Co. are acting as representatives, has severally agreed to purchase, the principal amount of Securities set forth opposite its name below.

| Underwriters | Principal Amount |
|---|---|
| Goldman, Sachs & Co. | $ 37,500,000 |
| Bear, Stearns & Co. | 2,500,000 |
| A. G. Becker Paribas Incorporated | 2,500,000 |
| Blyth Eastman Paine Webber Incorporated | 2,500,000 |
| Alex. Brown & Sons | 1,500,000 |
| Dain Bosworth Incorporated | 2,500,000 |
| Dillon, Read & Co. Inc. | 2,500,000 |
| Donaldson, Lufkin & Jenrette Securities Corporation | 2,500,000 |
| Drexel Burnham Lambert Incorporated | 2,500,000 |
| A. G. Edwards & Sons, Inc. | 1,500,000 |
| The First Boston Corporation | 3,500,000 |
| E. F. Hutton & Company Inc. | 2,500,000 |
| Kidder, Peabody & Co. Incorporated | 2,500,000 |
| Lazard Freres & Co. | 2,500,000 |
| Merrill Lynch, Pierce, Fenner & Smith Incorporated | 3,500,000 |
| Morgan Stanley & Co. Incorporated | 3,500,000 |
| Oppenheimer & Co., Inc. | 1,500,000 |
| Piper, Jaffray & Hopwood Incorporated | 2,500,000 |
| Prudential-Bache Securities Inc. | 2,500,000 |
| L. F. Rothschild, Unterberg, Towbin | 2,500,000 |
| Salomon Brothers Inc | 3,500,000 |
| Shearson/American Express Inc. | 2,500,000 |
| Smith Barney, Harris Upham & Co. Incorporated | 2,500,000 |
| Thomson McKinnon Securities Inc. | 1,500,000 |
| Wertheim & Co., Inc. | 2,500,000 |
| Dean Witter Reynolds Inc. | 2,500,000 |
| Total | $100,000,000 |

Under the terms and conditions of the Underwriting Agreement the Underwriters are committed to take and pay for all of the Securities, if any are taken.

The Underwriters propose to offer the Securities in part directly to retail purchasers at the initial public offering price set forth on the cover page of this Prospectus Supplement, and in part to certain securities dealers at such price less a concession of 0.50% of the principal amount. The Underwriters may allow, and such dealers may reallow, a concession not to exceed 0.25% of the principal amount to certain brokers and dealers. After the Securities are released for sale to the public, the offering price and other selling terms may from time to time be varied by the representatives.

### LEGAL OPINIONS

The validity of the Securities offered hereby is being passed upon for the Company by Faegre & Benson, 3400 IDS Center, Minneapolis, Minnesota 55402, and for the Underwriters by Sullivan & Cromwell, 125 Broad Street, New York, New York 10004, who may rely on Faegre & Benson as to matters of Minnesota law.

S-6

**FIGURE 14–3**

---

PROSPECTUS SUPPLEMENT

(To Prospectus dated December 28, 1983)

 *FINANCIAL*

## $50,000,000
# Norwest Financial, Inc.
## 9⅞% Senior Notes 1990 Series due June 15, 1990

---

Interest payable June 15 and December 15, commencing December 15, 1985.

---

The Notes are redeemable on or after June 15, 1989 at the option of the Company, in whole or in part, without premium.

---

THESE SECURITIES HAVE NOT BEEN APPROVED OR DISAPPROVED BY THE SECURITIES AND EXCHANGE COMMISSION NOR HAS THE COMMISSION PASSED UPON THE ACCURACY OR ADEQUACY OF THIS PROSPECTUS SUPPLEMENT OR THE PROSPECTUS TO WHICH IT RELATES. ANY REPRESENTATION TO THE CONTRARY IS A CRIMINAL OFFENSE.

|  | Price to Public(1) | Underwriting Discount | Proceeds to Company(1)(2) |
|---|---|---|---|
| Per Note........................ | 99.88% | .268% | 99.612% |
| Total ........................... | $49,940,000 | $134,000 | $49,806,000 |

(1) Plus accrued interest, if any, from July 18, 1985.

(2) Before deducting expenses payable by the Company estimated at $50,000.

---

The Notes are offered for delivery on or about July 18, 1985, subject to prior sale, when, as and if delivered to and accepted by Merrill Lynch, Pierce, Fenner & Smith Incorporated. Merrill Lynch, Pierce, Fenner & Smith Incorporated reserves the right to withdraw, cancel or modify such offer and to reject orders in whole or in part.

---

## Merrill Lynch Capital Markets

---

The date of this Prospectus Supplement is July 2, 1985.

## FIGURE 14-4

### UNDERWRITING

Under the terms of and subject to the conditions contained in an Underwriting Agreement dated July 2, 1985, Merrill Lynch, Pierce, Fenner & Smith Incorporated has agreed to purchase the Notes and the Company has agreed to sell the Notes to Merrill Lynch, Pierce, Fenner & Smith Incorporated.

Merrill Lynch, Pierce, Fenner & Smith Incorporated proposes initially to offer part of the Notes directly to the public at the public offering price set forth on the cover page hereof and part to dealers at a price which represents a concession not in excess of .20 of 1% of the principal amount. Merrill Lynch, Pierce, Fenner & Smith Incorporated may allow and such dealers may reallow a concession, not in excess of .125 of 1% of the principal amount, to certain other dealers. After the initial public offering, the public offering price and such concessions may be changed.

The Underwriting Agreement provides that the Company will indemnify Merrill Lynch, Pierce, Fenner & Smith Incorporated against certain civil liabilities, including liabilities under the Securities Act of 1933, as amended, or contribute to payments Merrill Lynch, Pierce, Fenner & Smith Incorporated may be required to make in respect thereof.

S-4

of the gross spread, which comes to about 23 percent. Such bought deals with tight spreads have become commonplace under Rule 415.

Under that same rule, the negotiated deal arrangement has been developed. In this arrangement, notes are marketed to syndicate members and by them to clients (Figure 14–5).

Finally, the Citicorp note (see Figure 14–6) was bid for competitively and, even though the gross spread was not especially thin (compare the .6 of 1 percent with the Norwest issue of .268), the syndicate certainly was—the manager carrying more than 80 percent of the total.

However, if all the major firms engage in deals like these (that is, with the manager carrying half the deal or more and with very short syndicates), deal diversification will simply involve fewer firms. For the firms that manage those deals, effective diversification among the deals still exists as long as sufficient capital is available to the major firms. Rule 415 has forced, quite inadvertently, many smaller and regional firms out of the syndicate game. On the other hand, major underwriting firms have felt the need to build their capital positions because they need to buy larger proportions of more issues and on short notice. Likewise, the pressure to build capital may also be responsible, at least in part, for the drive of more firms to switch from partnership to corporate organization.

## SYNDICATE RISK MANAGEMENT AND HEDGING

The syndicate manager and all syndicate members by necessity operate with price control on the upside. As long as the syndicate is maintained, they may not make sales at prices higher than the price to the public stated in the prospectus. If an unanticipated rise in security prices occurs after the new issue is priced and before the syndicate's distribution is complete, the syndicate will experience a reduction in risk but no increase in revenues; it only benefits because it sells out its long positions more rapidly. If, in order to support the new-issue price, the syndicate manager took a short position in the issue prior to the unforeseen price surge, he may have to cover the short (1) at a higher market price (that is, potentially at a loss) or (2) by exercising the Green Shoe option, if one was written into the prospectus. In case (1), he would reduce his gross flotation revenue by the extent of the net cost of the short cover.[8] In case (2), the aggregate revenue from the flotation would rise by somewhat less than 10 percent for the syndicate as a whole if, as is typical, the Green Shoe option is equal to 10 percent of the new issue and the short-cover operations carried some costs.

Suppose that market prices do not move up but move down. Instead of having the new issue go out the window, the flotation process now is slow going in the face of declining market prices. For all syndicate members, unsold inventories of the new issue rise to levels higher than desired.[9] This result involves, first, the acceptance of greater-than-before inventory price risks on larger inventories. Second, investment bankers (like all financial firms) carry a high-leverage capital structure; that is, they manage on a narrow base of equity capital. Charges against the capital base because of larger security inventories (or eventual capital losses) constrain firms' decision making and/or risk taking. With stronger expectations of market-price declines (or greater future risks), risk avoidance may become stronger or more widely held.

## Tactics

Accordingly, lead underwriters may resort to two types of actions to offset risk in flotations. *Tactical* actions refer to the specific flotation itself. The Green Shoe option is the most useful tactic in an unanticipated up market. In a volatile market with little strong direction, overallotment by the managing underwriter is probably the best marketing device. The managing underwriter offers added securities to syndicate members or members of the selling group with the expec-

---

[8] At the least, there would be an opportunity cost in that total revenues would be less than: (a) the share of gross spread (per security sold) times (b) the number sold by managers, syndicate members, or others.

[9] Suppose that, in order to place some of the new issue with institutional investors, syndicate members engage in preferential swap transactions. This could work as follows. They place a premium bid with an institution on security X taken in a swap for new issue Y; their report to the syndicate only shows as a Y transaction.

**FIGURE 14-5** _____

PROSPECTUS

## $125,000,000

# The Stop & Shop Companies, Inc.

### 10¾% Notes Due 1995

---

Interest Payable January 15 and July 15

---

The Notes may not be redeemed prior to July 15, 1992. On and after that date, the Notes are redeemable at the option of the Company, in whole or in part, at 100% of the principal amount thereof plus accrued interest to the redemption date. The Notes, which mature on July 15, 1995, are not entitled to any mandatory redemption or sinking fund provisions. See "Description of Notes."

---

Application has been made to list the Notes on the New York Stock Exchange.

---

THESE SECURITIES HAVE NOT BEEN APPROVED OR DISAPPROVED BY THE SECURITIES AND EXCHANGE COMMISSION NOR HAS THE COMMISSION PASSED UPON THE ACCURACY OR ADEQUACY OF THIS PROSPECTUS. ANY REPRESENTATION TO THE CONTRARY IS A CRIMINAL OFFENSE.

|  | Price to Public | Underwriting Discounts and Commissions (1) | Proceeds to Company (2) |
|---|---|---|---|
| Per Note | 99.75% | .70% | 99.05% |
| Total | $124,687,500 | $875,000 | $123,812,500 |

(1) The Company has agreed to indemnify the Underwriters with respect to certain liabilities, including liabilities under the Securities Act of 1933. See "Underwriting."

(2) Before deducting certain expenses payable by the Company estimated at $265,000.

---

The Notes are offered by the several Underwriters named herein subject to prior sale, to withdrawal, cancellation or modification of the offer without notice, to delivery to and acceptance by the Underwriters, and to certain further conditions. It is expected that delivery of the Notes will be made at the office of Shearson Lehman Brothers Inc., New York, New York, on or about July 16, 1985.

---

## Shearson Lehman Brothers Inc.

July 9, 1985

## FIGURE 14–5 *(concluded)*

indemnity satisfactory to it before it enforces the Indenture or the Notes. Subject to certain limitations, holders of a majority in principal amount of the Notes may direct the Trustee in its exercise of any trust or power. The Trustee may withhold from Noteholders notice of any continuing default (except a default in payment) if it determines that withholding notice is in their interests. The Company is required to file periodic reports with the Trustee as to the absence of default.

Directors, officers, employees or stockholders of the Company will not have any liability for any obligations of the Company under the Notes or the Indenture or for any claim based on, in respect of, or by reason of, such obligations or their creation. Each Noteholder by accepting a Note waives and releases all such liability. The waiver and release are part of the consideration for the issue of the Notes.

**The Trustee**

The First National Bank of Boston (the "Bank") will act as Trustee under the Indenture. Under an existing line of credit and a revolving loan agreement, the Company has available to it up to $70,000,000 from the Bank. The maximum principal amount outstanding under the line of credit since February 2, 1985 was $11,000,000. No borrowings are currently outstanding under the line of credit or the revolving loan agreement. The Bank also serves as the Transfer Agent for the Company's Common Stock and provides other customary commercial banking and fiduciary services for the Company. See also the note under "Capitalization."

### UNDERWRITING

The Underwriters, represented by Shearson Lehman Brothers Inc. (the "Representative"), have severally agreed, subject to the terms and conditions contained in the Underwriting Agreement, a copy of which is filed as an exhibit to the Registration Statement, to purchase from the Company the Notes offered hereby. The names of the several Underwriters and the principal amount of Notes to be purchased by each of them are as follows:

| Underwriter | Principal Amount of Notes |
|---|---:|
| Shearson Lehman Brothers Inc. | $ 44,900,000 |
| The First Boston Corporation | 4,500,000 |
| Goldman, Sachs & Co. | 4,500,000 |
| Merrill Lynch, Pierce, Fenner & Smith Incorporated | 4,500,000 |
| Morgan Stanley & Co. Incorporated | 4,500,000 |
| Salomon Brothers Inc | 4,500,000 |
| Bear, Stearns & Co. | 3,400,000 |
| Alex. Brown & Sons Incorporated | 3,400,000 |
| Dillon, Read & Co. Inc. | 3,400,000 |
| Donaldson, Lufkin & Jenrette Securities Corporation | 3,400,000 |
| Drexel Burnham Lambert Incorporated | 3,400,000 |
| E. F. Hutton & Company Inc. | 3,400,000 |
| Kidder, Peabody & Co. Incorporated | 3,400,000 |
| Lazard Frères & Co. | 3,400,000 |
| PaineWebber Incorporated | 3,400,000 |
| Prudential-Bache Securities Inc. | 3,400,000 |
| L. F. Rothschild, Unterberg, Towbin | 3,400,000 |
| Smith Barney, Harris Upham & Co. Incorporated | 3,400,000 |
| Wertheim & Co., Inc. | 3,400,000 |
| Dean Witter Reynolds Inc. | 3,400,000 |
| A. G. Edwards & Sons, Inc. | 2,000,000 |
| Oppenheimer & Co., Inc. | 2,000,000 |
| Prescott, Ball, Turben | 2,000,000 |
| Thomson McKinnon Securities Inc. | 2,000,000 |
| Tucker, Anthony & R. L. Day, Inc. | 2,000,000 |
| | $125,000,000 |

12

**FIGURE 14-6** _____

PROSPECTUS SUPPLEMENT
(To Prospectus dated May 2, 1985)

$150,000,000

# CITICORP ✚

## 11% Subordinated Notes Due August 1, 1995

Interest on the Subordinated Notes (the "Notes") is payable semiannually on February 1 and August 1, commencing February 1, 1986. The Notes will be subordinate and junior in right of payment to all Senior Indebtedness (as defined in the Prospectus) of Citicorp. The Notes are redeemable on and after August 1, 1990, at the option of Citicorp, in whole or in part, at their principal amount plus accrued interest.

THESE SECURITIES HAVE NOT BEEN APPROVED OR DISAPPROVED BY THE SECURITIES AND EXCHANGE COMMISSION NOR HAS THE COMMISSION PASSED UPON THE ACCURACY OR ADEQUACY OF THIS PROSPECTUS SUPPLEMENT OR THE PROSPECTUS. ANY REPRESENTATION TO THE CONTRARY IS A CRIMINAL OFFENSE.

|  | Price to Public(1) | Underwriting Discount | Proceeds to Citicorp(1)(2) |
|---|---|---|---|
| Per Note | 99.55% | .60% | 98.95% |
| Total | $149,325,000 | $900,000 | $148,425,000 |

(1) Plus accrued interest, if any, from July 30, 1985.

(2) Before deduction of expenses payable by Citicorp.

The Notes are offered severally by the Underwriters as specified herein subject to receipt and acceptance by them and subject to their right to reject orders in whole or in part. It is expected that the Notes will be ready for delivery at the offices of Goldman, Sachs & Co,. New York, New York, on or about July 30, 1985.

# Goldman, Sachs & Co.

The date of this Prospectus Supplement is July 23, 1985.

# FIGURE 14-6 *(concluded)*

## SUPPLEMENTAL DESCRIPTION OF NOTES

The Notes offered hereby will be limited to $150,000,000 aggregate principal amount and will mature on August 1, 1995. The Notes will be subordinate and junior in right of payment to all Senior Indebtedness (as defined in the Prospectus) of Citicorp. The Notes will bear interest from July 30, 1985 at the rate per annum shown on the front cover of this Prospectus Supplement, payable semiannually on February 1 and August 1 of each year, commencing February 1, 1986, and at maturity, to the person in whose name the Note (or any Predecessor Note) is registered at the close of business on the January 15 and July 15 next preceding such Interest Payment Date. The Notes will be issued in denominations of $1,000 or any integral multiple thereof.

The Notes offered hereby will not be subject to redemption prior to August 1, 1990. On and after such date they will be subject to redemption upon not less than 30 nor more than 60 days' notice by mail at any time, in whole or in part, at the election of Citicorp, at a redemption price equal to their principal amount plus accrued interest to the date of redemption. If less than all the Notes are to be redeemed, Notes will be selected by the Trustee by such method as it shall deem fair and appropriate and which may provide for selection for redemption of portions of the principal amount of any Note of a denomination larger than $1,000.

Reference is made to the Prospectus for a description of other terms of the Notes.

## UNDERWRITING

Subject to the terms and conditions set forth in the Underwriting Agreement, Citicorp has agreed to sell to each of the Underwriters named below, and each of the Underwriters, for whom Goldman, Sachs & Co. are acting as Representatives, has severally agreed to purchase, the principal amount of Notes set forth opposite its name:

| Underwriter | Principal Amount |
| --- | --- |
| Goldman, Sachs & Co. | $122,200,000 |
| Alex. Brown & Sons Incorporated | 2,700,000 |
| Daiwa Securities America Inc. | 2,700,000 |
| Drexel Burnham Lambert Incorporated | 2,700,000 |
| E. F. Hutton & Company Inc. | 2,700,000 |
| Keefe, Bruyette & Woods, Inc. | 2,700,000 |
| Kidder, Peabody & Co. Incorporated | 3,500,000 |
| The Nikko Securities Co. International, Inc. | 2,700,000 |
| Nomura Securities International, Inc. | 2,700,000 |
| M. A. Schapiro & Co., Inc. | 2,700,000 |
| Yamaichi International (America), Inc. | 2,700,000 |
| Total | $150,000,000 |

Citicorp has been advised by the Representatives that the several Underwriters propose initially to offer the Notes to the public at the public offering price set forth on the cover page of this Prospectus Supplement and to certain dealers at such price less a concession not in excess of .375% of the principal amount of the Notes. Underwriters may allow and such dealers may reallow a concession not in excess of .125% of such principal amount. After the initial public offering, the public offering price and such concessions may be changed.

Citicorp has agreed to indemnify the Underwriters against certain civil liabilities, including liabilities under the Securities Act of 1933.

See "Plan of Distribution" in the Prospectus for further information regarding the distribution of the Notes offered hereby.

S-8

tation that they will put forth a strong sales effort just because they have a chance to earn whatever share of the spread to which they are entitled and for a larger volume of securities. If, in the process, they place more securities by accepting more swaps at relatively attractive prices to the buyer of the new issue, they would be no more than fine-tuning the bid/ask spread while selling at the fixed price to the public.

In the flotation of new-equity issues, syndicate members may engage in what appear to be counterproductive actions, namely, selling into the syndicate manager's support bid in the market. Of course, even a relatively small firm who is an occasional syndicate member would never want to appear to be fouling the nest in this manner. It would hide the action by using a broker's broker (or more than one) to hide its identity. In turn, the syndicate manager, by keeping all the facts of actual syndicate sales and support operations to himself, tries to prevent information leaks regarding slow sales to keep such defections to a minimum. Large syndicate participants who are special-bracket firms (or those in the next bracket who frequently run syndicates), although tempted, may fear retaliatory actions by their peers if such actions are even suspected.

In turn, even the syndicate participants who do not expect to be managing syndicates are constrained from engaging in such self-protective actions too frequently. They know that cycles of slim stock offerings in down markets (when the temptation to bail out is strongest) are followed by surges in stock flotations in bull markets. Thus responsible syndicate behavior safeguards the prestige of syndicate participants and the occasional appearance in tombstone ads. In addition, it assures the small firm (and, even more important, its customers) of continuously available new merchandise. Because this process helps the distribution process generally, lead managers, in turn, may be constrained from disciplining syndicate members too obviously.

## Strategy

The group of special-bracket firms and all other important syndicate managers have the problem of temporarily becoming buyers of last resort for the offerings they manage. This proposition implies that they will be accumulating securities at those times when markets are less receptive or most unpredictable. For the major underwriters for whom maintenance of market share in the new-offering game is important, an accumulation of unsold securities when markets are difficult or uneasy may be implied. Moreover, the compulsion to maintain market share does not permit the luxury of making too many bids too far away from the markets. Inevitably, some inventories accumulate.

Suppose an underwriter wants to hedge a $1 million undesired inventory bond position. Even for a significant investment banking firm this would not be an unusually large or small amount considering that, as new-issue syndicates break up and positions are liquidated, new flotations are taken in. The hedge could be an offset to a revolving excess inventory.

Now suppose that, in a skittish market, nearby Treasury bond futures are trading at $65.[10] For a hedge value of 10 contracts of $100,000 par each, these constitute a market value of $650,000 with a par value of $1 million (for 8 percent U.S. governments with a maturity of about 15 years). Assuming a $20,000 initial margin requirement, the short sale of 10 bond futures contracts is equivalent to a short sale of $650,000 long governments on 97 percent margin. If market prices fall so that price quotations on futures decline from $65 to $64 (or by 1½ percent) the value of the 10 contracts (short) would rise by $10,000, a cash value that may be withdrawn from the account.

The cash value of the undesired $1 million inventory in the syndicate will probably have declined by the same amount that, if it were marked to market, would have reduced the firm's available capital by $10,000. If the cash gain from the futures short position is deposited into the firm's capital, the decline is exactly offset. Of course, there is a commission fee for this hedging transaction. Using the preceding transaction, the bid/ask spread per contract plus commission per round trip is about 2/32 of a point or approximately 1/10 of 1 percent. (The round-trip cost for 10 contracts would therefore be about $650.)

---

[10] The following data are taken from F. H. Trainer, Jr., "The Uses of Treasury Bond Futures in Fixed-Income Portfolio Management," *Financial Analysts Journal*, January–February 1983, pp. 28–29.

Finally, the question arises whether the breadth and depth of the futures market is great enough to accommodate hedging significant flotations volume. Suppose that the total volume of syndicate hedging was not 10 bond contracts but 1,000. For example, in August 1983, the number of September 1983 Treasury bond futures contracts outstanding was nearly 100,000, while estimated total daily trading volume came to about 90,000 contracts. That meant a short hedging position for 1,000 industry contracts came to about 1 percent of either near-term open interest or of daily trading volume, an amount not likely to raise price variances in futures market. Since 1983 these markets have further increased in depth.

## Other Syndicate Games—An Example

Prior to the pricing of an IPO, the managing underwriter gets indications of interest from institutional buyers and other major clients that add up to the full number of shares expected to be sold (1 million shares) plus the Green Shoe option (another 150,000 shares). The price range discussed with the client and known to the syndicate as well as the institutions was $9 to $11 per share. At that price range, the manager has a number of indications that the stock will be held by buyers if he can price it within the range.

Assume that the market experiences a sinking spell—the most-recent Fed report on the money supply raises fears of an impending rise in the discount rate. The managing underwriter is still committed to produce the shares for the buyers if they ask for them after pricing, but he now feels that the institutions, in view of bearish market price expectations, may prefer to trade the stock, rather than hold it. There may even be opinions in the syndicate department that some of the institutions may now be free riders in the deal rather than just traders.

The manager might go back to the client for permission to lower the price range by $1 (to $8–$10) in view of the chillier market climate. But the client had been attracted to the underwriter because *his* range ($9–$11) was better than that of another underwriter with whom the client had previously considered the deal. The client could argue that he was being played for a sucker by the second underwriter's higher price just to get the business. After all, he could argue, the M, M2, and M3 reports of the Fed are often substantially revised, and the manager should know the vagaries of prices in the markets since that is his business. What should the manager do?

The manager decides to continue with the offering as originally proposed ($9–$11 per share), but the greater price uncertainty in the marketplace requires more underwriting support. The manager knows the size of the demand in his book while he continues to evaluate the quality of that demand. He provides that added support by taking a naked short position in the market. (This short position is in addition to the covered short represented by the Green Shoe option.) As a result, the manager adds to the perceived market demand for the stock (which stands in the book in the form of indications of interest at 1,150,000 shares) another "synthetic" 150,000 market-share demand, which constitutes his naked short.

If he covers the naked short at a below-market price (because expectations of continued market-price declines are fulfilled), he will have helped to support the price and acted in his fiduciary function with respect to the issuer. If the market rises, the short cover will be more expensive, and the syndicate's expenses rise. As a result, the syndicate will produce a lesser return to its members but will have successfully sold the deal.[11]

In point of fact, the naked short is another aspect of the underwriting-insurance process. It is a premium paid on the equivalent of an accident policy. That policy is designed to cover the reduction in cash proceeds—the accident—that might have been brought about by an unfortunate timing event in the economy at large. And even though the premium paid adds to costs, these costs are spread over the syndicate as a whole.

## SUMMARY AND SOME NEW THOUGHTS ON AGENCY COSTS

The syndicate tactics indicated earlier reduce the riskiness of placing a particular issue with the public at the least time delay (overallotment) and least cost (Green Shoe option). Such

---

[11] On the other hand, the higher price per share on the issue will probably mean somewhat better underwriting revenues to the syndicate. In part, this offsets the higher short-cover costs.

tactics are designed to place the maximum portion of the offering with the public at the price fixed in the syndicate; these mechanisms could reduce the "unique" or "specific" risks of flotation per issue.

So much for specific flotations. The active syndicate participants in volatile markets and under the shelf registration rule will face continuous requests to place new issue bids at short notice. A clustering of such opportunities at times of temporary rate drops also reflects a risk clustering of surges of inventories of unsold securities priced above the current market. From the point of view of portfolio management (of unsold inventory), there is an unexpected result:

1. Portfolio structure (by securities) is not determined by the portfolio manager but by random issue of new securities (at the option of issuers) and the macroeconomic policies that influence reception.
2. Proportions of securities in portfolio are not based on low risk/high return tradeoff but by something more random that may approach its reverse if interest-rate volatility carries an upward bias. Under those circumstances, covariance of returns may become more positive, and portfolio variance may be rising.

To offset the rising systematic risk of unanticipated portfolio surges, short positions in futures markets may be established and maintained. In part, this procedure permits gross new-issue spreads to be maintained (even though systematic risk may be rising) as long as the transaction cost of developing a short hedge is relatively low. Another reason for the relative stability of gross spreads even as rising rate volatility raises portfolio risks is the economics of capital budgeting that reduce the volume of flotations (long-term) as rates rise and the cost of capital to the issuer rises.[12] Rising competition among underwriters for lesser volume of a new product (such as new securities) also holds down direct financing of higher inventory risks by larger gross spreads. Inevitably, then, the short hedge in the futures market becomes the more attractive the greater the perceived systematic risk.

---

[12] In part also, corporations with an inelastic demand for funds will find short-term financing substitutes.

## Agency Costs

The foregoing discussion could be reinterpreted as representing a special case of agency theory. Jensen-Meckling define an agency relationship as "...a contract under which one or more persons [the syndicate participant(s)[13]] engage another person (the agent) to perform some service on their behalf which involves delegating some decision-making authority to the agent. If both parties to the relationship are utility maximizers, there is good reason to believe that the agent will not always act in the best interests of the principal. The *principal* can limit divergences from his interest by establishing appropriate incentives for the agent and by incurring monitoring costs designed to limit the aberrant activities of the agent."[14]

In some interesting ways, the foregoing approach could be reversed. The relatively free hand given lead managers, their monopoly control over the information set (the book), and their use of syndicate tactics makes *managers* the agents of syndicate members. That point, as well as potential future role reversals among the syndicate members (where all the majors are syndicate managers as well as members some of the time), suggests that agency theory, when applied to syndicates, should be discussed in terms of "double agency."[15] Still, under Rule 415 the foregoing application of agency theory applies to the interrelationship among the syndicate members *only* and *not* to the relationship between the corporate (or other) issuers and the investment bankers. Once the corporation has sold the issue, it becomes the syndicate's risk and selling problem.

Monitoring costs may be small and monitoring itself quite effective in those cooperative enterprises where each member has a chance to be chairperson—that is, the monitor—some of the time. To the extent that one effect of Rule 415 has been the shorter syndicate and much heavier participation by managing underwriters, leading to the bought deal, monitoring costs are substantially reduced because nearly all syndicate mem-

---

[13] In the original article, that person is called the principal(s).

[14] M. C. Jensen and W. H. Meckling, "Theory of the Firm: Managerial Behavior and Ownership Structure," *Journal of Financial Economics* 3 (1976), p. 308, (italics in original).

[15] Jensen and Meckling also point out that agency costs "arise in any situation involving cooperative effort" (p. 309).

bers are now major underwriters. In fact, each syndicate member is sooner rather than later in a lead managership position. If major participants represent a small number acting in a well-defined market, information regarding performance *ex post* is available quickly, and the ability to retaliate is continuously present. For the few smaller firms left, behavior such as shirking or antigroup behavior can be controlled by threats—or only the fear—that future syndicate allocations will be still further reduced. The fact that the small number of major participants are always in the same markets and competing to win bids for the same merchandise helps enforce discipline among them.

The agency problem, as proposed by Jensen and Meckling and Jensen and Fama, is based on a long-term (if not permanent) separation in which the segregation of risk bearing and corporate managerial decision making is fixed (although it cannot be perfectly specified) in spite of the uncertainties in which these relationships obtain. On the other hand, the reality of continued role reversals in the syndicate game provides a functional remedy to the agency problem. Finally, the disclosure and underwriter liability provisions of the Securities Act of 1933 (Section 11)[16] offer potential direct remedies to corporate and other issuers if collusion is suspected in a given flotation. In any case, competitive bids and substitute flotation methods are always available if an issuer wants to assess alternative flotation costs.

---

[16] For further discussion see Chapter 13.

# PART IV

# Investment Bankers and Their Clients: Institutionalization Takes Command

Electronic trading has created a revolution in financial markets by breaking the barriers of scale, time, and space. At the trading level, broker-dealers have an increasing need for a large capital base. Only the largest investment banking firms will have the capacity to act as counterparts—that is, as dealers—for the increasingly larger trades done continuously by the world's largest institutional clients.

# 15

## Institutionalization

This section will detail the following dimensions to institutionalization:

1. Those involved in large-scale trading generally.
2. Block trading.
3. Merger-related activities.

**LARGE-SCALE TRADING:**
**INVESTMENT BANKERS AS DEALERS**

With the electronic marvels of instant communication came the demand to transfer vast sums just as quickly. Finding two large transactors who want to do exactly opposite sides of a single trade at the same time becomes less probable the larger the trade and the shorter the decision lag. And yet, high-speed communications are perhaps more likely to trigger professional and institutional-sized transactions than retail trades.

Until the late 1950s, the auction markets of the NYSE easily accommodated just about all transactions in common stock of listed firms, and floor trading arrangements were functionally related to the large number of generally offsetting small-scale orders. In that sense, the specialist system could readily absorb temporary price fluctuations and small random retail imbalances of supply and demand.

During the 1960s and 1970s, the stock market *became increasingly institutionalized.*[1] At that time, substantial upheavals occurred in both the broker-dealer industry and the NYSE and other exchanges because institutional-type trading could not be made to work in an essentially retail-type marketplace. For example, in the late 1960s, the NYSE could not cope with a transaction volume of 13 to 15 million shares *per day* and had to close one day a week to catch up with the paper work. In addition, some 100 firms were forced to leave the industry due to insufficient capital or insufficient capacity to deal with the transactions' volume, size, or record keeping. General dissatisfaction with some trading practices finally led to congressional action in providing investor insurance (SIPC) and negotiated commissions.[2]

In any case, the information network developed by and for institution-sized traders[3] led them to seek mechanisms away from the floor to trade positions. This meant that a dealer network had to be developed to serve the contra side; the participants were called block traders—the "upstairs" traders (as contrasted symbolically to "floor traders"). Of course, some block traders could provide a search process—that is, a large-scale brokerage function—where the equivalent of a "private placement" of a large secondary trade was done for a commission fee. The dozen or so investment banking firms that manage private placements or public syndicates also have the facilities to do block trades effectively.

The investor side of block trading is based on growing institutionalization of the savings process. The development of pension funds and their encouragement by legislation such as ERISA helped increase labor force demands for deferred lifetime compensation. Governmental efforts and institutional

---

[1] See for example, the multivolume report by the SEC, *Institutional Investor Study Report* 82d Congress, 1st Session, U.S. Government Printing Office (Washington, D.C.: 1971).

[2] For a more complete discussion, see E. Bloch and R. H. Schwartz, eds., *Impending Changes for Securities Markets* (Greenwich, Conn.: JAI Press, 1979).

[3] Access to Dow Jones and Reuters news wires is much too costly for retail traders but not for institutions.

arrangements designed to keep the process honest probably contributed too. In more recent years, Keogh and IRA accounts for middle-income individuals further added to the institutionalization of savings in firms that were not necessarily financial intermediaries with tightly constrained asset regulations.

When all the foregoing is multiplied by income growth related to rapid inflation and to the demand for portfolio performance to maintain the real value of capital, it is easy to explain how large amounts of funds began to accumulate and how fund managers at times wished to make substantial trades on short notice. Thus institutionalization of savings led to institutionalization of trading, and this required development of trading and risk-taking services on a large scale and at short notice.

Within the investment banking community the capacity to trade on a large scale is done by what SEC reports call national full-line firms and large investment banking houses, many of which are also the special-bracket firms that manage most of the major flotations (see Chapter 2). A synergistic relationship clearly exists between the skills and capacities required to do large-scale trading in secondary markets and syndicate management in primary markets. What, then, does it take to be a dealer in institutional-sized transactions, or a special-bracket firm? Why do some firms that are large in terms of assets or in trading activity not move to become special-bracket firms? Is it lack of competition or oligopolistic collusion?

Posing the question of whether there is competition (or its restraint) in the industry is not useful because the more fundamental problem is which firms have the ability continuously to be a *dealer* on a large scale. This requires the capacity to efficiently perform several not necessarily complementary services:

1. Secondary sales *in size.*
2. Pricing close to the market, (that is, relatively high price with small commission charge).[4]
3. Accepting inventory risks.

---

[4] As we shall indicate below, the unit charge for commissions tends to drop with size.

The first item, size, is the most fundamental aspect of special-bracket investment banking. It involves the capacity to find buyers for large blocks of stock or a large proportion of a bond issue and skill in setting prices that clear the market without leaving too large a residual to be inventoried. Adding in the narrowing of equity trading commissions (following May 1, 1975) results in a market environment in which the intermediary is expected to accept more risk for less return on some transactions while trading in size. Further, the willingness to make bids on a continuing basis for large-scale offerings at close-to-market prices is necessary to maintain membership in the club. All these members, by proving they belong by offering continuous large-scale *secondary* trading capacity, will, in consequence, be asked to make bids as lead underwriters for new issues as well. Two nearly inconsistent capacities are thus required to serve institutional investors:

1. Size.
2. Agility.

### SIZE

The size criterion alone would qualify a number of additional broker-dealer firms to belong to the SEC's groups of national full line or large investment banks. Why don't they? One possible answer is that although the New York-based and the NYSE regionals do participate in virtually the same markets as investment banking firms (and even at comparable *aggregate* volume), their average transaction size is closer to retail sized than wholesale sized. This difference in emphasis by the more retail-oriented firms, even those deemed to be large in total assets and in equity capital, involves them only occasionally with large-scale trades. In fact, they do their business with a somewhat different clientele than the more institution-oriented firms even though the merchandise traded may be the same for all.

In that sense, then, the difference between wholesale and retail is an analog to the block trader in IBM stock and the retail broker in IBM. Both use the same merchandise trading at similar prices. The big difference is that trade execution takes place in two separate markets for all practical purposes even though the consolidated NYSE tape may print virtually all block transactions.[5]

As a proxy for this proposition, consider the impact of negotiated commissions (since Mayday 1975) on both small-sized and large-scale traders as developed by an SEC study.[6] As shown by the bottom chart in Figure 15-1, commissions on large-scale trades for individual accounts as well as for institutions dropped by about 50 to 60 percent between early 1975 and the end of 1981. Commissions on small-sized trades (200 shares or less) dropped about 20 percent for institutions, while individuals were charged about the same at the beginning and the end of the period for trading less than 200 shares. Finally, institutions always paid less commission (as a share of the total trade) than did individuals, and the relative cost difference was the greater the *smaller* the transaction size. Moreover, comparing transaction costs at the beginning and end of the period studied shows that, for institutions, these costs have receded for all transactions. However, for individuals, transactions costs in the 1980s at the low-sized end are slightly higher than in 1975, while at the upper end, they are slightly lower. The market power of institutions has clearly dominated the establishment of transactions costs; this is borne out especially by direct comparison on the cost/principal value basis shown in the top chart in Figure 15-1.

## AGILITY

The element of the institutional trading process most difficult to illustrate is the ability to place large blocks of securities with institutional buyers without market dislocation. The bond markets, be they for U.S. governments or corporate or foreign issues, are largely institutional and over the counter.[7] As a result, little bond-trading information relevant to institutional transactions[8] is available, implying institutionalization of the markets from structural changes in equity trading.

---

[5] For further discussion of block trading see below.

[6] SEC Directorate of Economic and Policy Analysis, "Commission Rate Trends, 1975–1981" (Washington, D.C.: July 7, 1982), p. 5.

[7] Tax-exempt issues are somewhat less institutionalized, however.

[8] The information regarding bond trading on organized exchanges refers to only a tiny fraction of total transactions.

**FIGURE 15–1**
Effective Commission Rates versus Order Size, April 1975 and 4th
Quarter 1981

A. Commissions as a percent of principal value

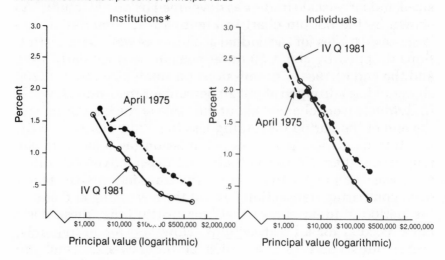

B. Commission cents per share

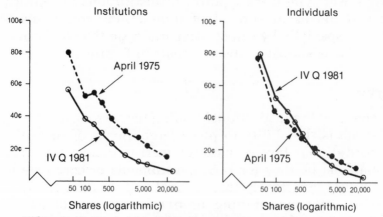

\*Where institutional and individual customers cannot be precisely identified, COD
business is defined as institutional and all other business as individual.

SOURCE: U.S. Securities and Exchange Commission, Directorate of Economic and
Policy Analysis, Survey of Commission Charges on Brokerage Transactions.

Table 15–1 indicates the two major methods of institutional trading performed through the NYSE:

1. Organized secondary offerings and other special methods.
2. Block trades.

The first set of secondaries indicated in the table uses the full panoply of mechanics that makes such offerings similar to a new issue: a formal prospectus is written, a syndicate of investment bankers is formed, and all other requirements of the securities act (as amended) are met. Block trades, on the other hand, are much simpler. A single investment banker (usually) is asked for a bid, and if that bid is deemed satisfactory by the seller,[9] the investment banker takes the responsibility to resell the shares he bid for or place those not sold in inventory.

The data shown in Table 15–1 are revealing. Through 1975, the annual volume of blocks sold came to about three quarters of a billion shares (half a billion in 1974, a recession year). Starting with 1976, block volume grew each year, reaching more than one fourth of all shares sold in 1979 and nearly 50 percent in 1983.

This proposition bears out the general point that the market organization of the NYSE and other exchanges is not necessary to block trading. Further, those wholesale methods crossed on to the retail floor, namely, secondary offerings and other special methods, are no longer a significant factor, while the more or less informal and quick-acting upstairs deals are currently the method of choice for large-scale transactions.

In fact, there is an analog here of instant secondaries—that is, block trades—to instant bond issues developed first through Form S-16 in 1980 and presently institutionalized by Rule 415 shelf registrations. And large upstairs block dealers and major lead underwriters for bonds tend to be the same firms.

## A Case Study

These arguments were brought out in almost textbook fashion by the second-largest block trade ever executed on the NYSE

---

[9] Nearly all block trades are sales.

**TABLE 15-1**
Large-Scale Trades on the NYSE by Secondary Offerings and by Block Trades, 1972–1983
(in number of transactions and by thousands of shares traded; % of total NYSE volume)

| Year | Secondary Offerings | | | Block Trades | | | |
|------|---------------------|--------|--------------|------------------|-----------|-----------------|-----------------|
| | Number of Trades | Shares | Average Size | Number of Trades | Shares | Average Size | % of NYSE Volume |
| 1972 | 154 | 65,067 | 423 | 31,207 | 766,406 | 25 | 18.5 |
| 1973 | 174 | 33,160 | 191 | 29,233 | 721,356 | 25 | 17.8 |
| 1974 | 57 | 7,243 | 127 | 23,200 | 549,387 | 24 | 15.6 |
| 1975 | 73 | 21,257 | 291 | 34,420 | 778,540 | 23 | 16.6 |
| 1976 | 69 | 20,341 | 295 | 47,632 | 1,001,254 | 21 | 18.7 |
| 1977 | 49 | 10,685 | 218 | 54,275 | 1,183,924 | 22 | 22.4 |
| 1978 | 34 | 11,285 | 332 | 75,036 | 1,646,905 | 22 | 22.9 |
| 1979 | 26 | 9,559 | 368 | 97,509 | 2,164,726 | 22 | 26.5 |
| 1980 | 34 | 18,611 | 547 | 133,597 | 3,311,132 | 25 | 29.2 |
| 1981 | 34 | 14,351 | 422 | 145,564 | 3,771,442 | 26 | 31.8 |
| 1982 | 72 | 39,047 | 542 | 254,707 | 6,742,481 | 26 | 41.0 |
| 1983 | 67 | 61,049 | 911 | 363,415 | 9,842,080 | 27 | 45.6 |

SOURCE: New York Stock Exchange, NYSE Fact Book 1984 (New York: 1984).

up to 1983, a deal that produced about $130 million for the seller.

One of the most-confusing and complex takeover-merger deals ever attempted involved, among others, Martin Marietta, the Bendix Corporation, and Allied Corporation (see Chapter 7). The outcome, after much sound and fury, was a takeover of Bendix by Allied. In the Bendix takeover, Allied Corporation acquired a huge block of stock (previously bought by Bendix) of RCA Corporation (5.4 million shares of common and 145,600 shares of preferred) that represented about 7.2 percent of RCA's ownership. Allied did not wish to acquire RCA or even a minority interest in that company—to the contrary, in early 1983, it wanted to reduce the substantial debt ($2.4 billion) it had taken on to finance the Bendix acquisition.

In late February 1983,[10] Allied "retained Oppenheimer & Co., Inc., for financial advice and assistance" but also talked to many other of the largest investment bankers "all of whom were interested in handling the RCA transaction." One of these firms (Lehman Brothers) proposed an underwriting-type deal for the sale of the block because one of the Lehman partners sat on the RCA board, and, in the opinion of legal advisers, a registered deal with SEC approval would be required. This would involve a two-day delay.

Allied decided not to delay. On Wednesday, March 30, the actual transaction crossed the tape as a block at $23.75 per share at 3:22 P.M., a few hours after Salomon Brothers had made a bid for the stock and a few weeks after Oppenheimer had attempted (unsuccessfully) to work the block. According to The New York Times (March 31, 1983), "John Gutfreund, Salomon's chairman, said that the investment house offered to buy the block without having lined up any customers, but strictly on the basis of its recent conviction that the public and institutional appetite for good-quality equities is much greater than we perceived it to be. He said that Salomon had agreed to buy the stock from Allied at 3:15 . . . and, after a blaze of phone calls by its 300-strong sales force, had resold all the common shares by 3:30."

---

[10]The following is based on "The Story Behind The Deal," Investment Dealer Digest, April 12, 1983.

The story further explained that about 90 percent of the buyers were domestic financial institutions, of which none took more than 500,000 shares.

The following client relationships may have been influenced by Salomon's move:

1. Salomon's power as an effective mover of large blocks was clearly enhanced.
2. Its service to Allied in so doing, by providing immediate liquidity to enable Allied to pay down its debt (partly raised to finance the takeover), emphasized point 1.
3. Last—and not least—to RCA the successful dispersion of a large minority position without a major price change helped to reinforce that firm's independence while, at the same time, not raising its cost of capital.

In The New York Times, industry analysts speculated, "Salomon may have earned about $2 million in commissions for its 15 minutes work." Strictly speaking, this is not an accurate statement since Salomon made most of its fee from the bid/ask spread of about 25 cents per share on the block trade. Moreover, the compensation was for risk taking (the risk that during the trade the price would not recede by more than the ¼ point spread) rather than for Salomon's work of making "a blaze of phone calls." Indeed, in the post mortems on the deal, the Investment Dealers Digest quoted an unnamed investment banker to the effect that a trading decision involving over 5 million shares of a firm (RCA) that had "experienced sustained earnings disappointments" included, of course, a sizable capital risk, "especially when you are talking about a risk bid in an open market when everyone is talking [on March 30, 1983] about a market correction."

Competitive forces in the market may take not only the form of providing a cheaper price to win an issue. As this study suggests, there may be competition in risk taking by the size of the transaction, with pricing determined essentially in a parallel (retail) market. The shift away from organized secondary transactions to block trades reflects growing institutionalization or, in operative terms, the demand by potential sellers to execute a trade.

# 16

## Market Making
## and Market Seeking:
## The Other Face of
## Institutionalization

In the half century since the appearance of Berle and Means's work that emphasized the split between corporate control and ownership, its influence has spread to legislation (for example, the Securities Act of 1933 and the Securities and Exchange Act of 1934) and a huge volume of academic work has been generated.[1] One of the best-known academic versions explores agency theory—the conflicts of interest between management and ownership. Fama and Jensen,[2] in a recent recasting of the theory, examined managerial efficiency in decision making by "decomposing" strategic decision making from operations management. In that version, a distinction is made between (a) decision initiation and implementation and (b) decision control through monitoring and choices made among proposals presented. Their argument concludes that, in modern complex organizations, these two functions will be separated. This line of analysis suggests that the internal

---

[1] See, for example, Jensen & Meckling, "Theory of the Firm: Managerial Behavior Agency Costs and Ownership Structure," *Journal of Financial Economics* 3 (1976), pp. 305–60; and R. H. Coase, "The Nature of the Firm," *Economica* 4 (1937).

[2] E. F. Fama and M. Jensen, "Separation of Ownership and Control," *Journal of Law and Economics*, June 1983, pp. 301–26.

organization of large and complex organizations is not only important but has a bearing on their economic performance as well.

## INSTITUTIONAL MARKET USERS: A SEEMING DIGRESSION ON PENSION FUNDS

The argument may be pushed further on the ownership side. The emphasis here is on the proposition that the management of wealth has undergone a split between ownership and management. Decisions regarding institutional portfolios are made by managers of wealth with minimal participation by the owners of wealth. This characteristic of wealth holding can be most readily assessed by a survey of pension funds.[3] By 1980 aggregate assets of *private* plans alone exceeded $400 billion, and *annual* contributions came to $70 billion (about 6 percent of annual wages and salaries).

The growth of these plans, with the related incentives for growth, is not unlike the agency theory story itself. Just as Berle and Means presented their insight into the separation of ownership and management from a long focus dating back to the 18th century, so the theory of employer-financed pension plans has been related by Alice Munnell to " . . . unilaterally provided gratuities that employers offered long-service employees in order to induce them to retire."[4] At present such paternalism has become institutionalized through the tax system because the tax code treats employer contributions more favorably than employee contributions.[5] In effect, this leads to a tax-induced preference for deferred wages to be invested by the employer prior to disbursement to employees, and hence pension plans tend to be *employer* controlled. In turn, that control is sometimes turned over to others, who then succeed

---

[3] The following is based on two important contributions to the literature by Alicia H. Munnell: (a) *The Economics of Private Pensions* (1982 Washington, D.C.: The Brookings Institution); and (b) "Who Should Manage the Assets of Collectively Bargained Plans," Federal Reserve Bank of Boston, *New England Economic Review*, July–August 1983.

[4] Munnell, "Who Should Manage the Assets," p. 20.

[5] Employer contributions and the income earned on them remain untaxed until benefits are distributed to the beneficiary. Conversely, employee contributions may be taxed at the source.

to the management of wealth. Industries that perform wealth-management services are insurance companies, bank trust departments, and investment managers.

Table 16–1 shows the distribution of asset management of employee benefit plans managed by 25 of the most important banks, insurance firms, and investment advisers. In that group, the top 4 are insurance companies, although the 25 break down into roughly similar proportions—about one third for each industry. The question now arises: If the growth of managed pension funds keeps rising, how does the separation of wealth management from wealth ownership influence pension fund governance? Or is there an influence?

Munnell shows the results of a survey (done by Greenwich Research Associates) of the pension managers of the 1,600 largest U.S. corporations to assess investment policies and constraints on these policies. Judged by the proportion of responses, the findings, in order of importance, were:

Constraints on managers:
a. Stock/bond ratio.
b. Minimum rate of return.
c. Limit on real estate investments.
d. Limit on foreign securities.
e. Limit on maximum holdings of one security.
f. Limit on minimum quality rating of any bond.

Discretion retained by managers:
a. Diversification of equities.
b. Volatility of equity portfolio.
c. Average maturity of bonds.
d. Turnover rate of bond portfolio.

Munnell asks the most significant question last, namely, how well have the financial managers done for the owners? She answers that "excessive emphasis on equity investment coupled with low rates of return has resulted in a very poor level of performance for pension portfolios."[6] She attributes these results to portfolio selections "not made solely on the basis of economic criteria," but rather, ". . . in the interests of

---

[6]Munnell, "Who Should Manage the Assets," p. 21.

**TABLE 16-1**

Total Assets and Assets of Employee Benefit Plans Managed by Top 25 Banks, Insurance Companies, and Investment Advisers, January 1983 (in billions)

| Institution | Total Trust Assets | Assets of Employee Benefit Plans |
|---|---|---|
| 1. Equitable Life | $ 45.4 | $ 32.6 |
| 2. Prudential Insurance | 66.7 | 27.4 |
| 3. Aetna Life | 32.1 | 23.9 |
| 4. Metropolitan Life | 50.2 | 21.1 |
| 5. Morgan Guaranty | 39.1 | 19.3 |
| 6. Bankers Trust Co. | 18.8 | 18.8 |
| 7. Travelers/TIMCO | 30.3 | 14.3 |
| 8. Alliance Capital | 13.5 | 13.2 |
| 9. Connecticut General/CIGNA | 28.6 | 12.7 |
| 10. Manufacturers Hanover | 21.6 | 12.6 |
| 11. Citicorp | 19.7 | 12.2 |
| 12. John Hancock | 21.7 | 11.1 |
| 13. State Street Research | 11.3 | 10.1 |
| 14. Jennison Associates | 9.0 | 9.0 |
| 15. Mellon Bank | 13.0 | 8.8 |
| 16. Chase Investors | 12.5 | 8.5 |
| 17. Fayez Sarofim & Co. | 8.8 | 8.5 |
| 18. Capital Guardian Trust | 8.3 | 8.3 |
| 19. Chemical Bank | 11.3 | 8.0 |
| 20. Batterymarch Financial | 8.0 | 7.9 |
| 21. Loomis Sayles | 9.7 | 7.5 |
| 22. Wells Fargo | 10.0 | 7.2 |
| 23. T. Rowe Price | 15.3 | 7.1 |
| 24. State Street Bank | 8.6 | 7.1 |
| 25. Bankers Life | 10.0 | 6.9 |
| Total | $523.5 | $324.1 |

SOURCE: "Investor Advisor Profiles," *Pensions & Investment Age*, April 4, 1983, p. 25.

corporate pension executives and the limited expertise of bank trust departments." This is not an acceptable or even an excusable result since pension fund inflows are generally stable and predictable and outflows are actuarially determined. In short, the corpus of these funds tends to be growing, and their net changes are predictable.

Still more curious is the apparent divergence between the portfolio behavior of life insurance firms on the one hand and banks and investment advisers on the other (see Table 16–2). Munnell blames one part of the difference—namely, banks'

**TABLE 16-2** _____
Distribution of Private Pension Assets Managed by Life Insurers and
Private Pension Assets Managed by Banks and Investment Advisers,
1982 (dollars in billions)

| Type of Assets | Managed by Life Insurers | | Managed by Banks and Investment Advisers | |
|---|---|---|---|---|
| | Amount | Percent | Amount | Percent |
| Cash and deposits | $ 1.8 | 0.8% | $ 12.4 | 3.6% |
| U.S. government securities | 13.3 | 5.9 | 54.5 | 15.8 |
| Corporate and other bonds | 83.1 | 37.0 | 68.2 | 19.8 |
| Stock | 23.8 | 10.6 | 198.6 | 57.6 |
| Mortgages | 56.6 | 25.2 | 4.3 | 1.2 |
| Other assets | 46.1 | 20.5 | 6.9 | 2.0 |
| Total assets | $224.7 | 100.0% | $344.9 | 100.0% |

SOURCE: Board of Governors of the Federal Reserve System. Flow of Funds Acounts.

lack of investments in mortgage-type assets and particularly in
nearly default risk-free envelope issues such as GNMAs—on
the lack of acquaintance with that product. While such an
excuse may be made, it is not a professional response. Among
the major trust companies that manage pension accounts,
some of the same banks mentioned in Table 16-1 are also
important GNMA dealers.[7]

Another example given by Munnell for poor stock portfolio performance cites Schotland's study comparing mutual-
fund performance with pension-fund performance. As Table
16-3 indicates, the comparison is exceedingly unfavorable to
pension-fund portfolios. Schotland attributes that result to the
phenomenon that "the client is the culprit." He argues that
investment managers of pension funds become too tightly
constrained by client guidelines, while the investment policies spelled out in the prospectus proposals of mutual funds
permit their portfolio managers more decision-making scope.

Other attempts at explaining the poor pension performance phenomenon point to too frequent shifts among man-

_____
[7] Perhaps one bank department does not know what the other department is (or is not) doing.

**TABLE 16-3**
Median Rate of Return for Equity Investments of A. G. Becker's Pension Fund Universe and Lipper's Equity Mutual Fund Universe and Percent of Each Sample with Returns below the Standard & Poor's (S&P) Index, 1961–1981 and Selected Subperiods

| Period | Annualized Median Rate of Return | | Percent of Sample with Returns below S&P Index | |
| | A. G. Becker Pension Funds | Lipper Mutual Funds | A. G. Becker Pension Funds | Lipper Mutual Funds |
| --- | --- | --- | --- | --- |
| 1961–1981 | 6.7% | 7.3% | 74% | 44% |
| 1972–1981 | 4.3 | 7.6 | 74 | 41 |
| 1977–1981 | 9.1 | 12.7 | 36 | 15 |
| 1979–1981 | 15.6 | 18.2 | 36 | 22 |
| 1981 | –5.0 | –1.6 | 49 | 33 |

SOURCE: Roy A. Schotland, "Why Mutual Funds Are Top Performers," Pensions & Investment Age, July 20, 1981, p. 13. Updated data provided by Professor Schotland and A. G. Becker, Inc.

agers in a futile attempt to beat average performance. (As in baseball, the cheapest way to appear to be doing something when approaching the cellar is to fire the manager.) And often, replacing one manager with a new one because the latter shows some recent success forces the new manager to continue previously successful investment policies to excess. By receiving too much money, such managers succeed only in bidding up prices as a way of replicating recent performance, which only drives rates of return back toward—or possibly even below—market averages. In Munnell's words, "corporations choosing pension management tend to hire high and fire low."[8] She says, further, " . . . the pursuit of short-term gains has caused corporate managers to engage in speculative timing practices and new untested approaches that promise immediate returns. This type of investment behavior has produced particularly poor results."[9]

In view of the foregoing critiques, the interference with pension wealth administration by corporate officials or the lack of experience with certain sectors of the capital markets by the presumed experts may be the main "culprits" in low performance. In a more general frame, an analysis could be developed using a new application of agency theory to financial, or wealth, management. Considering pensions as deferred wages (and deferred wages *are* wages), then the future pension beneficiary is the "owner" and the current portfolio manager is the "manager." There are two dimensions to this type of separation:

1. The *space* separation of the owner-worker from the policy making (within constraints) of the wealth manager and the added separation of the worker-beneficiary from the corporate official in deciding on:
   a. The portfolio manager.
   b. Change in the portfolio manager.
   c. Changes in the financial management of pension policies.
2. The *time* dimension that separates the current, usually automatic, purchase by the worker of a portfolio man-

---

[8] Munnell, "Who Should Manage the Assets," p. 25.
[9] Ibid., p. 24.

agement service from the pension manager and the eventual receipt of pension benefits based on unknown intermediate rates of return.

The diffuseness of that financial principal-agent relationship is further exacerbated by the fickleness of the connection between corporate trusteeship and its capacity to change agents (called portfolio managers). Some people may also have the misapprehension that the pension corpus representing deferred wages is the employer's contribution and thus not the employee-owner's money, causing further psychological barrier to effective monitoring, control, and so forth. If anything, the availability of the federal Pension Benefit Guaranty Corporation insurance scheme, while it provides some financial backstop, may, by offering psychological comfort, serve to further diffuse the owner-manager relationship.

## AGENCY THEORY: SOME FURTHER IMPLICATIONS

Suppose that pension-fund managers, trust managers, and other wealth managers begin to see that if they manage an increasingly large portion of the country's wealth for the actual owners they themselves, to an increasing extent, become a larger share of the financial market. To paraphrase Pogo, they will have met the market and discover that the market is them. They may even find that simply buying the market may be the only policy by which they can achieve at least average performance.

From this it follows that as their portfolios grow larger, wealth administrators have more rationale to acquire securities from large firms almost exclusively. This must be so for two reasons: (1) When buying more at a time than on average as employment rises, most pension funds would be in the market with a strong, predictable cash flow. (2) Likewise, markets can more readily absorb sell surges without excessively large price declines if sales occur in the more widely distributed security issues of large firms. Put slightly differently, the need to make very large amounts of purchases or sales at any one time forces these large institutions to acquire securities in the largest firms even if they wish to achieve only average performance.

For the wealth managers, in turn, carrying in their portfolios as well as trading a significant share of many of the largest and best-known corporations may make them the largest single owners—at least by proxy—in the original agency context. If a number of institutional investors achieve that position but find it unacceptable to participate in corporate governance, we may have still another and unforeseen split in the ownership-management or agency relationship.[10] If the institutions maintain voting neutrality, it may take a substantially *smaller* share of outside stockholders or takeover interests to achieve a controlling ownership position in even the largest firms. That is to say, the higher the proportion of institutional ownership that does not participate in corporate policy decisions, the lesser the proportion of ownership it takes to control even large corporations. Or, if and when institutions vote *with* management, the more difficult would be the monitoring by noninstitutional owners.

This seeming digression illustrates elements of investment institutionalization to which an important and different application of agency theory may be applied. Given the focus on investment banking, the shift to large-scale activities by investment banking firms in making markets was the necessary counterpart to financial institutionalization. What made that shift technologically feasible was the data-processing revolution that (1) generated enormous scale economies for large transactions and (2) provided further scale economies for information. The direction of that change was supported by tax subsidies to individuals shifting funds to institutional pension management as well as into IRAs and Keogh plans (a *demand-side* phenomenon).

---

[10]Pension fund managers may have several conflicts of interest in voting their shares:

a.  If they do not vote with management, they may lose the pension account.

b.  If they vote with management, a political question may be raised regarding a few pension managers "controlling" the corporate universe.

For a general discussion of this issue, see SEC, *Staff Report on Corporate Accountability*, Senate Committee on Banking, 96th Congress, 2nd Session (1980).

## DEMAND FOR WEALTH MANAGEMENT

The demand-side aspects of the split may be appreciated by examining the wealth management of large institutions. One example is the ownership distribution at year-end 1982 of one major security type, namely, corporate bonds. The three major industry groups held about two thirds of outstandings at the end of 1982, with the remaining eight major holder groups controlling the remaining one third.[11] (See Table 16–4.) What an examination of these and other asset-holding industries indicates is that the ownership-management split is becoming more important.

An even more direct piece of evidence can be found in the growth of large-scale *equity* trades (block trades) reported by the NYSE (see Table 16–5).

As shown by the last line of the table, block trades—the indicator for institutional activity—reached more than 40 percent in 1982. Since most block trades are arranged away from the floor, if the relative growth in that area continues at the present rate, in the space of just a few years the volume of institutional equity trading away from the floor may exceed that done on the floor. That would, of course, make the volume of NYSE stock trading more dealer than auction oriented.

## MERGERS AND PENSION FUND MANAGEMENT

Chapter 7 discussed investment banking firms' participation in mergers and takeovers. At this point it is useful to discuss what appears to be a side-issue, namely, the participation of pension fund managers in corporate governance—another unforeseen by-product of the current merger wave and of institutionalization.

Under the Employee Retirement Income Security Act of 1974 (ERISA), the manager of a pension fund is supposed to make decisions solely to benefit the interest of pension beneficiaries. Because one of the few good bets in merger analysis is

---

[11]Of those groups, the largest two are foreign (official and private at 9 percent) and the residual share presumed to be households (also 9 percent). The holdings of such assets by financial mutuals (discussed by Fama and Jensen) was only about 4 percent.

**TABLE 16-4**
Ownership of Corporate Bonds Year-End 1982 (dollars in billions)

| Ownership Group | Amount | Percentage |
|---|---|---|
| Life insurance companies | $197 | 35% |
| State and local retirement funds | 113 | 20 |
| Private noninsured pension funds | 66 | 12 |
| All others | 188 | 33 |
| Total | $564 | 100% |

SOURCE: Salomon Brothers.

**TABLE 16-5**
NYSE Large Block Transactions, Selected Years, 1968-1982

| Year | Number of Trades | Daily Average | Number of Shares (millions) | Proportion of Total Reported Volume |
|---|---|---|---|---|
| 1968 | 11,254 | 50 | 293 | 10.0 |
| 1973 | 29,233 | 116 | 722 | 17.8 |
| 1976 | 47,632 | 188 | 1,001 | 18.7 |
| 1978 | 75,036 | 298 | 1,647 | 22.9 |
| 1982 | 254,707 | 1,007 | 6,742 | 41.0 |

SOURCE: New York Stock Exchange, NYSE Fact Book 1983 (New York: 1983), p. 70.

that the largest share of GAIN (see Chapter 7) accrues to the *target* firm, pension-fund managers have tended to vote proxies *against* antitakeover amendments. An article in *Institutional Investor*[12] clearly indicates that recently many firms (and their CEOs) have put strong pressure on pension managers to vote *with* the management of target firms. In the words of the article, "Institutional investors generally oppose antitakeover amendments because they would rather sell shares to acquirers at healthy premiums" (p. 145). Of course, such sales also improve the manager's performance rating. The article suggests that antitakeover resolutions are now being passed by wide margins even though in 1985 institutions owned about

[12] "The Proxy Pressure on Pension Managers," *Institutional Investor*, July 1985, pp. 145-47.

75 percent of NYSE-listed stocks. The explanation offered is that a nonfavorable (to management) vote of a large pension-fund holding can be identified and that an implicit, or even explicit, threat to take away the management of the pension fund appears to be sufficient to induce compliance with management's policy rather than with fiduciary responsibility. Some of these reactions " . . . surfaced publicly at hearings that Robert Monks, administrator of the Department of Labor's Pension and Welfare Benefit Programs (PWBP) conducted. . . . [In those hearings] several money managers admitted they were periodically subjected to strong pressure from clients to approve shark repellants." [13]

Institutionalization has led to the need for large-scale trading and large-scale investing—and to large-scale conflicts of interest. The agency conflict now interposes not one but *two* layers of management between the owners (that is, beneficiaries) and the firm's policies. It appears that monitoring even by presumptive government regulators (PWBP) is not very effective. Institutionalization that interposes several layers of equity management between (1) the largely anonymous owners and (2) the corporation's management group has produced a profound change in agency relationships. One could deal with the overly simple assumption of individual owner and individual manager by the usual request for more research. But reality once again suggests otherwise. The knowledgeable players in the merger, takeover, and risk arbitrage games are doing exactly that research as applied to individual firms in the marketplace (see Chapter 7). In effect, that research may provide the most effective, if "hidden-hand," type of monitoring left in the age of institutionalization. And taking this argument one last step, even the possibility of a takeover may help to concentrate the minds of the managements of many listed firms.

## SUPPLY-SIDE FACTORS

Commercial bank trust departments and equity mutual funds (closed or open) have provided wealth management for a long

---

[13] Ibid., p. 147.

time. More recently, variable annuities of every kind further added to the menu of management arrangements offered to wealth owners.[14] In the last decade, still another type of wealth management was offered to wealth owners, the envelope security—that is, the refinancing of existing securities portfolios by a new and transferable instrument that traded separately in its own right. The best known transitional instrument of the management-ownership split is the GNMA bond. Here the management process involved less current management decision making than in more recent innovations, but the mechanism familiarized the public with trading envelope issues.

The true paradigm for the management-ownership split would be the money market mutual fund. That market opened up when short-term rates soared and the SEC permitted, in 1977, a new method of accounting (on a dollar-valuation basis) for money market funds. Within a relatively short period, a number of investment banking firms offered such services—particularly those firms that had strong retail accounts for other services beyond the money market fund. In fact, most supply-side factors relate to retail as opposed to institutional trading. And that retail orientation primarily provides some bank-type functions. Those functions may increasingly differentiate retail-oriented firms from the wholesale-institutional investment bankers whose major function is market making, especially on a large scale. There continues to be many reasons for having both types of firms.

The cash-management account developed by Merrill Lynch and others has had many versions, but in essence, originators also made available a cluster of financial services ancillary to such accounts and their owners. This may, for example, develop clientele loyalty to the extent that new-issue offerings can be made to retail customers in competition with institutional sales. More specifically, substitutes for large-scale institutional blocks in noncorporate issues could use the envelope-security system (otherwise called by names such as investment trusts) as a mechanism for placing new issues or portfolios of existing securities. This does not imply that

---

[14] Beyond this are all the other financial intermediaries, many of whom have recently received broader investment powers.

undesired inventories would thus be laid off by investment bankers since competition among money market funds, and the easy switch of customer assets among them, would require at least average performance as a goal from management.

Beyond this, within an investment banking firm, strong institutional sales and trading departments and equally strong managements of customer assets compete with each other for the scarce resources *within* the firm, namely, capital in human and financial form. It is unlikely that one department of any investment banking firm will assist another to its own detriment either in performance or in the earnings that may be claimed by the partner (or vice president) in charge.[15]

## MARKET SEEKING

This mysterious-seeming notion refers to wealth managers' need to find ways of selling large blocks of securities to make portfolio adjustments. Recall that the proportion of total securities outstanding so managed is rising. Consequently, the desire by wealth managers to sell blocks of stock or bonds of increasing size will occur more frequently and, if there is a drive toward average performance, may lead to large selling waves. In this manner, the switch by individuals to institutional wealth management suggests there will continue to be a decline of small trades whose once large number was more likely to be offsetting than institutional trades tend to be. Thus the rise in institutionalization leads to the rise in investment managers demand for block-trading services in the equity markets and large swaps in the bond markets. In broader terms, then, the separation of wealth management from ownership raises the demand for market-making counterpart services by dealers and an associated rise in institutional-sized risks taken by market makers. The growing need for that type of market-making service will be called market seeking—it is the necessary counterpart to institutionalization of wealth and its management.

---

[15]Even in terms of controlling the firm's capital, it is important to have generally acceptable performance data available to the management committee of the firm.

## PROGRAM TRADING

Still another product of the stock market's institutionalization is the set of hedge vehicles provided by the various exchanges, such as the Standard & Poor's 500 Stock Price Index. The original purpose of providing the index was to permit financial managers to hedge market risk. What was not foreseen was that an appropriately selected set of market stocks, and the hedge vehicle, were nearly perfect substitutes for another and could be used together as arbitrage vehicles. This is how "program trading," as it is called, was born.

In the view of many, program trading breeds volatility, especially when markets reach the "triple witching hour"— that is, the time when options and futures on stock price indexes expire. This occurs on the third Fridays of March, June, September, and December, but it may happen at other times as well. And the mechanism used is the simple short hedge even though the mechanics are complex: traders may buy a set of stocks that mimic the price index (say, the S&P 500) and sell short contracts in S&P 500 index futures. The idea is to profit from the spread because, at the market's close on the third Fridays of March, June, September, and December the spread disappears. If the market rises, the profit from the stocks more than compensates for the short sale of stock price futures; if the market falls, the reverse occurs. This is a classic (and riskless) form of arbitrage, not the risk arbitrage discussed in Chapter 8.

As institutionalization grows, the demand by large investors for market-making services will grow more than proportionately. This is so for the following reasons: In markets with rising prices, market-making services will be provided by a growing number of dealers. Conversely, in a down market, or a down market made more skittish by large selling waves of institutional-sized blocks, fewer market makers will be willing to deal in scale, thereby further widening the amplitude of price variance. At that time, the investment bankers who can survive, and even thrive, in that high-variance environment will be the industry leaders. And those leaders will also be the special-bracket firms in the new-issue market once that market revives after market-price risks decline. Market making is the name of every game.

# 17

## This Is the Last Chapter

But it is not the last word on investment banking. As we have noted in the preceding 16 chapters, because the industry has changed so much over the past 20 years and because it continues to change, no "last word" can ever be written for the hallmark of the industry has been an often swift and sometimes even creative response to change. And while change has been an unwelcome interruption for some firms, industry leaders have learned to accommodate it, and even to thrive. Among the leading firms many have generated change themselves by creating new value-added when the old mechanics or security designs offered returns no better than average.

For example, Table 17–1 lists the first 10 firms in the Department of Justice's 1947 antitrust complaint (in order of importance by percent of new-issue flotations). Perhaps the most useful way of assessing change since then, and the positive responses to change, is a brief review of how the industry has transformed itself. In the years since World War II, few leading firms have maintained their position. From the 1947 set of 10, only 4 remain in a leadership position today (Table 17–2). And among the largest 10

**TABLE 17–1** _____

| | |
|---|---|
| Morgan Stanley & Co. | 16% |
| First Boston Corporation | 13 |
| Dillon, Read & Co., Inc. | 7 |
| Kuhn, Loeb & Co. | 7 |
| Blyth & Co. | 4 |
| Smith, Barney & Co. | 4 |
| Lehman Brothers | 3 |
| Harriman, Ripley & Co., Inc. | 3 |
| Glore, Forgan & Co. | 2 |
| Kidder, Peabody & Co. | 2 |
| Total | 61% |

underwriters of corporate issues in 1985, only 2 of the first 4 firms were in that first leadership group. To be sure, some of the old names appear as part of the 1985 company names, but some have been merged so many times that they have vanished altogether (e.g., Kuhn Loeb).

Still another major organizational change has worked its way through the investment banking industry in the 1980s. Institutionalization of the marketplace has led to the need for financial firms to deal in size—and to deal in size the firms need capital in size. This they have achieved in the 1980s by infusions of funds from other firms (called takeovers in Table 17–3) or by going public.[1] And as Table 17–3 indicates, among the special-bracket firms only Goldman, Sachs & Co. remains organized as a partnership in June 1986.

The conclusion is straightforward: deregulation of financial markets and technological changes have supported the forces that drive the institutionalization of savings and investment.

The speed and cheapness of transaction processes not only permit large-scale trading immediately and at any time, but the process of innovation and the speed of transmission keep changing values in the marketplace. Deregulation of various interest-rate barriers, of barriers to entry, and even of commission levels for transactions have further accelerated the pace of change. And the above holds not just for the U.S. capital market but is increasingly true for

_____

[1] It may be hard to remember that Merrill Lynch was the first NYSE member whose stock was listed, on July 27, 1971.

TABLE 17-2 _____

## Leading Underwriters of Corporate Issues, 1985

| Corporate Underwriters | Flotation Amounts ($ billions) | Position |
|---|---|---|
| Salomon Brothers | $26.4 | 1 |
| First Boston | 20.3 | 2 |
| Merrill Lynch | 16.6 | 3 |
| Goldman Sachs | 15.7 | 4 |
| Drexel Burnham Lambert | 11.5 | 5 |
| Morgan Stanley | 10.0 | 6 |
| Shearson Lehman Brothers | 9.9 | 7 |
| Kidder Peabody | 4.1 | 8 |
| Paine Webber | 3.2 | 9 |
| Smith Barney, Harris Upham | 2.1 | 10 |

SOURCE: _Institutional Investor_, March 1986, p. 155

TABLE 17-3 _____

## Acquired or Publicly Held Firms

| Current Name of Firm | Date | Change in Status |
|---|---|---|
| Prudential-Bache Securities | March 1981 | Takeover |
| Shearson Lehman Brothers | June 1981* | Takeover |
|  | May 1984† | Takeover |
| Dean Witter Reynolds | December 1981 | Takeover |
| Salomon Brothers | March 1982 | Takeover |
| Rooney, Pace Group | October 1983 | Went public |
| Jefferies Group | October 1983 | Went public |
| L. F. Rothschild | March 1986 | Went public |
| Bear Stearns | October 1985 | Went public |
|  | May 1986 | Went public |
| Alex. Brown & Sons | February 1986 | Went public |
| Morgan, Stanley | March 1986 | Went public |
| Kidder, Peabody | May 1986 | Takeover |

*Shearson Loeb Rhodes absorbed by American Express.

†Lehman Brothers Kuhn Loeb absorbed by American Express.

those in other parts of the world. As this is written, trading in Toronto and New York has been consolidated, as has trading on a number of futures markets internationally. Further, as these freer markets develop, so does intermarket trading. Increasingly there is one world capital market in which all of the firms discussed in this book operate as a matter of course and as a strategy for survival. Their actions have been part and parcel of the greater coordination of market forces worldwide.

# Common Investment Banking and Financial Market Terms*

**Accrued interest** Interest due from the issue or from the last coupon date to the present on an interest-bearing security. The buyer of the security pays the quoted dollar price plus accrued interest.

**Active** A market in which there is much trading.

**Add-on rate** A specific rate of interest to be paid (in contrast to the rate on a discount security, such as a Treasury bill, that pays *no* interest).

**After-tax real rate of return** Money after-tax rate of return minus the inflation rate.

**Agencies** Federal agency securities.

**Agent** A firm that executes orders for or otherwise acts on behalf of another (the principal) and is subject to its control and authority. The agent may receive a fee or a commission.

**All-in cost** Total costs, explicit and other. Example: In a swap the all-in cost to a fixed income payer *plus* the pro rata share of flotation costs added to the rate.

---

*This glossary is adapted in part from the glossary in Marcia L. Stigum and Rene O. Branch, Jr., *Managing Bank Assets and Liabilities* (Homewood, Ill.: Dow Jones-Irwin, 1983), pp. 397–418.

**All or none (AON)** Requirement that none of an order be executed unless all of it can be executed at the specified price.

**Annual report** A yearly report to shareholders containing financial statements (balance sheets, income statement, source and application, and funds statement), auditor's statement, president's letter, and various other information.

**Arbitrage** Strictly defined, buying something where it is cheap and selling it where it is dear; for example, a bank buys three-month CD money in the U.S. market and sells three-month money at a higher rate in the Eurodollar market. In the money market, arbitrage often refers: (1) to a situation in which a trader buys one security and sells a similar security in the expectation that the spread in yields between the two instruments will narrow or widen to his profit, (2) to a swap between two similar issues based on an anticipated change in yield spreads, and (3) to situations where a higher return (or lower cost) can be achieved in the money market for one currency by utilizing another currency and swapping it on a fully hedged basis through the foreign exchange market.

**ARM (adjustable rate mortgage)** A type of mortgage in which the interest rate is periodically adjusted as market rates change.

**Arrearage** An overdue payment as in passed preferred dividends. If cumulative, arrearage must be made up before common dividends are resumed.

**Asked price** The price at which securities are offered.

**Auditor's statement** A letter from the auditor to the company and its shareholders in which the accounting firm certifies the propriety of the methods used to produce the firm's financial statements.

**Away** A trade, quote, or market that does not originate with the dealer in question; for example, "the bid is 98–10 away (from me)."

**Back up** (1) When yields rise and prices fall, the market is said to back up. (2) When an investor swaps out of one security into another of shorter current maturity (such as out of a two-year note into an 18-month note), he is said to back up.

**Bank discount rate** Yield basis on which short-term non-interest-bearing money market securities are quoted. A rate quoted on a discount basis understates bond equivalent yield. That must be calculated when comparing return against coupon securities.

**Bank line** A line of credit granted by a bank to a customer.

**Bank wire** A computer message system linking major banks. It is used not for effecting payments but as a mechanism to advise the receiving bank of some action that has occurred, such as the customer's payment of funds into that bank's account.

**Bankers' acceptance (BA)** A draft or bill of exchange accepted by a bank or trust company. The accepting institution guarantees payment of the bill.

**BANs** Bond anticipation notes are issued by states and municipalities to obtain interim financing for projects that will eventually be funded long term through the sale of a bond issue.

**Basis** (1) The number of days in the coupon period. (2) In commodities jargon, basis is the spread between a futures price and some other price. Money market participants talk about spread rather than basis.

**Basis point** One one hundredth of 1 percent.

**Basis price** The price expressed in terms of yield to maturity or annual rate of return.

**Bear market** A declining market or a period of pessimism when declines in the market are anticipated. (A way to remember: "bear down.")

**Bearer security** A security whose owner is not registered on the books of the issuer. A bearer security is payable to the holder.

**Best-efforts basis** Securities dealers do not underwrite a new issue but sell it on the basis of what can be sold.

**Bid price** The price offered for securities.

**Bills** Government debt securities issued on a discount basis by the U.S. Treasury for periods of one year or less (Treasury bills).

**Black/Scholes formula** An option pricing formula based on the assumption that a riskless hedge between an option and its underlying stock should yield the riskless return.

Black/Scholes asserts that option value is a function of the stock price, striking price, stock return volatility, riskless interest rate, and option term.

**Block** A large amount of securities, normally much more than what constitutes a round lot in the market in question. On the NYSE, a trade of 10,000 or more shares.

**Bond** A debt obligation (usually long term) in which the borrower promises to pay a set coupon rate until the issue matures, at which time the principal is repaid. Some bond issues are secured by a mortgage on a specific property, plant, or piece of equipment. See also **Debenture.**

**Bond swap** A technique for managing a bond portfolio by selling some bonds and buying others; may be designed for taxes, yields, or trading profits (also called asset swap).

**Book-entry securities** The Treasury and federal agencies are moving to a book-entry system in which securities are not represented by engraved pieces of paper but are maintained by financial institutions in computerized records of the securities they own as well as those they are holding for customers. In the case of other securities for which there is a book-entry system, engraved securities do exist somewhere in quite a few instances. These securities do not move from holder to holder but are usually kept in a central clearinghouse or by another agent.

**Book value** The value at which a debt security is shown on the holder's balance sheet. Book value is often acquisition cost ± amortization/accretion, which may differ markedly from market value. It can be further defined as "tax book," "accreted book," or "amortized book" value.

**Bridge financing** Interim financing of one sort or another.

**Bracketing** The group of underwriters in a syndication. The major investment banking firms come first, but they can be elsewhere. Other brackets are determined by participating underwriters' size and capacity to place securities.

**Broker** A broker brings buyers and sellers together for a commission paid by the initiator of the transaction or by both sides; he does not position. In the money market, brokers are active in markets in which banks buy and sell money and in interdealer markets.

**Broker call-loan rate or call-loan rate** The interest rate charged by banks for loans brokers use to support their margin loans to customers. The customer's margin loan rate is usually scaled up from the broker call-loan rate.

**Bull market** A period of optimism when increases in market prices are anticipated. (A way to remember: "bull ahead.")

**Buy-back** Another term for a repurchase agreement.

**Calendar** List of new bond issues scheduled to come to market soon.

**Call money** Interest-bearing bank deposits that can be withdrawn on 24-hours notice. Many Eurodeposits take the form of call money.

**Callable bond** A bond that the issuer has the right to redeem prior to maturity by paying some specified call price.

**Call protection** An indenture provision preventing a security (usually a bond or preferred stock) from being redeemed earlier than a certain time after its issue. Thus a 20-year bond might not be callable for the first 5 years after its issue.

**Carry** The interest cost of financing securities held. (See also **Negative carry** and **Positive carry.**)

**Cash flow** Reported profits plus depreciation, depletion, and amortization.

**Cash market** Traditionally, this term has been used to denote the market in which commodities were traded, for immediate delivery, against cash. Since the inception of futures markets for T bills and other debt securities, a distinction has been made between the cash markets in which these securities trade for immediate delivery and the futures markets in which they trade for future delivery.

**Cash settlement** In the money market, a transaction is said to be made for cash settlement if the securities purchased are delivered against payment in Fed funds on the same day the trade is made.

**CAPM (Capital Asset Pricing Model)** A theoretical relationship that explains returns as a function of the risk-free rate and market risk.

**Certificate of deposit (CD)** A time deposit with a specific maturity evidenced by a certificate. Large-denomination CDs are typically negotiable.

**CHIPS** The New York Clearing House's computerized Clearing House Interbank Payments System. Most Euro transactions are cleared and settled through CHIPS rather than over the Fed wire.

**Circle**   Underwriters, actual or potential as the case may be, often seek out and "circle" retail interest in a new issue before final pricing. The customer circled has basically made a commitment to purchase the note or bond or to purchase it if it comes at an agreed-on price. In the latter case, if the price is other than that stipulated, the customer supposedly has first offer at the actual price.

**Clear**   A trade carried out by the seller delivering securities and the buyer delivering funds in proper form. A trade that does not clear is said to fail.

**Clearinghouse funds**   Payments made through the New York Clearing House's computerized Clearing House Interbank Payments System. Clearinghouse debits and credits used to be settled in Fed funds on the first business day after clearing. Since October 1981, these debits and credits have been settled on the same day in Fed funds.

**Collateral**   An asset pledged to assure repayment of debt.

**Commercial paper**   An unsecured promissory note with a fixed maturity of no more than 270 days. Commercial paper is normally sold at a discount from face value.

**Commissions**   Fees charged by brokers for handling security trades.

**Committed facility (line of credit)**   A legal commitment undertaken by a bank to lend to a customer.

**Competitive bid**   (1) A bid tendered in a Treasury auction for a specific amount of securities at a specific yield or price. (2) Issuers such as municipal and public utilities often sell new issues by asking for competitive bids from one or more syndicates.

**Confirmation**   A memorandum to the other side of a trade describing all relevant data.

**Compound interest**   Returns are compounded by reinvesting one period's income to earn additional income the following period. Thus at 9 percent compounded annually, $100 will yield $9 the first year. In the following year, the 9 percent will be computed on $109 for a return of $9.81. In the third year the principal will have grown to $118.81 (100 + 9 + 9.81), and another 9 percent will add about $10.62. This process continues with the interest being applied to a larger and larger principal. Compounding may take place annually, as above, or more frequently.

**Compound value**   The end-period value of a sum earning a compounded return.

**Consortium banks**   A merchant banking subsidiary set up by several banks that may or may not be of the same nationality. Consortium banks are common in the Euromarket and are active in loan syndication.

**Convertible bond**   A bond containing a provision that permits conversion to the issuer's common stock at some fixed exchange ratio.

**Corporate bond equivalent**   See **Equivalent bond yield.**

**Corporate taxable equivalent**   The rate of return required on a par bond to produce the same after-tax yield to maturity that the premium or discount bond quoted would.

**Country risk**   See **Sovereign risk.**

**Coupon**   (1) The annual rate of interest on the bond's face value that a bond's issuer promises to pay the bondholder. (2) A certificate attached to a bond evidencing interest due on a payment date.

**Cover**   Eliminating a short position by buying the securities shorted.

**Covered interest arbitrage**   Investing dollars in an instrument denominated in a foreign currency and hedging the resulting foreign exchange risk by selling the proceeds of the investment forward for dollars.

**Credit risk**   The risk that an issuer of debt securities or a borrower may default on his obligations or that payment may not be made on the sale of a negotiable instrument. (See **Overnight delivery risk.**)

**Cross hedge**   Hedging a risk in a cash market security by buying or selling a futures contract for a different but similar instrument.

**CRTs**   Abbreviation for the cathode-ray tubes used to display market quotes.

**Current coupon**   A bond selling at or close to par; that is, a bond with a coupon close to the yield currently offered on new bonds of similar maturity and credit risk.

**Current issue**   In Treasury bills and notes, the most recently auctioned issue. Trading is more active in current issues than in off-the-run issues.

**Current maturity**   Current time to maturity on an outstanding note, bond, or other money market instrument; for example, a five-year note one year after issue has a current maturity of four years.

**Current yield**   Coupon payments on a security as a percentage of the security's market price. In many instances, the price should be gross of accrued interest, particularly on instruments where no coupon is left to be paid until maturity.

**Cushion bonds**   High-coupon bonds that sell at only a moderate premium because they are callable at a price below that at which a comparable noncallable bond would sell. Cushion bonds offer considerable downside protection in a falling market.

**Day trading**   Intraday trading in securities for profit as opposed to investing for profit.

**Dealer**   A dealer, as opposed to a broker, acts as a principal in all transactions, buying and selling for his own account.

**Dealer loan**   Overnight, collateralized loan made to a dealer financing his position by borrowing from a money market bank.

**Debenture**   A bond secured only by the general credit of the issuer.

**Debt leverage**   The amplification in the return earned on equity funds when an investment is financed partly with borrowed money.

**Debt securities**   IOUs created through loan-type transactions—commercial paper, bank CDs, bills, bonds, and other instruments.

**Default**   Failure to make timely payment of interest or principal on a debt security or to otherwise comply with the provisions of a bond indenture.

**Demand line of credit**   A bank line of credit that enables a customer to borrow on a daily or an on-demand basis.

**Direct paper**   Commercial paper sold directly by the issuer to investors.

**Direct placement**   Selling a new issue not by offering it for sale publicly but by placing it with one or several institutional investors.

**Discount basis**   See **Bank discount rate**.

**Discount bond**   A bond selling below par.

**Discount paper**   See **Discount securities.**

**Discount rate**   The rate of interest charged by the Fed to member banks that borrow at the discount window. The discount rate is an add-on rate.

**Discount securities**   Non-interest-bearing money market instruments that are issued at a discount and redeemed at maturity for full face value; for example, U.S. Treasury bills.

**Discount window**   A facility provided by the Fed enabling member banks to borrow reserves against collateral in the form of governments or acceptable paper.

**Disintermediation**   The investing of funds that would normally have been placed with a bank or other financial intermediary directly into debt securities issued by ultimate borrowers; for example, into bills or bonds.

**Distributed**   After a Treasury auction, there will be many new issues in dealers' hands. As those securities are sold to retail, the issue is said to be distributed.

**Diversification**   Dividing investment funds among a variety of securities offering independent returns.

**DM**   Deutsche (German) marks.

**Documented discount notes**   Commercial paper backed by normal bank lines plus a letter of credit from a bank stating that it will pay off the paper at maturity if the borrower does not. Such paper is also referred to as LOC (letter of credit) paper.

**Dollar bonds**   Municipal revenue bonds for which quotes are given in dollar prices. Not to be confused with U.S. Dollar bonds, a common term of reference in the Euro bond market.

**Dollar price of a bond**   The percentage of face value at which a bond is quoted.

**Don't know (DK, DKed)**   "Don't know the trade"—a street expression used whenever one party lacks knowledge of a trade or receives conflicting instructions from the other party (for example, with respect to payment).

**Due bill**   An instrument evidencing the obligation of a seller to deliver securities sold to the buyer. Occasionally used in the bill market.

**Dun & Bradstreet**   A firm that rates the creditworthiness of many borrowers and generates financial ratios on many industry groups.

**Duration**   The weighed average rate of return of a bond's principal and interest.

**Dutch auction**   An auction in which the lowest price necessary to sell the entire offering becomes the price at which all securities offered are sold. This technique has been used in Treasury auctions.

**Earnings per common share (EPS)**   The net income of a company—minus any preferred dividend requirements—divided by the number of outstanding common shares.

**Effective (or going effective)**   The SEC has finished examination of the offering statement and will permit the deal to take place.

**Efficient-market hypothesis**   The theory that the market correctly prices securities in light of the known relevant information. In its weak form, the hypothesis implies that past price and volume data (technical analysis) cannot be profitably used in stock selection. The semistrong form implies that no superior manipulation of public data can improve stock selection. In the hypothesis' strong form, even inside (nonpublic) information is thought to be reflected accurately in prices.

**Eligible bankers' acceptances**   In the BA market an acceptance may be referred to as eligible because it is acceptable by the Fed as collateral at the discount window and/or because the accepting bank can sell it without incurring a reserve requirement.

**Equity**   Net worth; assets minus liabilities. The stockholder's residual ownership position.

**Equivalent bond yield**   The annual yield on a short-term, non-interest-bearing security calculated so as to be comparable to yields quoted on coupon securities.

**Equivalent taxable yield**   The yield on a taxable security that would leave the investor with the same after-tax return he would earn by holding a tax-exempt municipal; for example, for an investor taxed at a 50 percent marginal rate, equivalent taxable yield on a muni note issued at 3 percent would be 6 percent.

**ERISA (Employee Retirement Income Security Act)**   A 1974 federal law that protects workers' pension funds.

**Euro bonds**   Bonds issued in Europe outside the confines of any national capital market. A Euro bond may or may not be denominated in the currency of the issuer.

**Euro CDs**   CDs issued by a U.S. bank branch or foreign bank located outside the United States. Almost all Euro CDs are issued in London.

**Euro lines**   Lines of credit granted by banks (foreign or foreign branches of U.S. banks) for Eurocurrencies.

**Eurocurrency deposits**   Deposits made in a bank or bank branch that is not located in the country in whose currency the deposit is denominated. Dollars deposited in a London bank are Eurodollars; German marks deposited there are Euromarks.

**Eurodollars**   U.S. dollars deposited in a U.S. bank branch or a foreign bank outside the United States.

**Exchange rate**   The price at which one currency trades for another.

**Exempt securities**   Instruments exempt from the registration requirements of the Securities Act of 1933 or the margin requirements of the Securities and Exchange Act of 1934. Such securities include governments, agencies, municipal securities, commercial paper, and private placements.

**Extension swap**   Extending maturity through a swap; for example, selling a two-year note and buying one with a slightly longer current maturity.

**Face value**   The maturity value of a bond or other debt instrument; sometimes referred to as the bond's par value.

**Fail**   A trade is said to fail if on settlement date either the seller fails to deliver the securities in proper form or the buyer fails to deliver the funds in proper form.

**FDIC (Federal Insurance Deposit Corporation)**   A federal agency that insures deposits at commercial banks up to $100,000.

**Fed funds**   See **Federal funds.**

**Fed (The Federal Reserve System)**   The federal government agency that exercises monetary policy through its control over banking system reserves.

**Federal Reserve Board of Governors**   The governing body of the Federal Reserve System. The seven members are appointed by the president for long and staggered terms.

**Fed wire**   A computer system linking member banks to the Fed; used for making interbank payments of Fed funds and for making deliveries of and payments for Treasury and agency securities.

**Federal credit agencies**  Agencies of the federal government set up to supply credit to various classes of institutions and individuals; for example, S&Ls, small business firms, students, farmers, farm cooperatives, and exporters.

**Federal Deposit Insurance Corporation (FDIC)**  A federal institution that insures bank deposits, currently up to $100,000 per deposit.

**Federal funds**  (1) Non-interest bearing deposits held by member banks at the Federal Reserve. (2) Used to denote "immediate available" funds in the clearing sense.

**Federal funds rate**  The rate of interest at which Fed funds are traded. This rate is influenced by the Federal Reserve through open-market operations.

**Federal Home Loan Banks (FHLB)**  The institutions that regulate and lend to savings and loan associations. The Federal Home Loan Banks play a role analogous to that played by the Federal Reserve banks vis-à-vis member commercial banks.

**Firm**  Refers to an order to buy or sell that can be executed without confirmation for some fixed period.

**Fixed dates**  In the Euromarket the standard periods for which Euros are traded (one month out to a year) are referred to as the fixed dates.

**Fixed pricing**  The way an IPO is priced. The night before the offering the managing underwriters price the deal. The underwriters up to a certain time after the deal is priced each have the right to reject being an underwriter.

**Fixed-rate loan**  A loan on which the rate paid by the borrower is fixed for the life of the loan.

**Flat trades**  (1) A bond in default trades flat; that is, the price quoted covers both principal and unpaid accrued interest. (2) Any security that trades without accrued interest or at a price that includes accrued interest is said to trade flat.

**Floating-rate note**  A note that pays an interest rate tied to current money market rates. The holder may have the right to demand redemption at par on specified dates.

**Floating supply**  The amount of securities believed to be available for immediate purchase; that is, in the hands of dealers and investors wanting to sell.

**Flower bonds**   Government bonds that are acceptable at par in payment of federal estate taxes when owned by the decedent at the time of death.

**Footings**   A British expression for the bottom line of an institution's balance sheet; total assets equal total liabilities plus net worth.

**Foreign bond**   A bond issued by a nondomestic borrower in the domestic capital market.

**Foreign exchange rate**   The price at which one currency trades for another.

**Foreign exchange risk**   The risk that a long or short position in a foreign currency might, due to an adverse movement in the relevant exchange rate, will have to be closed out at a loss. The long or short position may arise out of a financial or commercial transaction.

**Forward Fed funds**   Fed funds traded for future delivery.

**Forward market**   A market in which participants agree to trade some commodity, security, or foreign exchange at a fixed price at some future date.

**Forward rate**   The rate at which forward transactions in some specific maturity are being made; for example, the dollar price at which DM can be bought for delivery three months hence.

**Free reserves**   Excess reserves minus member bank borrowings at the Fed.

**Full-coupon bond**   A bond with a coupon equal to the going market rate and consequently selling at or near par.

**Futures market**   A market in which contracts for future delivery of a commodity or a security are bought and sold.

**Gap**   A mismatch between the maturities of a bank's assets and liabilities.

**Gapping**   Mismatching the maturities of a bank's assets and liabilities, usually by borrowing short and lending long.

**General obligation bond**   Municipal securities secured by the issuer's pledge of its full faith, credit, and taxing power.

**Give up**   The loss in yield that occurs when a block of bonds is swapped for another block of lower-coupon bonds. Can also be applied to the sharing of commission income by one broker with another (pre-1975).

**Glass-Steagall Act**   A 1933 federal act requiring the separation of commercial and investment banking.

**GNMA (Government National Mortgage Association)**   A government agency that provides special assistance on selected types of mortgages. Its securities are backed both by its mortgage portfolios and by the general credit of the government.

**Go-around**   When the Fed offers to buy securities, to sell securities, to do repos, or to do reverses, it solicits competitive bids or offers, as the case may be, from all primary dealers. This procedure is known as a go-around.

**Golden parachute**   A very generous termination agreement for upper management; takes effect if control of the firm shifts.

**Good delivery**   A delivery in which everything—endorsement, any necessary attached legal papers, and so on—is in order.

**Governments**   Negotiable U.S. Treasury securities.

**Green Shoe**   Overallotment option granted by the company to the managing underwriter to purchase an additional 10 to 15 percent of the offering if needed. This option has to be exercised less than eight days after the deal. For IPOs there is a Green Shoe option in almost every deal. This gives the manager extra flexibility in creating the proper environment for the offering.

**Greenmail**   The practice of acquiring a large percentage of a firm's stock and then threatening to take over the firm unless management buys you out at a premium.

**Gross spread**   The difference between the price that the issuer receives for its securities and the price that investors pay for them. This spread equals the selling concession plus the management and underwriting fees.

**Haircut**   Wall Street jargon for ratio of equity capital (relative to borrowed funds) required of members of organized exchanges. That ratio rises with the riskiness of the assets held. The ratio is set by self-regulating organizations for their members.

**Handle**   The whole-dollar price of a bid or offer is referred to as the handle. For example, if a security is quoted 101-10 bid and 101-11 offered, 101 is the handle. Traders are assumed to know the handle, so a trader would quote that market to another by saying he was at 10-11. (The 10 and 11 refer to 32nds.)

**Hedge**   To reduce risk (1) by taking a position in futures equal and opposite to an existing or anticipated cash position or (2) by shorting a security similar to one in which a long position has been established.

**Histogram**   A bar chart displaying a probability distribution in which the assigned probabilities add up to 100 percent.

**Hit**   A dealer who agrees to sell at the bid price quoted by another dealer is said to hit that bid.

**In the box**   This means that a dealer has a wire receipt for securities indicating that effective delivery on them has been made. This jargon is a holdover from the time when Treasuries took the form of physical securities and were stored in a rack.

**Indenture of a bond**   A legal statement spelling out the obligations of the bond issuer and the rights of the bondholder.

**Insider trading**   Buying or selling by persons having access to nonpublic information relating to the company in question.

**Institutional pot**   That portion of the underwriting that has been set aside to satisfy the demands from major institutional investors.

**Interest rate exposure**   Risk of gain or loss to which an institution is exposed due to possible changes in interest-rate levels.

**IPO**   Initial public offering.

**Joint account**   An agreement between two or more firms to share risk and financing responsibility in purchasing or underwriting securities.

**Junk bonds**   High-risk bonds that have low credit ratings or are in default.

**Keogh account**   A retirement account that allows self-employed individuals to set aside (1984) up to $30,000 or 20 percent of their income into a tax-sheltered fund.

**Lettered stock**   Newly issued stock sold at a discount to large investors prior to a public offering of the same issue.

Lettered stock buyers agree not to sell their shares for a prespecified period. SEC Rule 144 restricts such sales.

**Leverage**   See **Debt leverage.**

**Leveraged lease**   The lessor provides only a minor portion of the cost of the leased equipment, borrowing the rest from another lender.

**LIBOR**   The London Interbank Offered Rate on Eurodollar deposits traded between banks. There is a different LIBOR rate for each deposit maturity. Different banks may quote slightly different LIBOR rates because they use different reference banks.

**Lifting a leg**   Closing out one side of a long-short arbitrage before the other is closed.

**Line of credit**   An arrangement by which a bank agrees to lend to the line holder during some specified period any amount up to the full amount of the line.

**Liquidity**   A liquid asset is one that can be converted easily and rapidly into cash without a substantial loss of value. In the money market, a security is said to be liquid if the spread between the bid and asked prices is narrow and reasonable size can be done at those quotes.

**Liquidity diversification**   Investing in a variety of maturities to reduce the price risk to which holding long bonds exposes the investor.

**Liquidity risk**   In banking, the risk that monies needed to fund may not be available in sufficient quantities at some future date. Implies an imbalance in committed maturities of assets and liabilities.

**Long**   (1) Owning a debt security, stock, or other asset. (2) Owning more than one has contracted to deliver.

**Long bonds**   Bonds with a long current maturity.

**Long coupons**   (1) Bonds or notes with a long current maturity. (2) A bond on which one of the coupon periods, usually the first, is longer than the others or longer than standard.

**Long hedge**   The purchase of a futures contract to lock in the yield at which the person stands ready to buy and sell.

**Make a market**   A dealer is said to make a market when he quotes bid and offered prices at which he stands ready to buy and sell (i.e., price making).

**Manager bills and delivers**   The managing underwriter actually confirms the securities sold on behalf of the other underwriters and delivers the new stock for those underwriters. The buyer only receives one piece of paper rather than 100 different pieces of paper with orders on them.

**Manager and co-manager**   The manager's responsibility is to control the books, road shows, and prospectus. The co-manager might only have one responsibility and that is to sell X amount of stock.

**Margin**   Borrowing to finance a portion of a securities purchase. The Fed regulates the extent of margin borrowing by setting the margin rate (according to Regulations T and U). If a 60 percent rate is set, $10,000 worth of stock may be purchased with up to $4,000 of borrowed money. Only listed and some large OTC companies' securities qualify for margin loans.

**Marginal tax rate**   The tax rate that would have to be paid on an additional dollar of taxable income earned.

**Market value**   The price at which a security is trading and could presumably be purchased or sold.

**Marketability**   A negotiable security is said to have good marketability if there is an active secondary market in which it can easily be resold.

**Mark-to-market**   Practice of recomputing equity position in a margin account (stock or futures) on a daily basis. May also refer to bond valuation as rates change.

**Merchant bank**   A British term for a bank that specializes not in lending out its own funds but in providing various financial services such as accepting bills arising out of trade, underwriting new issues, and providing advice on acquisitions, mergers, foreign exchange, and portfolio management.

**Mismatch**   A mismatch between the interest rate maturities of a bank's assets and liabilities. See also **Gap** and **Unmatched book**.

**Money market**   The market in which short-term debt instruments (such as bills, commercial paper, and bankers' acceptances) are issued and traded.

**Money market (center) bank**   A bank that is one of the nation's largest and consequently plays an active and important role in every sector of the money market.

**Money market fund**  A mutual fund that invests solely in money market instruments.

**Money rate of return**  The annual money return as a percentage of asset value.

**Money supply definitions currently used by the Fed**
  M-1:  Currency plus demand deposits and other checkable deposits.
  M-2:  M-1 plus overnight RPs and money market funds and savings and small (less than $100,000) time deposits.
  M-3:  M-2 plus large time deposits and term RPs.

**Mortgage-backed security**  A debt instrument representing a share of, for example, GNMA pass-throughs, or backed by FNMA bonds; a pool of mortgages.

**Mortgage bond**  A bond secured by a lien on property, equipment, or other real assets.

**Multicurrency clause**  Such a clause on a Euro loan permits the borrower to switch from one currency to another on a rollover date.

**Municipal (muni) notes**  Short-term notes issued by municipalities in anticipation of tax receipts, proceeds from a bond issue, or other revenues.

**Municipals**  Securities issued by state and local governments and their agencies.

**Naked position**  A long or short position that is not hedged.

**NASD (National Association of Security Dealers)**  The self-regulator of the OTC market and umbrella group for all broker-dealers.

**NASDAQ (National Association of Security Dealers Automated Quotations)**  The name applied to stock quotation machines of NASD.

**National banks**  National banks are federally chartered banks that are subject to supervision by the Comptroller of the Currency. State banks, in contrast, are state chartered and state regulated.

**Negative carry**  The net cost incurred when the cost of carry exceeds the yield on the securities being financed.

**Negotiable certificate of deposit**  A large-denomination (generally $1 million) CD that can be sold but cannot be cashed in before maturity.

**Negotiated sale**  A situation in which the terms of an offering are determined by negotiation between the issuer and the underwriter rather than through competitive bidding by underwriting groups.

**New-issues market**  The market in which a new issue of securities is first sold to investors.

**New money**  In a Treasury refunding, the amount by which the par value of the securities offered exceeds that of those maturing.

**Noncompetitive bid**  In a Treasury auction, bidding for a specific amount of securities at the price, whatever it may turn out to be, equal to the average price of the accepted competitive bid.

**Nonperforming loan**  A loan on which interest is not paid as it accrues. Since banks are examined only periodically, a nonperforming loan may or may not be classified.

**Note**  Coupon issues with a relatively short original maturity are often called notes. Muni notes, however, have maturities ranging from a month to a year and pay interest only at maturity. Treasury notes are coupon securities that have an original maturity of up to 10 years.

**NOW (negotiable order of withdrawal) accounts**  These amount to checking accounts on which depository institutions (banks and thrifts) may pay a rate of interest.

**Odd lot**  Less than a round lot.

**Off-the-run issue**  In Treasuries and agencies, an issue that is not included in dealer or broker runs. With bills and notes, normally only current issues are quoted.

**Offer**  Price asked by a seller of securities.

**One-sided (one-way) market**  A market in which only one side, the bid or the asked, is quoted or firm.

**Open book**  See **Unmatched book.**

**Open repo**  A repo with no definite term. The agreement is made on a day-to-day basis, and either the borrower or the lender may choose to terminate. The rate paid is higher than on an overnight repo and is subject to adjustment if rates move.

**Opportunity cost**  The cost of pursuing one course of action measured in terms of the forgone return offered by the most-attractive alternative.

**Option**  (1) **Call option:**  A contract sold for a price that gives the holder the right to buy from the writer of the option, over a specified period, a specified amount of securities at a specified price. (2) **Put option:** A contract sold for a price that gives the holder the right to sell to the writer of the contract, over a specified period, a specified amount of securities at a specified price.

**Original maturity** The maturity at issue. For example, a five-year note has an original maturity at issue of five years; one year later it has a current maturity of four years.

**Over-the-counter (OTC) market** Market created by dealer trading as opposed to the auction market prevailing on organized exchanges.

**Overnight delivery risk** A risk brought about because differences in time zones between settlement centers require that payment or delivery on one side of a transaction be made without knowing until the next day whether funds have been received in account on the other side. Particularly apparent where delivery takes place in Europe for payment of dollars in New York.

**Pac-Man defense** A tactic used to avoid takeover by attempting to take over the attacking firm.

**Paper** Money market instruments, commercial paper, and other.

**Paper gain (loss)** Unrealized capital gain (loss) on securities held in portfolio, based on a comparison of current market price and original cost.

**Par** (1) Price of 100 percent. (2) The principal amount at which the issuer of a debt security contracts to redeem that security at maturity, *face value*.

**Par bond** A bond selling at par.

**Pass-through** A mortgage-backed security on which payment of interest and principal on the underlying mortgages are passed through to the security holder by an agent.

**Paydown** In a Treasury refunding, the amount by which the par value of the securities maturing exceeds that of those sold.

**Pay-up** (1) The loss of cash resulting from a swap into higher-price bonds. (2) The need (or willingness) of a bank or other borrower to pay a higher rate to get funds.

**P/E ratio** The stock price relative to the most recent 12-month earnings per share.

**Pickup** The gain in yield that occurs when a block of bonds is swapped for another block of higher-coupon bonds.

**Picture**   The bid and asked prices quoted by a broker for a given security.

**Placement**   A bank depositing Eurodollars with or selling Eurodollars to another bank is often said to be making a placement.

**Plus**   Dealers in governments normally quote bids and offers in 32nds. To quote a bid or offer in 64ths, they use pluses; for example, a dealer who bids 4 + is bidding the handle plus $4/32$ + $1/64$, which equals the handle plus 9/64.

**PNs**   Project notes are issued by municipalities to finance federally sponsored programs in urban renewal and housing. They are guaranteed by the U.S. Department of Housing and Urban Development.

**Point**   (1) 100 basis points = 1 percent. (2) One percent of the face value of a note or bond. (3) In the foreign exchange market, the lowest level at which the currency is priced. Example: One point is the difference between sterling prices of $1.8080 and $1.8081.

**Poison pill**   An antitakeover defense in which a new diluting security is issued to existing shareholders if control of the firm is about to shift.

**Portfolio**   The collection of securities held by an investor.

**Position**   (1) To go long or short in a security. (2) The amount of securities owned (long position) or owed (short position).

**Positive carry**   The net gain earned when the cost of carry is less than the yield on the securities being financed.

**Preemptive rights**   Shareholder rights to maintain their proportional share of their firm by subscribing proportionally to any new stock issue.

**Premium**   (1) The amount by which the price of an issue being traded exceeds the issue's par value. (2) The amount that must be paid in excess of par to call or refund an issue before maturity. (3) In money market parlance, the fact that a particular bank's CDs trade at a rate higher than others of its class or that a bank has to pay up to acquire funds.

**Premium bond**   A bond selling above par.

**Prepayment**   A payment made ahead of the scheduled payment date.

**Present value**   The value of a future sum or sums discounted by the appropriate discount rate, or factor (D.F.).

**Presold issue**   An issue that is sold out before the coupon announcement.

**Price risk**   The risk that a debt security's price may change due to a rise or fall in the going level of interest rates.

**Prime rate**   The rate at which banks lend to their best (prime) customers. The all-in cost of a bank loan to a prime credit equals the prime rate plus the cost of holding compensating balances.

**Principal**   (1) The face amount or par value of a debt security. (2) A person who acts as a dealer buying and selling for his own account.

**Private placement**   An issue that is offered to a single or a few investors as opposed to being publicly offered. Private placements do not have to be registered with the SEC.

**Prospectus**   A detailed statement prepared by an issuer and filed with the SEC prior to the sale of a new issue. The prospectus gives detailed information on the issue's condition and prospects.

**Put**   See **Option.**

**Put bond**   A bond with an indenture provision allowing it to be sold back to the issuer at a prespecified price.

**RANs (Revenue anticipation notes**   These are issued by states and municipalities to finance current expenditures in anticipation of the future receipt of nontax revenues.

**Rate risk**   In banking, the risk that profits may decline or losses occur because a rise in interest rates forces up the cost of funding fixed-rate loans or other fixed-rate assets.

**Ratings**   An evaluation given by Moody's, Standard & Poor's, Fitch, or other rating services of a security's credit worthiness.

**Real market**   The bid and offer prices at which a dealer could do size. Quotes in the brokers' market may reflect not the real market but pictures painted by dealers playing trading games.

**Reallowance**   On a new issue distribution, members of the NASD may buy and sell from each other at the reallowance concession. NASD members are able to buy and sell securities at a discount from one another.

**Red herring**  A preliminary prospectus containing all the information required by the Securities and Exchange Commission except the offering price and coupon of a new issue.

**Refunding**  Redemption of securities by funds raised through the sale of a new issue.

**Registered bond**  A bond whose owner is registered with the issuer.

**Regular-way settlement**  In the money and bond markets, the regular basis on which some security trades are settled is that delivery of the securities purchased is made against payment in Fed funds on the day following the transaction.

**Registration statement**  A statement that must be filed with the SEC before a security is offered for sale. The statement must contain all materially relevant information relating to the offering. A similar type of statement is required when a firm's shares are listed.

**Regulation Q**  A Fed rule that limits interest rates that bank and thrifts can pay on certain types of deposits/investments. Deregulation has largely eliminated the regulation's effect.

**Regulation T**  A Fed rule that governs credit to brokers and dealers for security purchases.

**Regulation U**  A Fed rule that governs margin credit limits.

**Reinvestment rate**  (1) The rate at which an investor assumes interest payments made on a debt security can be reinvested over the life of that security. (2) The rate at which funds from a maturity or sale of a security can be reinvested. Often used in comparison to give-up yield.

**Relative value**  The attractiveness—measured in terms of risk, liquidity, and return—of one instrument relative to another or for a given instrument of one maturity relative to another.

**Reopen an issue**  The Treasury, when it wants to sell additional securities, will occasionally sell more of an existing issue (reopen it) rather than offer a new issue.

**Repo**  See **Repurchase agreement.**

**Repurchase agreement (RP or repo)**   A holder of securities sells these securities to an investor with an agreement to repurchase them at a fixed price on a fixed date. The security buyer in effect lends the seller money for the period of the agreement, and the terms of the agreement are structured to compensate him for this. Dealers use RP extensively to finance their positions. Exception: When the Fed is said to be doing RP, it is lending money; that is, increasing bank reserves.

**Reserve requirements**   The percentages of different types of deposits that member banks are required to hold on deposit at the Fed, or in currency.

**Retail**   Individual and institutional customers as opposed to dealers and brokers.

**Revenue bond**   A municipal bond secured by revenue from tolls, user charges, or rents derived from the facility financed.

**Reverse**   See **Reverse repurchase agreement.**

**Reverse repurchase agreement**   Most typically, a repurchase agreement initiated by the lender of funds. Reverses are used by dealers to borrow securities they have shorted. Exception: When the Fed is said to be doing reverses, it is borrowing money; that is, absorbing reserves.

**Revolver**   See **Revolving line of credit.**

**Revolving line of credit**   A bank line of credit on which the customer pays a commitment fee and can take down and repay funds according to his needs. Normally the line involves a firm commitment from the bank for a period of several years.

**Right**   A security allowing shareholders to acquire new stock at a prespecified price over a prespecified period. Rights are generally issued proportional to the number of shares currently held and are normally exercisable at a specified price, usually below the current market. Rights usually trade in a secondary market after they are issued.

**Risk**   The degree of uncertainty of the return on an asset.

**Risk arbitrage**   Taking offsetting positions in the securities of an acquisition candidate and its would-be acquirer.

**Roll over**   Reinvest funds received from a maturing security in a new issue of the same or a similar security.

**Rollover**   Most term loans in the Euromarket are made on a rollover basis, which means that the loan is periodically repriced at an agreed spread over the appropriate, currently prevailing LIBOR rate.

**Round lot**   In the money market, round lot refers to the minimum amount for which dealers' quotes are good. This may range from $100,000 to $5 million, depending on the size and liquidity of the issue traded. On the NYSE, this is 100 shares.

**RP**   See **Repurchase agreement.**

**Rule 415**   An SEC rule allowing shelf registration of a security which may then be sold periodically without separate registrations of each part.

**Run**   A run consists of a series of bid and asked for quotes for different maturities. Dealers give to and ask for runs from each other.

**Running the books, or book-running manager**   The manager who has total control over an offering (usually appears on the upper left of the list of underwriters in a tombstone advertisement).

**S&L**   See **Savings and loan association.**

**Safekeep**   For a fee, banks will safekeep (that is, hold in their vault, clip coupons on, and present for payment at maturity) bonds and money market instruments.

**Sale repurchase agreement**   See **Repurchase agreement.**

**Savings and loan association**   A federal- or state-chartered institution that accepts savings deposits and invests the bulk of the funds thus received in mortgages.

**Savings deposit**   An interest-bearing deposit at a savings institution that has no specific maturity.

**Scale**   A bank that offers to pay different rates of interest on CDs of varying maturities is said to post a scale. Commercial paper issuers also post scales.

**Seasoned issue**   An issue that has been well distributed and trades well in the secondary market.

**Secondary distribution**   A large public securities offering made outside the usual exchange or OTC market (often underwritten). Those making the offering wish to sell more of the security than they believe can be easily absorbed by the market's usual channels. A secondary offering spreads out the period for absorption.

**Secondary market**   The market in which previously issued securities are traded.

**Sector**   A group of securities that are similar with respect to maturity, type, rating, and/or coupon.

**Securities and Exchange Commission (SEC)**   An agency created by Congress to protect investors in securities transactions by administering securities legislation.

**Selling concession**   The portion of the gross spread that brokers receive for selling underwritten securities.

**Selling group**   Those firms that are not members of the underwriting group who want to participate on a registered distribution.

**Serial bonds**   A bond issue in which maturities are staggered over a number of years.

**Settle**   See **Clear.**

**Settlement date**   The date on which a trade is cleared by delivery of securities against funds. The settlement date may be the trade date or a later date.

**Shell branch**   A foreign branch—usually in a tax haven—which engages in Eurocurrency business but is run out of a head office.

**Shop**   In street jargon, a money market or bond dealership.

**Shopping**   Seeking to obtain the best bid or offer available by calling a number of dealers and/or brokers.

**Short**   A market participant assumes a short position by selling a security he does not own. The seller makes delivery by borrowing the security sold or reversing it in. (See also **Short sale.**)

**Short bonds**   Bonds with a short current maturity.

**Short book**   See **Unmatched book.**

**Short coupons**   Bonds or notes with a short current maturity.

**Short hedge**   The sale of a futures contract to hedge, for example, a position in cash securities or an anticipated borrowing need.

**Short sale**   The sale of securities not owned by the seller in the expectation that the price of these securities will fall or as part of an arbitrage. A short sale must eventually be covered by a purchase of the securities sold.

**Sinking fund**   Indentures on corporate issues often require that the issuer make annual payments to a sinking fund, the proceeds of which are used to retire randomly selected bonds in the issue. Another type of sinking fund permits the issuer to retire the bond by a market purchase.

**Size** Large in size, as in "size offering" or "in there for size." What constitutes size varies with the sector of the market.

**Sovereign risk** The special risk, if any, that attaches to a security (or deposit or loan) because the borrower's country of residence differs from that of the investor's. Also referred to as country risk.

**Specialist** An exchange member who makes a market in listed securities.

**Spot market** The market for immediate as opposed to future delivery. In the spot market for foreign exchange, settlement is two business days ahead.

**Spot rate** The price prevailing in the spot market.

**Spread** (1) The difference between bid and asked prices on a security. (2) The difference between yields on or prices of two securities of differing sorts or differing maturities. (3) In underwriting, the difference between the price realized by the issuer and the price paid by the investor. (4) The difference between two prices or two rates. What a commodities trader would refer to as the basis.

**Spreading** In the futures market, buying one futures contract and selling a nearby one to profit from an anticipated narrowing or widening of the spread over time.

**Stabilization** Maintaining an orderly market at or below the offering price. A managing underwriter can be a buyer of the deal's stock in, for example, a cold market. This helps to stabilize the price of the stock. One other way of stabilizing the price of the stock is by going short.

**Stop-out price** The lowest price (highest yield) accepted by the Treasury in an auction of a new issue.

**Street** The brokers, dealers, and other knowledgeable members of the financial community; from the Wall Street financial community.

**Subject** Refers to a bid or offer that cannot be executed without confirmation from the customer.

**Subordinated debenture** The claims of holders of this issue rank after those of holders of various other unsecured debts incurred by the issuer.

**Swap** (1) In securities, selling one issue and buying another. (2) In foreign exchange, buying a currency spot and simultaneously selling it forward. (3) In liability swaps, exchanging fixed for variable liabilities.

**Swap rate** In the foreign exchange market, the difference between the spot and forward rates at which a currency is traded.

**Swing line** See **Demand line of credit.**

**Switch** British English for a swap; that is, buying a currency spot and selling it forward.

**Syndicate** A group of investment bankers organized to underwrite a new issue or secondary offering.

**TABs (tax anticipation bills)** Special bills that the Treasury occasionally issues. They mature on corporate quarterly income tax dates and can be used at face value by corporations to pay their tax liabilities.

**Tail** (1) The difference between the average price in Treasury auctions and the stop-out price. (2) A future money market instrument (one available some period hence) created by buying an existing instrument and financing the initial portion of its life with a term RP.

**Take** (1) A dealer or customer who agrees to buy at another dealer's offered price is said to take that offer. (2) Eurobankers speak of taking deposits rather than buying money.

**Take-out** (1) A cash surplus generated by the sale of one block of securities and the purchase of another; for example, selling a block of bonds at 99 and buying another block at 95. (2) A bid made to the seller of a security that is designed (and generally agreed) to take him out of the market.

**Takeover bid** A tender offer designed to acquire a sufficient number of shares to achieve working control of the target firm.

**Taking a view** A London expression for forming an opinion as to where interest rates are going and acting on it.

**TANs** Tax anticipation notes issued by states or municipalities to finance current operations in anticipation of future tax receipts.

**Technical condition of a market** Demand and supply factors affecting price, in particular the net position—long or short—of dealers.

**Tender offer** An offer to purchase a large block of securities made outside the general market in which the securities are traded (exchanges, OTC).

**Term bonds**   A bond issue in which all bonds mature at the same time.

**Term Fed funds**   Fed funds sold for a period of time longer than overnight.

**Term loan**   A loan extended by a bank for more than the normal 90-day period. A term loan might run five years or more.

**Term RP (repo)**   RP borrowings for a period longer than overnight, may be 30, 60, or even 90 days.

**Thin market**   A market in which trading volume is low and in which consequently bid and asked quotes are wide and the liquidity of the instrument traded is low.

**Tight market**   A tight market, as opposed to a thin market, is one in which volume is large, trading is active and highly competitive, and spreads between bid and ask prices are narrow.

**Time deposit**   An interest-bearing deposit at a savings institution that has a specific maturity.

**Trade date**   The date on which a transaction is initiated. The settlement date may be the trade date or a later date.

**Trade on top of**   Trade at a narrow or no spread in basis points to some other instrument.

**Treasury bill**   A non-interest-bearing discount security issued by the U.S. Treasury to finance the national debt. Most bills are issued to mature in three months, six months, or one year.

**Trustee**   A bank or other third party which administers the provisions of a bond indenture or of an asset portfolio.

**TT&L account**   A Treasury tax and loan account at a bank.

**Turnaround**   Securities bought and sold for settlement on the same day.

**Turnaround time**   The time available or needed to effect a turnaround.

**Two-sided market**   A market in which both bid and asked prices, good for the standard unit of trading, are quoted.

**Two-way market**   A market in which both a bid and an asked price are quoted.

**Underwriter**   A dealer who purchases new issues from the issuer and distributes them to investors. Underwriting is one function of an investment banker.

**Unmatched book**   If the average maturity of a bank's liabilities is less than that of its assets, it is said to be running an unmatched book. The term is commonly used in the Euromarket. Equivalent expressions are open book and short book.

**Value date**   Refers to the delivery date of funds traded in the market for Eurodollar deposits and foreign exchange. Normally it is on spot transactions two days after a transaction is agreed on and the future date in the case of a forward foreign exchange trade.

**Variable-price security**   A security, such as stocks and bonds, that sells at a fluctuating, market-determined price.

**Variable-rate CDs**   Short-term CDs that pay interest periodically on *roll* dates; on each roll date the coupon on the CD is adjusted to reflect current market rates.

**Variable-rate loan**   Loan made at an interest rate that fluctuates with the prime. (See also **Floating rate note.**)

**Venture capital**   Risk capital extended to start-up or small going concerns.

**Visible supply**   New muni bond issues scheduled to come to market within the next 30 days.

**Warrants**   Certificates offering the right to purchase stock in a company at a specified time over a specified period.

**When-issued trades**   Typically there is a lag between the time a new bond is announced and sold and the time it is actually issued. During this interval, the security trades "wi"—"when, as, if issued."

**Wi**   When, as, if issued. See **When-issued trades.**

**Wi wi**   T bills trade on a wi basis between the day they are auctioned and the day settlement is made. Bills traded before they are auctioned are said to be traded wi wi.

**Wire house**   An exchange member electronically linked to an exchange.

**Without**   If 70 were bid in the market and there was no offer, the quote would be "70 bid without." The expression *without* indicates a one-way market.

**Yankee bond**   A foreign bond issued in the U.S. market, payable in dollars, and registered with the SEC.

**Yankee CD**   A CD issued in the domestic market (typically in New York) by a branch of a foreign bank.

**Yield curve**   A graph showing, for securities that all expose the investor to the same credit risk, the relationship at a given point in time between yield and current maturity. Yield curves are typically drawn using yields on governments of various maturities.

**Yield to maturity**   The rate of return yielded by a debt security held to maturity when both interest payments and the investor's capital gain or loss on the security are taken into account.

**Zero coupon**   A security sold at a discount whose interest rate is determined by a rise in value per unit of time; its maturity value equals par.

# Index